IET CONTROL ENGINEERING SERIES 89

Control-Based Operating System Design

Other volumes in this series:

Control-Based Operating System Design

Alberto Leva, Martina Maggio,
Allessandro Vittorio Papdopoulos
and Federico Terraneo

The Institution of Engineering and Technology

Published by The Institution of Engineering and Technology, London, United Kingdom

The Institution of Engineering and Technology is registered as a Charity in England & Wales (no. 211014) and Scotland (no. SC038698).

© 2013 The Institution of Engineering and Technology

First published 2013

The Institution of Engineering and Technology
Michael Faraday House
Six Hills Way, Stevenage
Herts, SG1 2AY, United Kingdom

www.theiet.org

British Library Cataloguing in Publication Data
A catalogue record for this product is available from the British Library

ISBN 978-1-84919-609-3 (hardback)
ISBN 978-1-84919-610-9 (PDF)

Typeset in India by MPS Limited
Printed in the UK by CPI Group (UK) Ltd, Croydon

To Clara and Aurora, with love.
(A.L.)

To my parents, for their unconditioned love.
(M.M.)

To my grandfather, my parents, my sister, Ettore and Anna.
(A.V.P.)

To my father and my mother, for their support.
(F.T.)

It was stated at the outset,
that this system would not be here, and at once, perfected.
You cannot but plainly see that I have kept my word.
But I now leave my cetological System standing thus unfinished,
even as the great Cathedral of Cologne was left,
with the cranes still standing upon the top of the uncompleted tower.
For small erections may be finished by their first architects;
grand ones, true ones, ever leave the copestone to posterity.
God keep me from ever completing anything.
This whole book is but a draught—nay, but the draught of a draught.
Oh, Time, Strength, Cash, and Patience!
H. Melville, Moby Dick, 32

Contents

List of trademarks

- Fortran is a trademark of Lahey Computer Systems Inc.
- Linux is a registered trademark of Linus Torvalds.
- Mac OS X is a registered trademark of Apple Computer Corporation.
- POSIX is a registered trademark of the IEEE.
- UNIX is a registered trademark of The Open Group.
- Scilab is a registered trademark of Inria.
- VAX and VMS are trademarks of Digital Equipment Corp.
- Windows is a trademark of Microsoft Corp.

All other trademarks, registered trademarks and names are the property of their respective owners.

Preface

Most often, a research topic becomes the subject of books when it is approaching maturity, and a significant *corpus* of results and applications is available.

As suggested in the introductory quote, the story of this book is quite different. When we started approaching the design (not just the control) of operating system components in a system-theoretical manner, we were in fact quite surprised how sparingly the computer science and the control community have been interacting so far, at least in the sense described herein. Crudely, after a few years of research on the matter, we decided to write this book because we are convinced that the proposed approach is an important step forward with respect to present design practices, but to explain why and how clearly enough, too much space is required to comply with any other form of publication.

As such, this book is indeed 'but the draught of a draught'. Its main purpose is to sketch out a research path that can be reasonably expected to last for several years, providing some results to justify the required effort.

To this end, we decided to include some chapters on systems and control theory. These are in no sense to be thought of as a course on the matter. On the contrary, we tried to present only what is needed to follow and understand our proposals, addressing essentially a computer scientist who has little or no knowledge on the systems and control theory. The only constraint we adhered to is to provide a consistent treatise without conceptual jumps, but no doubt a number of important subjects are here omitted. For the convenience of the reader coming from the control community, on the other hand, we briefly present each addressed object and problem, thus reporting ideas and facts that for the computer scientist are totally obvious. We hope that this helps both types of reader feel comfortable with the text.

In the book we also provide some results, basically addressing a collection of problems that traditionally are not viewed from the control standpoint, to show the insight and simplicity enhancements that such a viewpoint conversely yields.

Overall, the book is organised as follows:

- Chapter 1 provides a general introduction to the addressed matter and motivates the adopted approach, also by means of a very synthetic historical analysis.
- Chapter 2 introduces the few required basic elements of systems theory, as anticipated. This chapter and the following Chapter 4 end with a 'problems' section, to allow the interested reader to verify his/her acquisition of the illustrated concepts.

- Chapter 3 applies the modelling-related ideas of Chapter 2 to the particular domain addressed herein, evidencing its peculiarities. Some introductory examples are reported and commented on.
- Chapter 4 deals with the required basic elements of *control* theory, adopting an attitude, and consequently an organisation, analogous to those of Chapter 2.
- Chapter 5 deals with task scheduling. A general dynamic model is proposed, and based on that, a methodology is presented to design a scheduler along the control-based paradigm. Said methodology is then applied, leading to two scheduling algorithms, that are comparatively tested with respect to classical (non-control-based) ones.
- Chapter 6 addresses the problem of memory management, and proposes for it too a control-based solution. Simulation results are presented and commented on, to evidence the obtained advantages.
- Chapter 7 presents, limiting again the scope to the bare essential, some control techniques – more advanced than those of Chapter 4 – that are used in the following one. In particular, the chapter deals with Model Predictive Control and model identification, and ends with a 'problems' section for the same reason as Chapters 2 and 4.
- Chapter 8 treats more in general the resource allocation problem. Thanks to the adoption of more a high-level viewpoint with respect to the previous chapters, here a design methodology is sketched out and supported, that can be used as a *modus operandi* when addressing numerous problems that appear quite different from the application point of view, but in the context of the systems theory have a definitely uniform mathematical structure.
- Chapter 9 applies the ideas presented so far to power-aware resource management. Apart from discussing another interesting application case, the main point here is to evidence how a control-based design attitude is naturally keen to host problems with very different requirements.
- Chapter 10 presents the Miosix kernel, i.e., the nucleus of an operating system that is being developed along the proposed approach. Motivations for developing an *ad hoc* kernel are provided, the realised functionalities are described, and future developments are outlined.
- Chapter 11, after all the different issues touched in the previous ones, suggests a way of casting them into a unitary view conceptually connected to that of 'cyber-physical' systems, thereby discussing – as a work in progress – some further ways in which a control-theoretical point of view can be helpful for design, analysis and assessment.

Chapters not related to introducing systems and control theory material do not have a 'problems' section for quite apparent reasons. The interested reader is, however, encouraged to try out the presented solutions, and also to use the approach to design and test his/her own ones, based, e.g., on the Miosix kernel, and the code examples reported in Appendix A. In particular, the reader – especially the computer scientist – is encouraged to use dynamic models for design, and to test the devised solutions by means of dynamic simulation.

Among the functionalities of the typical operating system, scheduling receives in this book quite significantly a dominant attention. This choice was dictated basically by two reasons. The first is that scheduling is undoubtedly a core functionality, and in some sense maybe the most important one. The second is that we wanted to present a complete solution, illustrating the proposed approach from the modelling phase till the realisation of the necessary code, so as to show the importance of giving the design process a system-theoretical flavour wherever possible and applicable. Quite intuitively, doing the same for all the functionalities mentioned and addressed in the book would have lead to a lengthy treatise with numerous repetitions. The abstraction and re-interpretation capabilities of the reader, in our opinion, can certainly suffice to allow him/her to re-apply the proposed ideas in different contexts, and for this reason only some guidelines for such re-applications are provided.

On the same front, several components that are considered part of an operating system – e.g., the file system – are not treated at all. In fact, as the book title, we might as well have chosen 'Control-based *kernel and operating system services* design'. On one hand doing so would probably have better reflected the detailed book content, but on the other we have the impression that it would have somehow limited the view on the potentialities of the proposed approach. We hope that after going through the book, the reader can share with us the belief that once a kernel and its services are designed and assessed as suggested, the rest of the operating system can rely on them and take profit of said design in quite a straightforward manner. The concluding remarks of Chapter 11 will further deal with this particular topic.

The book attempts to maintain an intermediate attitude between presenting solutions, which should help the computer scientist appreciate the usefulness of the approach, and evidencing the need for a more methodologically grounded treatise of some issues that tend to be considered, especially in the control community, as implementation-related matter of facts.

The authors are not sure at all that the best compromise between those two attitudes was here found, but hope that the effort will be appreciated, and even more important, that the *necessity* of such an effort will be acknowledged. Of course, the establishment of both a comprehensive 'systems and control theory for computer science' and of the consequent engineering principles is a formidable task, of which we do not claim here to present but the very initial steps.

We correspondingly understand that the perspective shift here proposed is significant indeed, and although we did our best to keep in mind implementation-related facts, we expect that besides some certainties, the matter exposed herein will most likely give rise to discussions. We hope that this happens, because the solutions proposed here can surely be improved, and doing this together would culturally enrich both the computer and the control community.

In fact, we believe that the foreseen convergence of the two communities just mentioned not only is highly beneficial for both, but given the steady complexity increase experience in virtually any domain related to computing systems at large, it may well become a necessity not so far in the future. As such, we strongly hope that this work, despite the undoubted imperfections of a research path that started out quite recently, can not only allow to appreciate some nice results, but above all foster a more strict inter-domain cooperation.

Alberto Leva
Martina Maggio
Alessandro Vittorio Papadopoulos
Federico Terraneo

December 2012

Acknowledgements

We would like to express our gratitude to the many people who helped us through this book; to all those who provided support, talked things over, read, wrote, offered comments, allowed us to quote their remarks and assisted in the editing, proofreading and design.

This book contains our personal views on Control-Theoretical Design of Operating Systems, and our opinions were influenced by various sources. To start, we would like to thank our colleagues, who have contributed to shape our mind and to the design and implementation of some of the work presented in the following pages. During an early stage of development, Carlo Alberto Furia and Paola Spoletini provided very useful insight and comments on the scheduling problem. The resource allocation problem was extensively discussed with Anant Agarwal, Marco Domenico Santambrogio and Jacopo Panerati, whom we thank for their invaluable help; also the help of Sara Negro was important in this respect. A lot of the inspiration for this book came from Henry Hoffmann's work on the Application Heartbeat and SEEC project. His contribution — both theoretical and practical — was inestimable and we would never have written this book without his support. Riccardo Scattolini helped with his long experience, particularly by reviewing the chapters on basis systems and control theory, and many other colleagues involved in Automatic Control (the list would really be long) contributed with discussions and suggestions. Finally, we would like to thank Antonio Filieri and Carlo Ghezzi. Even if the research we carried on together has no place in this book, our interaction cleared our mind and allowed us to face problems with a different mindset.

We would like to express a final comprehensive thank to all the people involved in this research: even if some of them was left out from this short section, this does not mean that his/her contribution was less valuable. Indeed, without the help of so vast a group, this book simply would not exist.

Chapter 1

Introduction

Until some years ago, computers occupied a well-delimited part of our world, and life. Now, this is not true anymore. If we take as definition of computer the broadest one of 'some digital circuitry providing a Turing-complete instruction set, in some way programmed to execute some task, and interacting with outside through interfaces and peripheral devices', we shall see immediately that computers are everywhere. And even restricting the definition to 'some processors executing some software and interacting with a memory and peripherals', the *scenario* remains more or less the same.

Traditionally, a computer is thought of as a set of hardware devices, the major role among them being played by one or more microprocessors, on which some software runs. In turn, software can be very broadly distinguished in two layers. Nearest to the user stands the *application* software, be it a word processor, a web browser, a CAD package, or whatever. Between application software and hardware is conversely the *operating system*, on which this book is focused.

In a few words, the operating system takes care of making the hardware available to the application software in an orderly manner. It manages the file system, the memory, the network and the various peripherals, coordinates the execution of the different application programs running in multitasking, guarantees that each of them can access the needed resources by suitably resolving conflicts, and performs numerous other tasks that it would be lengthy and inessential to list in this introduction.

Also in this respect, in the last years significant changes can be observed. The level of complexity reached by modern software is really impressive, due mostly to the need of fulfilling multiple and possibly conflicting requirements. Software has firstly and obviously to serve the purpose it was designed for, be it word processing, video, mathematics, or whatever. But modern software needs conceiving for an architecturally heterogeneous hardware and for highly variable environmental conditions, and it must preserve its functionalities while at the same time optimising the usage of power and resources. For example, the same code may run on a network server, a laptop computer, or a mobile phone. In the first case, the main problem might be how to coordinate with (many) other applications so as to prevent the hardware from reaching critical temperatures [1]. In the second case, one could essentially want to optimise power consumption [2] when running on battery. In the third case, power constraints are typically stricter, and thus network usage could be delayed to group packets together, so as to consume the network adapter initialisation power only once [3,4].

Also, software has to cope with hardware evolutions (from single- to multi-processor contexts, for example) and not only preserve its functionalities, but allow for the redesign required to exploit the new hardware in an orderly and effective way.

Given their role as sketched above, operating systems are significantly complicated by such increasing needs – so significantly, in the authors' opinion, to evidence the need for a new design paradigm.

As a significant example of the complexity increase just sketched, consider the Linux scheduler. In kernel version 2.4.37.10, all the scheduler code was contained in a single file 1397 lines long. In kernel version 2.6.39.4, the scheduler code is spread among 13 files for a total length of 17, 598 lines.[1]

When a core, long-lasting and generally well-established functionality, like scheduling is for an operating system, 'explodes' by an order of magnitude in one year, as in the example above, it must be concluded that not only complexity is increasing, but changes in the design conditions can have abrupt and dramatic effects on the *rate* of that increase. A possible reason for that is that current design practices are in some sense 'not systematic enough', and it is advisable to reconsider them.

From a solely classical software engineering point of view, possible responses to this challenge are at present sought as *self-adaptive* [5] or *autonomic* [6] computing, where an adaptation *loop* is introduced to conform to different operating *scenarii*. However, designing a loop for self-adaptive systems is not a trivial task, and *in the computer science context alone* there are no well-assessed techniques for this purpose. The use of the control theory is often envisaged as a viable solution to design self-aware and adaptive computing systems [7]. However, there are still unsolved issues that prevent control-theoretical design to be widely adopted [8]. The aim of this work is to solve some of the reported (and other) issues, and more in general to propose a *fully* control-theoretical design of operating systems, integrating with concepts and results coming from the computer science domain, but not refraining from discussions and possible modifications of non-systemic design practices.

The so envisaged integration is in fact necessary but not at all easy indeed. Some reasons reside in the different lexicons of the 'computer' and the 'control' communities, where the same term could have very different meanings ('process', 'parameter', 'adaptation' and even 'feedback' are notable examples, although impossible to fully discuss at this point). However, the ultimate reason resides – in the opinion of the authors – in the parallel but separate evolution that the two communities had in time. To explain and motivate the presented work, it is then also useful to briefly go through those 'two parallel stories' and then, elaborating on them, to discuss motivations and advantages of the use of feedback control not *around*, but *inside* the components of an operating system.

In doing so, for brevity, we shall use terms that are typical of the jargons of each of the two communities, and thus may not be familiar to the specialist of the other one.

---

[1] Those information can be easily retrieved from http://www.kernel.org/. A kernel geek may object that this is due to the introduction of multi-core processors. However, in the following of this book it should become clear that from an engineering standpoint this is not the key fact.

The reader in this situation may therefore want to return on the following sections after reading the rest of the book.

1.1 Βίοι παράλληλοι (two parallel stories)[2]

The first story to sketch is that of the modern (feedback) control theory, a part of which is illustrated, in a very simplified manner for apparent reasons, in Figure 1.1. Locating its beginning in time would involve a huge discussion, apparently outside the scope of this work. Suffice thus to say that the principle of feedback was probably already known by the Greeks in the classical period and by the Arabs in the middle age, but said knowledge was substantially unconscious, i.e., no mathematical theory was available to ground it. In fact, till the burst of the Industrial Revolution, designing feedback systems was a trial-and-error process, relying entirely on engineering experience and intuition – indeed, more of an art than a science.

Only in the mid-1800s did mathematics come into play, the first problem addressed being that of analysing the stability of feedback systems. From that point of view, a historical work is that by the British astronomer G. B. Airy at Greenwich [9], who first formalised the idea of *instability* as a possible outcome of an improper feedback design. The work by Airy, and other similar ones, provided an application for the research by mathematicians such as Lagrange and Hamilton on the use of equations to analyse the motion of dynamic systems. The jargon of the modern control theory had thus started forming, differential equations were the mathematical tool of election, and the continuous-time domain was the natural *arena* for both theory and applications.

In terms of differential equations, J. C. Maxwell analysed the stability of the well-known Watt's governor. By linearising the differential equations of motion, he proved that the system is 'stable'[3] if its eigenvalues have negative real part [10]. With the paper just quoted, it is common opinion that the theory of control systems

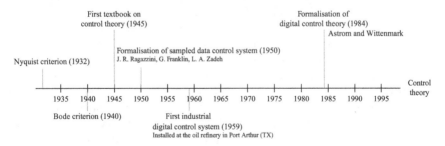

Figure 1.1   Control theory evolution – simplified timeline

---

[2] Βίοι παράλληλοι (Parallel lives) is a work by Plutarch, where biographies of famous personalities are presented and commented on in couples (a Greek and a Roman), i.e., 'in parallel'.
[3] Details on 'asymptotic' and 'simple' stability came later on.

had been established. Then came a deeper analysis on stability, the Routh criterion [11], the Lyapunov stability theory [12], the frequency domain with Nyquist [13] and Bode [14], and much more.

The continuous-time control theory is therefore far older than its *modern* engineering uses. Along the idea of 'feedback design as more an art than a science' stated above, the numerous attempts to use controls in the industry, up to more or less the beginning of the eighteenth century, can in fact be considered as still essentially empirical. Examples are the windmill fantail invented in 1745 by the British blacksmith E. Lee, the temperature regulator developed in 1777 by Bonnemain and later on applied to industrial furnaces, and so forth. In the twentieth century, on the other hand, when first mass communications – the name 'Bell Laboratories' is known worldwide – and then the World War II suddenly presented tough challenges to engineering, the continuous-time theory was there and quite mature: the first *textbooks* on control were near to appearing [15], but top-notch engineers and researchers already knew the methods, although slide rules and graphical constructions were the typical problem solution tools, and needless to say, any realisation was analogue or even 'hardware' in the most ancient sense of the term, e.g., mechanical or pneumatic. From those pioneering times on, in any case, the idea that 'a plant had to be conceived having control in mind' started emerging, and the mathematical tools used for control design paved themselves a parallel way into plant *design*, so that the two can nowadays be treated, whenever convenient, as a single compound entity. This is called 'process/control co-design', and is still a matter of research. Anyway, if a substantially unidirectional path is followed, by first designing (most of) the plant and then going for control, system-theoretical concepts remain a unitary framework for both activities.

If we now consider the theory and the modern engineering use of *digital* control and computers, the story more or less reverses. Early computers first entered the scene, around the late 1940s, as a means to solve design equations offline, and only the advent of the microprocessor made it possible to use them in control *online*: in fact, the first real industrial *digital* control system is by common opinion that installed in 1959 at the oil refinery in Port Arthur, Texas.

As a consequence, the growth of the digital control theory was (at least in part) fostered by the availability of computers, not vice versa. Said growth took origin by the theory of sampled data systems, developed in the 1950s by scientists such as J. R. Ragazzini, G. Franklin and L. A. Zadeh [16,17], and further expanded in the 1960s by the works of E. I. Jury, B. C. Kuo and others, see, e.g., [18] for a survey. At the same time, the work on chemical plants control in the previous years (recall the Port Arthur experience) and the growth of the nuclear industry, provided further motivations for the development of 'innovative instrumentation' (this was the term used at that time) with digital technology. The result was a number of theoretical studies on digital control that, however, took some decades before reaching a firmly established status, see, e.g., the comprehensive work by Åström and Wittenmark in 1984 [19]. Hence, it seems quite clear that in the mainstream control literature, digital computers have been treated as a means to solve problems, but right from the beginning they were not designed as 'objects to be controlled' themselves.

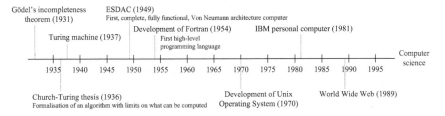

Figure 1.2   Computer science evolution – simplified timeline

The second story to sketch is that of modern computing, shown (again, very synthetically) in Figure 1.2. The mathematical foundations of modern computer science began to be laid by Kurt Gödel with his *incompleteness theorem*, in 1931 [20]. In this theorem, he showed that there were limits to what could be proved and disproved within a formal system. In the meantime, in 1936, Alan Turing [21] and Alonzo Church [22] independently – and also together – introduced the *formalisation of an algorithm*, with limits on what can be computed, and a 'purely mechanical' model for computing. These topics are covered by what is now called the Church–Turing thesis, a hypothesis about the nature of 'mechanical' calculation devices, such as electronic computers. The thesis claims that any calculation that is possible, can be performed by an algorithm running on a computer, provided that sufficient time and storage space are available. Turing also included in the thesis a description of his *Turing machine*. The Turing machine is the first formal model which is able to describe the behaviour of a computing system. And while such systems were becoming more and more complex, yet the Turing machine remained the only available formal model.

Anyway, the dawn of computer science is considered to be the year 1949, when Maurice Wilkes and a team at Cambridge University executed the first stored program on the *EDSAC* computer, which used paper tape input-output. Based on ideas from John von Neumann about stored-program computers, the EDSAC was in fact the first complete, fully functional von Neumann architecture computer [23]. In 1950, Britain's National Physical Laboratory completed *Pilot ACE*, a small-scale programmable computer, with 800 vacuum tubes, and mercury delay lines for its main memory, based on Turing's philosophy [24]. In 1954, the development of *FORTRAN* (FORmula TRANslation), the first high-level programming language, was started by John Backus and his team at IBM.

In 1970, the development of the *UNIX operating system* started, and in 1971 the first *microprocessor* (the 4004, realised by a team at Intel) was released. The first international connections to *ARPANET* [25] were established in 1972. ARPANET later became the basis for what we now call the Internet. In 1974, the *first personal computer* to be commercially released (the MCM/70) was built by Micro Computer Machines in Canada, while only later, in 1981, IBM announced their *IBM Personal Computer*, and 100,000 orders were taken by Christmas. In the same year, the TCP/IP protocol was established. In 1989, the *World Wide Web* was invented by Tim Berners-Lee, who wanted to use hypertext to make documents and information seamlessly accessible over different kinds of computers and systems, and wherever they might be in the world [26].

1.2   Control-based design as a means for convergence

Crudely speaking, one could well say that the operating system 'controls the computer', making it serve the application software requirements.

Having this in mind and relating the two parallel stories just told, consider the control of anything but a computer (a power plant, a robot or whatever else). Even a quick glance at the corresponding history shows that any 'modern' design for the controlled object ultimately relies on techniques that were established when the control theory had already produced the main results required to ground said design. For example, to size a physical component that is natively described by differential equations, the part of the control theory naturally coming into play is the continuous-time one, and most of the necessary results were already available when performance requirements started becoming so tight to require component and system design to account for dynamics. In one word, in any domain but computing systems, when the designer had to look for some control-theoretical tool, such a tool was more or less available, formally assessed, and ready for use.

Consider now the computers domain, and it will immediately become evident that the situation is totally different. The theory of digital control is far more recent than the continuous-time one, and the dawn of its development more or less coincides in time with the advent itself of digital computers. In fact, the development of the digital control theory, and even more of modern control sciences such as that of discrete-events systems, are historically in parallel with the development of computers and computer science: both started out approximately in the '40s of the last century, and some relevant results, e.g., on discrete-event systems, are even more recent; consider for example the historical Ph.D., thesis of C. A. Petri [27]. Again in one word, for the design of computing systems, no off-the-shelf well established tool has been available for a long time.

Of course, the *scenario* just sketched out is very simplistic. Nonetheless, in the authors' opinion it catches the big picture, and which is more, its consequences are evident. Despite many issues concerning the design and management of computers are control problems in nature, they were not treated as such for many years, owing to the scarce maturity of the available control-theoretical tools, let alone the consequent difficulties in agreeing a shared lexicon for the control and the computer science communities. As a result, many parts of existing systems, even critical ones like schedulers, were (and are) designed directly as algorithms, so that representing them as dynamic systems is extremely difficult. And which is worse, the design practices established by such habits in the computing system domain make such difficulties increase in time. Summarising, due to the unavailability of reliable control-related tool, in computing systems many solutions were devised based on heuristics, and that tradition is progressively consolidating: "Scheduling has gotten increasingly ad hoc over the years. 1960s papers very math heavy, now mostly 'tweak and see'" [28].

It must be made absolutely clear that the considerations reported so far imply no criticism at all to previous research on operating systems design. To be even more explicit, the authors are convinced that the work done by scientists in that domain, in the absence of a consolidated theory in the sense sketched above, is simply fantastic. Nonetheless, the authors also believe that as complexity increases, a boundary will eventually be (and possibly is nowadays being) trespassed, beyond which a systematic approach – in the system-theoretical sense – becomes a necessity.

In fact, in an attempt to bridge the two worlds, part of the scientific community has attempted to develop modelling formalisms capable of representing the complexity of computing systems, and to use the so obtained models for posing and solving the convenient control problems [29].

Therefore, in the literature a significant number of contributions can be found on 'control of computing systems', see, e.g., [7] and the papers quoted therein. However, those contributions almost invariantly refer to situations where some control loop is closed around an *existing* and *already functional* system, in order to guarantee the achievement of some properties. Examples can be found in several domains, starting from process scheduling, up to quality of service, and so forth.

If this approach is taken, the computing system is treated exactly the same as the 'process' is in control design problems referring to other domains when the unidirectional *modus operandi* is adopted, i.e., first the plant to be controlled is sized and designed, and then control is considered. To qualify the same approach in the field addressed herein, we could thus say that works of this type start from a system that is already functional, and *add* a control layer *on top* of it to achieve some improvement. This is what we call here 'using control *around* an operating system component'.

On the other hand, as anticipated, in recent years a steadily increasing interest has been encountered in the control community by the idea of process/control co-design [30–32], where the controller and the process are designed together and cooperatively, rather than in separate phases. In principle, doing so allows to jointly treat the choice and sizing of process components, and the design of a control strategy. This fosters better an attainment of goals that inherently refer to the overall system, not to the process and the controller individually. Historical grounding and strong support to the statement above can be found by quoting from a famous paper [33] by Ziegler and Nichols, who wrote

'In the application of automatic controllers, it is important to realize that controller and process form a unit; credit or discredit for results obtained are attributable to one as much as the other. A poor controller is often able to perform acceptably on a process, which is easily controlled. The finest controller made, when applied to a miserably designed process, may not deliver the desired performance. True, on badly designed processes, advanced controllers are able to eke out better results than older models, but on these processes there is a definite end-point which can be approached by the instrumentation and it falls short of perfection.'

Curiously enough, as will be pointed out and investigated in the following, computers – and in particular operating systems – natively provide a domain of election for process/control co-design, but on so promising a topic, the literature is significantly silent.

This further proves that an effort is required to fill the gap, and in the opinion of the authors, to do so it is necessary to abandon the idea of 'closing loops around already functional systems'. To describe as dynamic systems things that were conceived as algorithms, very complex and articulated formalisms are invariantly required (discrete-event systems, aggregates of queue networks, and more). Controlling such models is correspondingly complex, not easy to implement in real systems and potentially inefficient. And even more important, this way of reasoning may easily conceal the real nature of the phenomenon to be controlled, because the computing system and the contained heuristics very often (maybe unconsciously) already close some loops around it.

The research presented herein intends somehow to reverse the perspective. To explain with an introductory example, suppose that some 'phenomenon' (e.g., the concurrent execution of a pool of tasks) is at present ruled by some algorithm (e.g., a scheduler designed with some heuristics). The 'old' idea is to model somehow that algorithm, and then possibly control the so obtained model. The 'new' idea adopted herein is to forget about the present algorithm, describe and control the phenomenon in a system-theoretical framework, and then have the new algorithm naturally arise as the implementation of the so obtained controller (model).

To clarify once more and add some additional detail, consider the following control problem:

> A certain number of *tanks* need receiving a given amount of *fluid* within a specified period. Once each of them has received enough *fluid*, be it within the deadline or not, it *is emptied* and put in a waiting state, and starts over asking for the same amount of *fluid* at the beginning of the next period. *Tanks* are managed in a certain number of queues depending on their priority level, and when moved from a queue to another, they enter the latter in the last position. At any given time only one of them can receive *fluid*, and is selected as the first one of the highest-priority queue that is not in the waiting state. To ensure that each *tank* receives enough *fluid* within its period, a control mechanism is to be introduced having as control variables the *tank* priorities.

When confronted with a problem posed this way, no doubt that any control engineer would in the first place ask if it is possible to get rid of queues and priorities, and have access, as the control variables, to the (on-off) fluid valve opening times for the tanks that in turn have to be fed. In other words he/she would ask for a less 'miserably designed' process – in the sense of [33] – than the proposed one, or the control results will probably be poor, and its design almost surely cumbersome and hard to assess.

Now, just replace some terms in the problem above.

> A certain number of *processes* need receiving a given amount of *CPU time* within a specified period. Once each of them has received enough *CPU time*,

be it within the deadline or not, it *has the CPU time count reset* and is put in a waiting state, and starts over asking for the same amount of *CPU time* at the beginning of the next period. *Processes* are managed in a certain number of queues depending on their priority level, and when moved from a queue to another, they enter the latter in the last position. At any given time only one of them can receive *CPU time*, and is selected as the first one of the highest-priority queue that is not in the waiting state. To ensure that each *process* receives enough *CPU time* within its period, a control mechanism is to be introduced having as control variables the *process* priorities.

As can be easily seen, this is just taking standard 'dynamic priority multilevel scheduling' as the plant, and 'closing a loop around the plant as is'. Conversely, and differently from the mainstream literature, our approach is the same as that of the control engineer mentioned above. If the effort is made to identify what really cannot be changed (the mass balance for each tank, the equation 'accumulated CPU time equals previous value for it plus amount used in this period' for each scheduled process), then the 'plant physics' just contains the 'core phenomenon' that rules it. Despite the numerous works on control of computing systems, only a very few ones attempt to address the control theoretical *design* of computing systems, and as a result, a design framework as unitary and simple as possible is quite difficult to envisage. This is hence a definitely novel research area with respect to the mainstream literature.

The advantages of said approach are evident in terms of interpretation of the involved quantities and parameters, and also of different and additional potentialities with respect to those offered by classical techniques adopted in the computer science domain. In fact, not only static properties (typical of the computer science analysis) but also dynamic ones (typical of the control theory domain) can be formally proven, such as settling time, disturbance rejection, stability and so on.

In fact, when the problem formulation is translated into an equation based model and a controller is subsequently designed, the resulting system can be analysed in terms of standard control-theoretical indicators, like steady-state error and settling time, to the advantage of a well-grounded assessment without the need for extensive simulations. And even when simulation is needed, this can be done at any level of detail with methods and tools provided by the systems theory, without the need, e.g., to describe the target architecture if this is not required to answer the questions for which simulation is being used (see Section 3.2 for details on this relevant point). Apparently enough, adopting this *modus operandi* normally improves the performance of the controlled system, since those aspects are taken into account yet in the design phase of the controller. This is not possible when such systems are not designed in a control-theoretical way. The rest of the book is devoted to building upon this idea.

Chapter 2

A byte of systems theory

This chapter provides the barely essential system-theoretical foundations for the rest of the book. Basically, its goal is to introduce the notion of *dynamic system* and one of its simplest specialisations, namely the discrete-time linear time-invariant case. Of course the reader with expertise on the subject can safely skip the chapter, and no doubt in the opposite case he/she will find it largely incomplete. On the other hand, however, the reader coming from a computer science research path may not possess this fundamental concept. To overcome such a problem, the choice was here made to provide just the most important ideas in a manner deliberately abstracted from their utilisation, with just some proof sketches when relevant, and having the sole purpose of maintaining a consistent treatise. In Chapter 3, those ideas are applied to describe some problems of interest, and the so obtained models are subsequently used for control-based design. Needless to say, the authors hope that even so short a discussion can stimulate interest. If this is the case, plenty of books are available that offer a complete vision on the matter: a notable – and introductory – text is for example [34].

2.1 Dynamic systems

In this context, a *system* is a mathematical description of some phenomena. A system, also called a *model*, is created for basically three purposes:

- replicating its behaviour by turning it into a computer algorithm and running the corresponding code, which is *simulation*,
- determining whether or not it enjoys some properties, discussed later on, which is *analysis*,
- and deciding how to act on it so that a desired behaviour be obtained also in the presence of possible unforeseen environmental changes or *disturbances*, which is *control*.

We are here interested in *quantitative* models, i.e., we assume that the behaviour of the phenomena of interest is described by a convenient set of *variables* evolving over time, also called *signals*. Depending on the physics of the modelled phenomena, it will be possible to prescribe the value of some variables from outside the system, and these will be *inputs*. Other variables will conversely evolve in time as dictated by the system itself, and these will be *outputs*.

In some cases, knowledge of the inputs over a given time span is sufficient to know the outputs in the same time span. For example, if a resistor is connected in parallel to a voltage generator – thus, installed so that voltage be the input – then the current flowing through it – i.e., the output – in the same time span is fully determined.

In other cases, however, this is not true. For example, consider a buffer (and suppose for simplicity that it never gets emptied nor overflows). If the rates of element insertion and extraction over a time span are prescribed from outside – thus, they are inputs – and known, this is not sufficient to determine the buffer occupation – that we can consider the measurement of interest, thus the output – at any instant of the same span, unless also the *initial value* of that quantity is known.

Definition 2.1. A system (or model) for which knowledge of the inputs over a certain time span is not sufficient to know the outputs over the same span is called a *dynamic system*. The quantities the initial values of which must be known in order to know the outputs, are called the system's *state variables*, and collectively form the system's *state vector*, or *state* for short.

Note that in the buffer example state and output coincide, but this is just incidental. In fact the selection of the state variable(s) is in general not unique; however – as the cases treated later on will show – there is always a 'natural' choice of those variables, that comes quite evident to the analyst. Given the simple models used herein, we can thus avoid further discussions on this aspect.

It is very important to notice that the dynamic character of a system is intimately tied to the presence in that system of some *storage*. For example, if in a time span of one second a water tank has been receiving an inlet flowrate of two litres per second, then the water content at the end of the period will be two litres more than at the beginning. In other words, to know the water content at the end of the period, it is necessary to know the flowrate – an input, as it is prescribed from the outside – and also the amount of water *stored* in the tank at the beginning of the period. It is conversely irrelevant what the story of the storage has been before: if this is the water content at the beginning of the period and this is the flowrate, then this is the water content at the end. In more complex cases identifying the nature of the storage may not be immediate, but invariantly a dynamic system has to store something in order to have a state.

In some cases it is convenient to consider time as a real-valued entity. This typically happens when modelling 'strictly physical' phenomena, like, e.g., mechanical or thermal ones (the water tank example above was brutalised a bit to serve its purpose in the context of this discussion). Such an assumption gives rise to *continuous-time* dynamic systems, that are not necessary for this treatise. In other cases, conversely, time is better thought of as evolving by *steps* associated to an integer *(time) index*. This leads to *discrete-time* dynamic systems, which are a fundamental tool for our purposes.

Note that 'having time evolve by steps' does not imply here that those steps have the same duration in the continuous (or, maybe better for this discussion, 'physical') time. Since this makes the use of discrete-time system made herein a bit unusual with respect to a relevant part of the control-related literature, a short discussion is in order.

In most control domains, but not that addressed here, problems start out in the continuous time – i.e., where virtually any physical phenomenon lives – and end up in the first place with some controller designed as a continuous-time dynamic system (how this is done is irrelevant now). Then, to realise said controller, some algorithm needs creating that periodically computes the inputs to be fed to the controlled system so as to achieve the desired outputs. To do that, the continuous-time controller model is turned – as an intermediate step – into a discrete-time one, where, however, a unity increment of the time index k is thought to correspond to the elapsing of a fixed amount $h \in \mathbb{R}^+$ of the continuous time t, i.e., $t = kh$.

Systems like that just described are not only discrete-time. They do have a relationship to some continuous-time one, which they attempt to replicate, and for this reason they are also called *sampled-signals* systems. Sticking to the example, the system with the controller realised as an algorithm should ideally replicate that in which the controller was realised (e.g., with analogue electronics) in the continuous time, where it was in fact designed and assessed.

In our context, this is not necessarily true, as most often everything can be done in the discrete time directly, equally often with k counting the interventions of some controller – e.g., a resource allocator – that do not occur with constant period. As such, the systems used here are discrete-time but not sampled-signals, and unless explicitly noted, there is no relationship between the increment of k and some fixed time span.

2.1.1 State-space representation

Given the preliminary considerations above, the most general form of dynamic system employed herein reads

$$\begin{cases} x(k) = f(x(k-1), u(k-1), k-1) \\ y(k) = g(x(k), u(k), k) \end{cases} \tag{2.1}$$

where k is the integer time index, frequently also called the *discrete time*, $u(k) \in \mathbb{R}$ is the input, $y(k) \in \mathbb{R}$ the output, and $x(k) \in \mathbb{R}^n$ the state. Note that we are assuming $u(k)$ and $y(k)$ to be real scalars, i.e., we are limiting the scope to single input, single output (SISO) systems; we shall generalise to the multiple input, multiple output (MIMO) case later on. Also in the SISO case, however, $x(k)$ is in general a vector: its dimension n is called the system's *order*, and the vector space $\mathbb{R}^n$ in which $x(k)$ lives is the *state space*.

When a unitary increment of k corresponds to the elapsing of a fixed continuous time span T_s, a discrete-time system is termed a *sampled-signals* one. For example, if a buffer's inlet and outlet rates – $u_i(k)$ and $u_o(k)$, respectively – are varied only at each T_s, and step k is assumed correspondent to the continuous time interval $[(k-1)T_s, kT_s)$, then the dynamic model having as output the buffer occupation $o(k)$ is a specialisation of (2.1) in the form

$$o(k) = o(k-1) + T_s (u_i(k-1) - u_o(k-1)) \tag{2.2}$$

In such cases, calling k the discrete time is particularly appropriate. If conversely we consider an application in a multitasking system, that at the generic kth activation is allotted by the operating system a CPU reservation time $b(k)$, assuming a perfectly timely preemption makes its accumulated CPU time $T_{CPU}(k)$ ruled by

$$T_{CPU}(k) = T_{CPU}(k-1) + b(k-1) \tag{2.3}$$

where k is properly an index and not a 'time', since in general activations are not equally spaced. Apparently, (2.3) is just a discrete-time system, while (2.2) is sampled-signals.

In (2.1), the first equation is called the *state equation*. Its distinctive character is the presence of two subsequent values for the time index, which makes it a *difference equation*. The state equation gives the system memory of the past, as the same $u(k-1)$ will in general produce a different $x(k)$ depending on what $x(k-1)$ was, i.e., of the history of the system up to $k-1$, that $x(k-1)$ fully represents. It is worth anticipating that dynamic systems are a powerful mathematical formalism to represent the capability of an object to react to the same input in different ways depending on its 'condition', by rigorously casting the last concept into that of state. As we shall see and exploit throughout the book, such different reactions can be governed, and the idea of *state-dependent behaviour* comes thus to help formalising, in many cases of interest, the generic one of 'adaptiveness'.

The second equation in (2.1) is called the *output equation* and is synchronous, i.e., only one value of the time index is present. The output equation basically dictates what one wants to see of the system, while its dynamic character is entirely contained in the state equation.

Coming back to the main subject of this section, it is now the time to introduce a few more definitions.

Definition 2.2. If both f and g do not depend explicitly on the discrete time, the system is *time-invariant* (*time-varying* otherwise) and is written as

$$\begin{cases} x(k) = f(x(k-1), u(k-1)) \\ y(k) = g(x(k), u(k)) \end{cases} \tag{2.4}$$

Definition 2.3. If both f and g are linear in x and u, the system is *linear* (*nonlinear* otherwise) and reads

$$\begin{cases} x(k) = A(k)x(k-1) + b(k)u(k-1) \\ y(k) = c(k)x(k) + d(k)u(k) \end{cases} \tag{2.5}$$

where $A(k)$ is an $n \times n$ matrix, and in the SISO case the dimensions of $b(k)$ and $c(k)$ are respectively $n \times 1$ and $1 \times n$, while $d(k)$ is scalar ($x(k)$ is a column vector, thus $n \times 1$).

For a better comprehension of several following concepts, observe in (2.5) the time indices: at step k first the 'current' state is determined based on the 'last' state and input, and then the current output is obtained from the current state and input, all being done with the current matrices.

Definition 2.4. If g does not depend on u, the system is *strictly proper* (*non-strictly proper* otherwise) and takes the form

$$\begin{cases} x(k) = f(x(k-1), u(k-1), k-1) \\ y(k) = g(x(k), k) \end{cases} \tag{2.6}$$

meaning that the input influences the output only through the state, and as a consequence, with a one-step delay.

Definition 2.5. A linear and time-invariant (LTI) system is expressed as

$$\begin{cases} x(k) = Ax(k-1) + bu(k-1) \\ y(k) = cx(k) + du(k) \end{cases} \tag{2.7}$$

where A, b, c and d are constant. The system is also strictly proper iff $d = 0$.

LTI systems are very important, because for them a very strong theory is available. We shall cast problems in the LTI framework wherever possible.

2.1.2 Motion, equilibrium, stability

Consider the time-invariant system (2.4) – the presented concepts can be generalised, but doing so would unnecessarily complicate this introductory chapter.

Notice that the time invariance allows us to put the origin of the time axis wherever we choose to, and 0 is the most natural choice that will be adopted in the following:

Definition 2.6. Knowledge of $x(0)$ and $u(k)$ for $k \geq 0$ apparently provides knowledge of $x(k)$ and $y(k)$ for $k \geq 0$. These are respectively called the *state motion* and the *output motion* produced by $x(0)$ and $u(k)$, $k \geq 0$.

Now, and again with reference to (2.4), suppose that the input is kept constant, i.e., $u(k) = \bar{u} \; \forall k \geq 0$.

Definition 2.7. If there exist some state vectors $\bar{x}$ such that $x(0) = \bar{x}$ and $u(k) = \bar{u}$, $k \geq 0$, produce the constant state motion $x(k) = \bar{x}$, $k \geq 0$, then those vectors are called *equilibrium states* corresponding to the constant input $\bar{u}$.

To find the possible equilibrium states (also *equilibria* for short) for a given $\bar{u}$, it is then necessary to impose that $x(k) = x(k-1) \; \forall k$, i.e., to solve for $\bar{x}$ the equation

$$\bar{x} = f(\bar{x}, \bar{u}) \tag{2.8}$$

If then the expression $g(\bar{x}, \bar{u})$ does not lose significance – which is possible from an abstractly mathematical standpoint but can be excluded in any model of practical interest for us – the result is the *equilibrium output(s)* corresponding to the constant input $\bar{u}$.

It is very important to understand that the existence of an equilibrium $\bar{x}$ (for a constant input $\bar{u}$) *only* means that if the system starts out with exactly the initial state $\bar{x}$ and u is kept to $\bar{u}$, then x does not move at all. Nothing can be deduced on what happens if the initial state is different from $\bar{x}$, no matter how small the said difference may be. This is a matter of *stability*, discussed below.

To enter the subject, let us first talk about stability of equilibria. To this end, let $\bar{x}$ be an equilibrium for system (2.4) corresponding to the constant input $\bar{u}$, and denote by $x_\Delta(k)$ the *perturbed motion* produced by $\bar{u}$ and the perturbed initial state $x(0) = \bar{x} + \Delta\bar{x}$ (notice that in general $x_\Delta(k)$ will not be constant).

Definition 2.8. If, denoting by $||x||$ the norm[1] of vector x,

$$\forall \varepsilon > 0 \; \exists \delta_\varepsilon > 0 \; : \; ||\Delta\bar{x}|| < \delta_\varepsilon \Rightarrow ||x_\Delta(k) - \bar{x}|| < \varepsilon \; \forall k \geq 0 \tag{2.9}$$

then the equilibrium $(\bar{x}, \bar{u})$ is said to be *stable*.

In other words, an equilibrium is stable if, no matter how close one wants the *entire* perturbed motion to remain to that equilibrium, it is possible to find a maximum distance of the initial state from the equilibrium one such that the desire is fulfilled.

Definition 2.9. If an equilibrium $(\bar{x}, \bar{u})$ is stable as per Definition 2.8, and *in addition*

$$\lim_{k \to \infty} ||x_\Delta(k) - \bar{x}|| = 0 \tag{2.10}$$

then the equilibrium is said to be *asymptotically stable*.

Asymptotic stability thus implies stability, while the opposite is apparently false.

Definition 2.10. If for an equilibrium stability as per Definition 2.8 does not hold true, the equilibrium is said to be *unstable*.

With suitable reformulations, Definitions 2.8 through 2.10 can be extended to the stability of motions instead of equilibria, but this is not of interest for us. More important is to examine how the ideas of motion and equilibrium, and therefore the same definitions above, specialise to the LTI case.

2.2 The linear time-invariant (LTI) case

2.2.1 Motion and equilibrium

Let us begin with motion. Considering the LTI system (2.7) and given $x(0)$ and $u(k)$, $k \geq 0$, it is immediate to compute

---

[1] Stability conditions may depend on the particular norm chosen, but the matter would stray from the scope of this book. For our purposes, the reader can think of $||x||$ as the Euclidean norm.

$$x(1) = Ax(0) + bu(0)$$
$$x(2) = Ax(1) + bu(1) = A^2x(0) + Abu(0) + bu(1) \tag{2.11}$$
$$x(3) = Ax(2) + bu(2) = A^3x(0) + A^2bu(0) + Abu(1) + bu(2)$$
$$\cdots$$

that easily generalises to the *Lagrange state formula*

$$x(k) = A^k x(0) + \sum_{h=0}^{k-1} A^{k-h-1} bu(h) \tag{2.12}$$

This reveals a first relevant peculiarity of LTI systems: the state motion $x(k)$ can be viewed as the sum of a *free motion* $x_F(k)$ and an *induced motion* $x_I(k)$, expressed as

$$x_F(k) = A^k x(0), \quad x_I(k) = \sum_{h=0}^{k-1} A^{k-h-1} bu(h) \tag{2.13}$$

where the free motion depends linearly only on $x(0)$ and not on u, while the induced motion depends linearly only on u and not on $x(0)$. It is then immediate to extend (2.12) to the output. This too is the sum of a free motion $y_F(k)$ and an induced one $y_I(k)$, with the same characteristics and mutual relationship as for the state ones, given by

$$y_F(k) = cA^k x(0), \quad y_I(k) = c \sum_{h=0}^{k-1} A^{k-h-1} bu(h) + du(k) \tag{2.14}$$

The facts just mentioned are of great relevance for control, as discussed in Chapter 4. Coming now to equilibrium, for the LTI system (2.7), (2.8) takes the form

$$\bar{x} = A\bar{x} + b\bar{u} \tag{2.15}$$

Thus, if one is not an eigenvalue of A (i.e., if $I - A$, where I is the identity matrix of dimension n, is nonsingular), there exists the only equilibrium

$$\bar{x} = (I - A)^{-1} b\bar{u} \tag{2.16}$$

while in the opposite case, either there is no equilibrium, or there are infinite ones. This is another important peculiarity, as nonlinear systems can have a finite number of equilibria, different from zero and one. Also, in the LTI case, if a certain $\bar{u}$ produces zero, one or infinite equilibria, the same is true for any other $\bar{u}$ (which, again, is not true for the nonlinear case). Finally, in LTI systems, for each equilibrium state there surely exists one equilibrium output $\bar{y} = c\bar{x} + d\bar{u}$.

2.2.2 Stability

Consider again the LTI system (2.7), and let $(\bar{x}, \bar{u})$ be an equilibrium for it. Applying (2.12) leads to write

$$\bar{x} = A^k \bar{x} + \sum_{h=0}^{k-1} A^{k-h-1} b\bar{u} \tag{2.17}$$

while the perturbed motion $x_\Delta(k)$ produced by $\bar{u}$ and $x(0) = \bar{x} + \Delta\bar{x}$ is

$$x_\Delta(k) = A^k(\bar{x} + \Delta\bar{x}) + \sum_{h=0}^{k-1} A^{k-h-1}b\bar{u} \tag{2.18}$$

Subtracting (2.17) from (2.18) thus yields

$$x_\Delta(k) - \bar{x} = A^k\Delta\bar{x} \tag{2.19}$$

which is a very important relashionship, as it states that the way $x_\Delta(k)$ moves with respect to $\bar{x}$ does not depend on $\bar{x}$. That is, differently from the nonlinear case, there cannot be equilibria with different stability characteristics. Stability is here a property of the system, not of the individual equilibria.

Moreover, for $k \to \infty$, $||x_\Delta(k) - \bar{x}||$ converges to zero for any $\Delta\bar{x}$ iff A^k converges to a zero matrix, while the same norm diverges at least for some $\Delta\bar{x}$ (equilibrium and stability are related but distinct concepts, remember) if some elements of A^k do. Finally, if A^k neither converges to zero nor diverges, the same will happen to $||x_\Delta(k) - \bar{x}||$. In synthesis, then, not only in the LTI case stability is a property of the system, but everything concerning stability only depends on matrix A, also called the *dynamic matrix*.

This allows for a strong stability theory, apparently, but discussing the matter is outside our scope. Suffice to say that the following can be proven:

- An LTI system with dynamic matrix A is asymptotically stable iff all the eigenvalues of A have magnitude less than one, or 'are inside the unit circle' of the complex plane (that centred in the origin and with unity radius).
- The same system is unstable if (but not only if) at least one eigenvalue of A has magnitude greater than one.
- If all the eigenvalues of A have magnitude less than or equal to one, and there exists at least one eigenvalue with unity magnitude, the system can be either unstable or stable (but not asymptotically) depending on conditions that we cannot treat herein.

In this respect, it can be anticipated that for control purposes we shall invariantly want to impose asymptotic stability, however, hence the conditions above are enough for us. To briefly explain why, it is convenient to point out two interesting properties of asymptotically stable (LTI) systems.

Property 2.1. *An asymptotically stable system has one and only one equilibrium for each constant input.*

Proof. If there were zero or infinite equilibria (no other case is possible) for the same constant input, A would have at least one unit eigenvalue – recall (2.16) – contrary to the asymptotic stability condition. □

Property 2.2. *The state and output free motions of an asymptotically stable system converge to zero (norm) for $k \to \infty$.*

Proof. The asymptotic stability condition states that for $k \rightarrow \infty$, A^k converges to a zero matrix. □

As a consequence, asymptotically stable systems 'forget their initial condition' so that, when its effect has practically disappeared, they can be entirely driven by the input. As can already be guessed, and will become even more clear after going through Chapter 4, this is a very important property (not to say, a necessity) for every control system.

2.3   Input-output representation of LTI systems

In state space form, an LTI SISO system is described by the quadruplet (A, b, c, d). In this section, we shall introduce an alternative representation, more useful for control-related elaborations.

2.3.1   The $\mathcal{Z}$ transform

Consider a real discrete-time signal $v(k)$, defined for $k \geq 0$ (or, equivalently for our purposes, null for $k < 0$). Its $\mathcal{Z}$ transform is defined as

$$V(z) = \mathcal{Z}[v(k)] := \sum_{k=0}^{\infty} v(k) z^{-k} \tag{2.20}$$

where z is a complex variable.[2] From now on, the convention will be taken to denote the $\mathcal{Z}$ transform of a signal with the corresponding uppercase letter.

It is not our goal here to discuss the mathematical properties of the $\mathcal{Z}$ transform, except for two that are very relevant for the analysis and control of LTI discrete-time dynamic systems.

Property 2.3. *The $\mathcal{Z}$ transform is a linear operator, i.e., given two signals $v_1(k)$ and $v_2(k)$, and two arbitrary real numbers α_1 and α_2,*

$$\mathcal{Z}[\alpha_1 v_1(k) + \alpha_2 v_2(k)] = \alpha_1 \mathcal{Z}[v_1(k)] + \alpha_2 \mathcal{Z}[v_2(k)] \tag{2.21}$$

Proof. Immediate from (2.20). □

Property 2.4. *This is called the 'one-step advance' property, and relates the $\mathcal{Z}$ transform of $v(k + 1)$ to that of $v(k)$. Precisely,*

$$\mathcal{Z}[v(k + 1)] = z\mathcal{Z}[v(k)] - zv(0) \tag{2.22}$$

---

[2] Strictly speaking, some technical hypotheses should be introduced for the existence of (2.20); however, these are not relevant for our purposes.

Proof. Writing the expression of $\mathcal{Z}[v(k+1)]$ and then adding and subtracting $zv(0)$, one readily obtains

$$
\begin{aligned}
\mathcal{Z}[v(k+1)] &= \sum_{k=0}^{\infty} v(k+1)z^{-k} \\
&= v(1) + v(2)z^{-1} + v(3)z^{-2} \ldots + zv(0) - zv(0) \\
&= z(v(0) + v(1)z^{-1} + v(2)z^{-2} \ldots) - zv(0) \\
&= z \sum_{k=0}^{\infty} v(k)z^{-k} - zv(0) \\
&= z\mathcal{Z}[v(k)] - zv(0)
\end{aligned}
\tag{2.23}
$$

□

As such, z can be called the *one-step advance operator*. Also, in a way similar to property 2.4, it can be proven that

$$
\mathcal{Z}[v(k-1)] = z^{-1}\mathcal{Z}[v(k)]
\tag{2.24}
$$

which is why z^{-1} is called the *one-step delay operator*.

2.3.2 *The transfer function*

Consider the LTI system (2.7), and apply the $\mathcal{Z}$ transform to both sides of the state and output equation. Recalling properties 2.3 and 2.4, and the uppercase convention for $\mathcal{Z}$ transforms, this yields

$$
\begin{cases}
zX(z) - zx(0) = AX(z) + bU(z) \\
\qquad\quad Y(z) = cX(z) + dU(z)
\end{cases}
\tag{2.25}
$$

thus

$$
Y(z) = c(zI - A)^{-1}zx(0) + (c(zI - A)^{-1}b + d)U(z)
\tag{2.26}
$$

where the two terms on the right-hand side are respectively the $\mathcal{Z}$ transforms of the free and induced motion of y. Denoting the latter with $Y_I(z)$, it can be noticed that the ratio $Y_I(z)/U(z)$ does not depend on the input signal, but only on the system matrices. As such, the following definition can be given:

Definition 2.11. The complex function

$$
G(z) = c(zI - A)^{-1}b + d
\tag{2.27}
$$

of the complex variable z is the *transfer function* of the LTI system described in the state space by (A, b, c, d).

The system in input-output form is thus represented by writing

$$
G(z) = \frac{Y(z)}{U(z)}
\tag{2.28}
$$

which means that its transfer function is $G(z)$, and the output $y(k)$ induced by the input $u(k)$ is computed – in the $\mathcal{Z}$ transform domain – by means of (2.28).

It is immediate to see that $G(z)$ is the ratio of two polynomials in z, i.e., $G(z) = G_N(z)/G_D(z)$. The denominator $G_D(z)$ is the characteristic polynomial of A, thus its roots – hereinafter, the *poles* of $G(z)$ – are eigenvalues of A; also, the degree of $G_D(z) - \#G_D$ for short – equals the system's order n. The numerator $G_N(z)$ – the roots of which are called the *zeroes* of $G(z)$ – has conversely a maximum degree of n, as $G(z)$ can be written as $\widetilde{G}_N(z)/D(z) + d$, where $\widetilde{G}_N(z)$ is a linear combination of the complementary minors of A, all of which have degree $n - 1$; more precisely, then, $G_N(z)$ and $G_D(z)$ have both degree n iff $d \neq 0$. Observe that a system cannot have more zeroes than poles. This is dictated by the considerations above, but has also a very intuitive interpretation: if a system had more zeroes than poles, its output would depend on future inputs, which is clearly non-physical. Not having more zeroes than poles is thus frequently termed the *realisability condition* for a dynamic system.

In addition, it may happen that some root of $G_D(z)$ is also a root of $G_N(z)$. In that case, in the computation of $G(z)$, a *(zero/pole) cancellation* is said to occur. It is still true that $\#G_N \leq \#G_D$ and $\#G_N = \#G_D$ iff $d \neq 0$, but in this case $\#G_D < n$ and some eigenvalues (at least one) of A do not show up also as a pole of $G(z)$. If a cancelled eigenvalue is inside the unit circle, the cancellation is called *non-critical*, since one can safely discuss the stability of the system by observing the poles of $G(z)$ instead of the eigenvalues of A. In the opposite case the cancellation is *critical*, as studying the system's stability based on the poles of $G(z)$ is apparently incorrect. In any case, the presence of cancellations implies that the system has some *hidden parts*, i.e., some 'internal' dynamics that cannot be influenced by the input, or do not evidence themselves on the output, or both, so that the system is said not to be completely *controllable* and/or *observable*. Discussing the matter in detail would be too long for this book, however, hence only some words will be spent on it when relevant for the control problems to be addressed.

Based on the transfer function, a system can be characterised in ways that are extremely handy for control. This is the subject of the following Sections 2.4 and 2.5.

2.3.3   Block diagrams

An LTI SISO system with input $u(k)$, output $y(k)$ and transfer function $G(z)$, can be represented graphically as in Figure 2.1, left, where the box is called *block*. Also, summation expressions can be represented as in Figure 2.1, right, the shown element

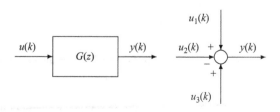

Figure 2.1   Basic elements of LTI block diagrams

being termed a *summation node*. The reported example means $y(k) = u_1(k) - u_2(k) + u_3(k)$, and generalisation is obvious. In summation nodes plus signs are sometimes omitted. Incidentally, recall that by definition of transfer function the left part of Figure 2.1 means that $Y(z) = G(z)U(z)$, but it is common practice to adopt a mixed $k - z$ notation and also write, equivalently, $y(k) = G(z)u(k)$.

By connecting elements such as those in Figure 2.1 one has thus the possibility of representing multivariable systems as *interconnections* of SISO ones, i.e., as *block diagrams*. Arrows indicate causality, thereby, e.g., qualifying $u(k)$ as exogenously determined from the point of view of the phenomena described by $G(z)$. However, it is extremely important to bear in mind that the same arrows do *not* imply that the mentioned block 'receives' $u(k)$ and 'produces' $y(k)$. Such an interpretation would be correct in the case of a data flow diagram, but *a block diagram is not a data flow diagram*. A block diagram contains dynamic systems, which in turn contain equations, not assignments, and connecting an input to an output means adding a further *equation* stating their equality, not that one receives the value of the other.

Block diagrams can be manipulated (we shall see some examples in the following) so as to compute the transfer function from a certain input to a certain output. To this end, we evidence here in figure three main (and for our purposes the only relevant) simplification operations.

2.3.3.1   Series connection

Two blocks are in *series* (or *cascade*) when the output of the first is the input of the second (generalising to more than two blocks is obvious).

Starting from Figure 2.2, we want to compute the compound transfer function $G(z)$ from $u(k)$ to $y(k)$. The two blocks correspond to the two equations $y_1(k) = G_1(z)u_1(k)$ and $y_2(k) = G_2(z)u_2(k)$. Also, the inner connection states that $u_2(k) = y_1(k)$, while the input and output of $G(z)$ are $u(k) = u_1(k)$ and $y(k) = y_2(k)$, respectively. Putting all equations together and eliminating all variables but $u(k)$ and $y(k)$, we easily obtain $y(k) = G_2(z)G_1(z)u(k)$. Thus, the transfer function of the series of the two blocks is

$$G(z) = G_2(z)G_1(z) \tag{2.29}$$

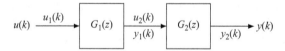

Figure 2.2   *Series or cascade connection*

2.3.3.2   Parallel connection

Two blocks are in *parallel* when their inputs are all equal and their outputs are summed together (here too, generalising to more than two blocks and different signs in the sum is straightforward).

Starting from Figure 2.3, we want again to compute the compound transfer function $G(z)$ from $u(k)$ to $y(k)$. The two blocks correspond to the same two equations of the series case, while the connection equations are $u(k) = u_1(k)$, $u(k) = u_2(k)$

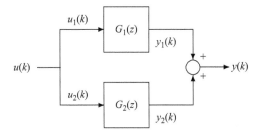

Figure 2.3 Parallel connection

and $y(k) = y_1(k) + y_2(k)$. Proceeding as above we have $y(k) = (G_1(z) + G_2(z))u(k)$. Thus, the transfer function of the parallel of the two blocks is

$$G(z) = G_1(z) + G_2(z) \tag{2.30}$$

2.3.3.3 Feedback (loop) connection

The two blocks in Figure 2.4 form a *feedback loop*, the term 'feedback' indicating that the input of each block in the loop depends on its output. In the loop, the transfer functions $G_{ff}(z)$ and $G_{fb}(z)$ are called, respectively, the *forward path* and the *feedback path*, while the product of all functions around the loop, disregarding the minus sign at the feedback summation node, is called the *(open) loop transfer function*. This function is traditionally denoted by $L(z)$, and equals here $G_{ff}(z)G_{fb}(z)$.

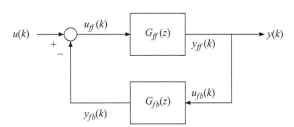

Figure 2.4 Feedback connection

To compute the compound transfer function $G(z)$ from $u(k)$ to $y(k)$, we write again the blocks' and the connection equations, obtaining

$$\begin{cases} y_{ff}(k) = G_{ff}(z)u_{ff}(k) \\ y_{fb}(k) = G_{fb}(z)u_{fb}(k) \\ u_{ff}(k) = u(k) - y_{fb}(k) \\ y(k) = y_{ff}(k) \\ u_{fb}(k) = y_{ff}(k) \end{cases} \tag{2.31}$$

that proceeding as in the two previous cases yields

$$G(z) = \frac{G_{ff}(z)}{1 + G_{ff}(z)G_{fb}(z)} \tag{2.32}$$

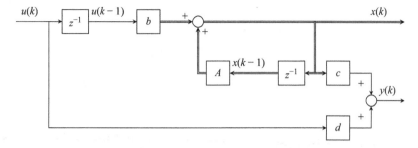

Figure 2.5   An LTI system as a block diagram

Note that any LTI system in the form (2.7) is naturally transformed into a block diagram containing only constant (matrix) gains, summation nodes and delay blocks, i.e., z^{-1} terms. Such a block diagram has a feedback structure, and takes the general form of Figure 2.5, where double lines indicate vector signals.

2.4   The frequency response

Representing LTI systems in transfer function form provides particular insight on how those systems 'filter' their input to produce the output. To this end, the notion of *frequency response* needs introducing.

2.4.1   Definition

Consider an LTI SISO system described in the state space by (A, b, c, d) subjected to an exponential input $u(k) = Ue^{\lambda k}, k \geq 0$, and the following question: does there exist an initial state $x_e(0)$ such that the *total* state motion (free plus induced) too has a pure exponential aspect, i.e., $x(k) = x_e(0)e^{\lambda k}$? To answer, it suffices to constrain such a motion to fulfil the system's state equation, thus solving

$$x_e(0)e^{\lambda(k+1)} = Ax_e(0)e^{\lambda k} + bUe^{\lambda k} \tag{2.33}$$

for $x_e(0)$. Dividing by $e^{\lambda k}$ and rearranging provides

$$(e^{\lambda}I - A)x_e(0) = bU \tag{2.34}$$

thus the required state exists and is unique iff e^{λ} is not an eigenvalue of A, and under said condition takes the value $(e^{\lambda}I - A)^{-1}bU$. Correspondingly, the motion of y is

$$\begin{aligned}
y(k) &= cx(k) + du(k) \\
&= c(e^{\lambda}I - A)^{-1}bUe^{\lambda k} + dUe^{\lambda k} \\
&= (c(e^{\lambda}I - A)^{-1}b + d)Ue^{\lambda k} \\
&= G(e^{\lambda})Ue^{\lambda k} \tag{2.35}
\end{aligned}$$

which evidences the role of the transfer function.

Now, suppose that a sinusoidal input $u(k) = \sin(\theta k)$ is applied, where $\theta \in [0, \pi]$ is the *angular frequency*,[3] and consider the following question: does there exist an initial state $x_s(0)$ such that the *total* state motion (free plus induced) too has a pure sinusoidal aspect? To answer, since obviously

$$\sin(\theta k) = \frac{e^{J\theta k} - e^{-J\theta k}}{2J} \tag{2.36}$$

and in force of the system linearity, one can just apply twice the reasoning made for the exponential case, and then combine the results. Defining $u_+(k) = e^{J\theta k}$ and $u_-(k) = e^{-J\theta k}$, if $e^{\mp J\theta}$ are not eigenvalues of A, then there exist two unique initial states causing $u_+(k)$ and $u_-(k)$ to respectively produce $y_+(k) = G(e^{J\theta})e^{J\theta k}$ and $y_-(k) = G(e^{-J\theta})e^{-J\theta k}$. Furthermore $G(e^{J\theta})$ and $G(e^{-J\theta})$ are easily shown to be complex conjugates, thus

$$\begin{aligned} y_+(k) &= |G(e^{J\theta})|e^{\arg(G(e^{J\theta}))}e^{J\theta k} \\ y_-(k) &= |G(e^{J\theta})|e^{-\arg(G(e^{J\theta}))}e^{-J\theta k} \end{aligned} \tag{2.37}$$

Putting it all together, iff $e^{\mp J\theta}$ are not eigenvalues of A, there exists a unique initial state (inessential to express for our purposes) such that

$$\begin{aligned} y(k) &= \frac{y_+(k) - y_-(k)}{2J} \\ &= \frac{|G(e^{J\theta})|e^{\arg(G(e^{J\theta}))}e^{J\theta k} - |G(e^{J\theta})|e^{-\arg(G(e^{J\theta}))}e^{-J\theta k}}{2J} \\ &= |G(e^{J\theta})|\frac{e^{J(\theta k + \arg(G(e^{J\theta})))} - e^{-J(\theta k + \arg(G(e^{J\theta})))}}{2J} \\ &= |G(e^{J\theta})| \sin(\theta k + \arg(G(e^{J\theta}))) \end{aligned} \tag{2.38}$$

Note, incidentally, that the system's stability properties never came into play in this discussion.

Definition 2.12. The complex function $G(e^{J\theta})$ of the real variable $\theta \in [0, \pi]$, is the *frequency response* of the system with transfer function $G(z)$.

It is easy to see that $G(e^{J\theta})$ is 2π-periodic, and $G(e^{J(2\pi-\theta)})$ is the complex conjugate of $G(e^{J\theta})$. Thus, $G(e^{J\theta})$ is completely determined by knowledge of it for $\theta \in [0, \pi]$.

2.4.2 Interpretation and use

The reasoning path of the previous section is summarised in the so-called *fundamental frequency response theorem* below.

---

[3] Since $\sin((2h\pi + \theta)k) = \sin(\theta k)$ and $\sin((2h\pi - \theta)k) = -\sin(\theta k)$ for any integer h, all signals of interest can be represented with the indicated range of θ.

Theorem 2.1. *Given a SISO LTI discrete-time dynamic system with transfer function $G(z)$ subject for $k \geq 0$ to a sinusoidal input $u(k) = U \sin(\theta k), \theta \in [0, \pi]$,*

1. *if $e^{\mp J\theta}$ are not eigenvalues of A, then there exists a unique initial state such that the produced output is*

$$y(k) = U|G(e^{J\theta})| \sin(\theta k + \arg(G(e^{J\theta}))), \qquad k \geq 0 \tag{2.39}$$

2. *if in addition the system is asymptotically stable, then for any initial state*

$$y(k) \to U|G(e^{J\theta})| \sin(\theta k + \arg(G(e^{J\theta}))) \tag{2.40}$$

for $k \to \infty$

Proof (sketch). Proposition 1 was already (synthetically) proven by construction, see (2.33)–(2.38). As for proposition 2, recall that the free motion of an asymptotically stable system converges to zero in norm for $k \to \infty$. □

Since we are here interested in control systems, where asymptotic stability is always to be ensured, we can take as 'response' of the system to a sinusoidal signal the asymptotic one, when the initial state effects have vanished. In this respect, the frequency response magnitude and argument indicate how a sinusoidal component of an input signal appears on the output, quantifying the undergone amplification (or attenuation) and phase shift. That is why the frequency response is said to qualify a system 'in the frequency domain', showing for example – anticipating the content of Chapter 4 – how capable it is of rejecting 'slowly' or 'rapidly' variable disturbances, how fast a reference output can vary for the actual one to follow it accurately enough, and so forth. Also, observe that under our hypotheses, an LTI system will respond to a $\mathcal{Z}$-transformable input with certain frequency components, by producing an output with the same components, just amplified and phase-shifted. This is not true for other types of systems.

Example 2.1. Consider the LTI dynamic system with transfer function $G(z) = 0.4/(z - 0.6)$, and determine the frequency range $\Theta \subseteq [0, \pi]$ such that an input signal $u(k) = U \sin(\theta k), \theta \in \Theta$, asymptotically produces an output $y(k)$ of amplitude not greater than $\alpha U, \alpha < 1$.

Solution. The considered system is asymptotically stable and – as a consequence – cannot have the unity-magnitude complex numbers $e^{\mp J\theta}$ as eigenvalues. Thus, for any initial state, $y(k)$ will asymptotically converge to a sinusoid. The amplitude of that sinusoid, in force of Theorem 2.1, will be $U|G(e^{J\theta})|$, which means that Θ is the set $\{\theta : 0 \leq \theta \leq \pi, |G(e^{J\theta})| < \alpha\}$. Bringing in the particular $G(z)$ we have

$$\left| \frac{0.4}{e^{J\theta} - 0.6} \right| < \alpha \tag{2.41}$$

and thus, omitting trivial computations,

$$\frac{2}{17 - 15 \cos \theta} < \alpha, \qquad 0 \leq \theta \leq \pi \tag{2.42}$$

which provides

$$\arccos\left(\frac{17}{15} - \frac{2}{15\alpha}\right) \leq \theta \leq \pi \tag{2.43}$$

For example, $\alpha = 0.5$ gives approximately $0.522 \leq \theta \leq \pi$. Needless to say, however, with even a slightly more complex $G(z)$ a numerical solution would be in order. $\qquad\square$

2.5 Time domain responses

Beside the frequency domain characterisation, a dynamic system can also be qualified based on the 'shape' of its response to some typical signals in the time domain, starting from zero initial state. The two signals most frequently used for such a purpose are the (discrete) *impulse* and *step* ones, respectively, defined as

$$\text{imp}(k) = \begin{cases} 1 & k = 0 \\ 0 & k \neq 0 \end{cases} \qquad \text{step}(k) = \begin{cases} 1 & k \geq 0 \\ 0 & k < 0 \end{cases} \tag{2.44}$$

The reasons for the importance of signals (2.44) are numerous. In the first place, their $\mathcal{Z}$ transforms have two notable expressions, as

$$\mathcal{Z}[\text{imp}(k)] = \sum_{k=0}^{\infty} \text{imp}(k)z^{-k} = 1 + 0 + 0\ldots \quad = 1$$

$$\mathcal{Z}[\text{step}(k)] = \sum_{k=0}^{\infty} \text{step}(k)z^{-k} = 1 + z^{-1} + z^{-2}\ldots = \frac{z}{z-1} \tag{2.45}$$

where strictly speaking the latter holds only for $|z| > 1$, but deepening the discussion to such technical issues would stray from the scope of this book. As a consequence, the impulse and the step responses have simple relationships with the system's transfer function, or in other words, assigning the impulse or step response of a system is a straightforward and intuitive way to assign its transfer function. Second, any signal can be viewed as a sum of infinite impulses, i.e.,

$$v(k) = \sum_{i=0}^{\infty} v(i)\,\text{imp}(k-i), \qquad \forall v(k),\, k \geq 0 \tag{2.46}$$

or equivalently of infinite steps, as

$$v(k) = \sum_{i=0}^{\infty} (v(i) - v(i-1))\,\text{step}(k-i), \qquad \forall v(k),\, k \geq 0 \tag{2.47}$$

where $v(-1) = 0$ is assumed; hence, which is some sense is just another viewpoint on the matter, knowing the impulse (or step) response of a system means knowing its – induced – response to any signal. Finally, accepting for a moment more suggestive than rigorous a terminology, the impulse and the step are the extremisations of a 'short-' or a 'long-lasting' signal respectively, so that a system capable of responding satisfactorily to both – whatever is meant for that, also in the light of the following Chapter 4 – is expected to provide a good behaviour in the face of most signals of possible interest. Let us now start the analysis from the impulse response, and immediately notice – see (2.45) – that its $\mathcal{Z}$ transform is the system's transfer function itself. This leads us to introduce a useful partition of dynamic systems into finite impulse response (FIR) and infinite impulse response (IIR) ones.

2.5.1   Impulse response of FIR systems

Consider an LTI SISO system of order n without hidden parts – as it is invariantly to be assumed when a system is specified directly as a transfer function – and suppose that its transfer function $G(z)$ has all the poles in the origin, which by the way implies asymptotic stability, i.e.,

$$G(z) = \frac{G_N(z)}{z^n} = \frac{1}{z^n} \sum_{i=0}^{n} b_i z^{n-i} \tag{2.48}$$

with $G_N(0) \neq 0$. Since (2.48) can be immediately rewritten as

$$G(z) = \sum_{i=0}^{n} b_i z^{-i} \tag{2.49}$$

its impulse response is directly provided by the numerator coefficients, i.e., starting from $k = 0$, it is the sequence $b_0, b_1, \ldots, b_n, 0, 0, \ldots$, and so on. That is, the impulse response has a finite duration given by n and then settles to zero, whence the name 'FIR'.

2.5.2   Impulse response of IIR systems

Consider an LTI SISO system of order n without hidden parts, and suppose that all its eigenvalues – or in this case equivalently, the poles of its transfer function $G(z)$ – are real and distinct. This makes the following treatise not general, but sufficient for our purposes. Denoting by p_i the generic pole of $G(z)$, one can immediately write

$$G(z) = r_0 + \sum_{i=1}^{n} \frac{r_i}{z - p_i} \tag{2.50}$$

where the r_i real numbers are the poles' residuals, and $r_0 \neq 0$ iff the relative degree of $G(z)$ is zero. As such, given the system's linearity, we can restrict our study to the elementary case

$$G_i(z) = \frac{r_i}{z - p_i} \tag{2.51}$$

Since it can be shown by applying the $\mathcal{Z}$ transform definition (an exercise left to the reader) that

$$\mathcal{Z}\left[r p^k\right] = \frac{rz}{z - p} \tag{2.52}$$

then the impulse response of (2.51) is immediately expressed as $y_i(k) = r_i p_i^{k-1}$ or, more precisely,

$$y_i(k) = \begin{cases} 0 & k = 0 \\ r_i p_i^{k-1} & k = 1, 2, \ldots \end{cases} \tag{2.53}$$

Considering that the impulse response of $G_0(z) = r_0$ is clearly $r_0 \, \text{imp}(k)$, the overall impulse response of $G(z)$ is

$$y_i(k) = \begin{cases} r_0 & k = 0 \\ \displaystyle\sum_{i=1}^{n} r_i p_i^{k-1} & k = 1, 2, \ldots \end{cases} \tag{2.54}$$

that is, the sum of n exponential terms, each one's qualitative behaviour depending on the corresponding p_i, which in our restriction to real poles means

- convergent to zero if $|p_i| < 1$, monotonically if $p_i > 0$ and with alternate signs if $p_i < 0$,
- constant if $p_i = 1$,
- indefinitely oscillating with constant magnitude and alternate signs if $p_i = -1$,
- diverging if $|p_i| > 1$, monotonically if $p_i > 0$ and with alternate signs if $p_i < 0$.

Now, concentrate on asymptotically stable systems and suppose that one of the (real) p_i has significantly larger a magnitude than all of the others.[4] If this is the case, the exponential terms originated by the other poles will vanish, as k increases, much more rapidly than that of p_i. The pole p_i is then said to be the *dominant pole*, meaning that 'from some k on' the response of the entire $G(z)$ becomes indistinguishable from that of the sole $r_i/(z - p_i)$.

In this case, the impulse response has an infinite duration – whence the name 'IIR' – and settles to zero exponentially (note that if a dominant pole is present, then it is quite easy on its basis to figure out the settling time scale). Referring to this case, and indicating with $\bar{p}$ the dominant pole and with $\bar{r}$ its residual, one can thus define an α-*settling time* as the number of steps required for the (unit) impulse response magnitude to fall – and remain – below α, $\alpha > 0$. Such a time k_α, of course measured in steps, is then obtained by solving

$$\left| \bar{r} \, \bar{p}^{k_\alpha - 1} \right| = \alpha \tag{2.55}$$

with respect to k_α, thus yielding

$$k_\alpha = 1 + \frac{\log(\alpha / |\bar{r}|)}{\log |\bar{p}|} \tag{2.56}$$

where, if a physical interpretation is required, the result of (2.56) has to be rounded up to the next integer.

---

[4] For the sake of correctness we should also suppose that there is no zero in the vicinity of that pole, but for our purposes we can safely neglect this fact, at least for the moment.

2.5.3   Step response of FIR and IIR systems

From (2.44), we can observe that

$$\text{step}(k) = \sum_{j=0}^{k} \text{imp}(j) \tag{2.57}$$

or equivalently

$$\text{step}(k) = \text{step}(k-1) + \text{imp}(k) \tag{2.58}$$

Thus, indicating with $S(z)$ and $I(z)$ the $\mathcal{Z}$ transforms of the step and the impulse, respectively, in transfer function terms one obtains

$$\frac{S(z)}{I(z)} = \frac{z}{z-1} \tag{2.59}$$

The transfer function just written is that of the *discrete integrator* – a concept on which we shall return later on. In this sense, we can say that the step response of a system is just the integral of its impulse response.

A FIR system like (2.48) will therefore exhibit as unit step response the sequence b_0, $b_0 + b_1$, ..., $b_0 + b_1 + \cdots + b_n$, $b_0 + b_1 + \cdots + b_n$, and so on, still 'exhausting' in n steps but this time converging to the final value $G(1)$ instead of zero.

An asymptotically stable IIR system (we neglect other cases here for brevity) will conversely still have a step response composed of exponential terms, converging to $G(1)$, and possibly dominated by some pole. An α-settling time can still be defined, in the same manner used to obtain (2.56), by just considering the distance of the response from $G(1)$ instead of zero. Incidentally, the step response of an asymptotically stable system (IIR or FIR) converges for $k \rightarrow \infty$ to $G(1)$, which is why $G(1)$ is called the system's *gain*.

2.6   Concluding remarks

The reader now possesses the notion of dynamic system, essentially limited to the discrete-time LTI case, and the basic concepts to describe and analyse such a system. Most important, it should be clear (albeit preliminarily) that the notion of state is a viable way to mathematically characterise the idea of 'different reactions to the same stimulus'. Chapter 3 applies the ideas introduced here to create models of computing system components in a way that is quite different from what is typically meant by 'model' in the computer science domain, but – as shown in the subsequent chapters – is very well suited for their design along the approach followed in this book.

2.7   Problems

Problem 2.1. *Given the system with input u and output y described in state space form by*

$$A = \begin{bmatrix} 1.2 & 1.4 \\ -0.7 & -0.9 \end{bmatrix}, \quad b = \begin{bmatrix} 1 \\ 2 \end{bmatrix}, \quad c = \begin{bmatrix} 0 & 1 \end{bmatrix}, \quad d = 0$$

1. *determine its stability properties,*
2. *compute its transfer function G(z) and determine if hidden parts exist,*
3. *compute the first four values (k = 0, 1, 2, 3) of its response to the input u(k) =*
   2 step (k) + imp (k − 1), having as initial condition x(0) = [2 1]′.

Problem 2.2. *Given the system with input u and output y described in state space form by*

$$A = \begin{bmatrix} 0.2 & 0 \\ 0 & 0.2 \end{bmatrix}, \quad b = \begin{bmatrix} 1 \\ 1 \end{bmatrix}, \quad c = \begin{bmatrix} 3 & 2 \end{bmatrix}, \quad d = 0$$

compute the transfer function G(z) = Y(z)/U(z), determine if hidden parts are present, and interpret the result. Hint: it can be useful to transform the system into a block diagram by evidencing the individual variables (i.e., without vector signals).

Problem 2.3. *Same as Problem 2.2 but with*

$$A = \begin{bmatrix} -0.1 & 0 \\ 0 & 0.5 \end{bmatrix}, \quad b = \begin{bmatrix} 10 \\ 0.1 \end{bmatrix}, \quad c = \begin{bmatrix} 0 & 2 \end{bmatrix}, \quad d = 0$$

Problem 2.4. *Given the system with transfer function*

$$G(z) = \frac{z - 0.3}{(z - 1)(z - 0.5)}$$

express the magnitude of its frequency response as a function of the angular frequency θ.

Problem 2.5. *Given the FIR system with transfer function*

$$G(z) = \frac{(z - 0.1)(z - 0.2)(z - 0.3)}{z^4}$$

compute its response to a unit step input.

Problem 2.6. *Given the asymptotically stable IIR system with transfer function*

$$G(z) = \frac{0.5}{z + 0.6}$$

subject to the input u(k) = 3 step (k), determine how many steps it takes for its output y(k) to reach 95% of its final value.

Chapter 3

Modelling for computing systems

This chapter, based on the concept of dynamic system as provided in Chapter 2, starts giving the considerations expressed in Section 1.2 a mathematical sense.

Anticipating the content of Chapter 4, a *control system* is composed of a *controlled system*, or *plant*, and a *controller*. Most often the latter senses some quantities from the former, and decides what actions to take based on said measurements, and some specification of the desired behaviour. Deferring the treatise of this matter to the mentioned Chapter 4, we can, however, already schematise the situation as shown in Figure 3.1.

The standard control design procedure is to build a model for $\mathcal{P}$ in the form of a dynamic system, then obtain a model in the same form for $\mathcal{C}$ and finally turn the latter into control algorithms.

The usefulness of modelling in a view to control a system is testified by a huge literature, both in general [34] and in the particular domain addressed herein [7,35]. Here we would like to point out some peculiarities that can be observed when the system to be controlled is a computer as seen by an operating system, instead of a 'plant' in the common sense of the term.

In virtually any domain but computing systems, $\mathcal{P}$ and $\mathcal{C}$ are heterogeneous objects with well-defined boundaries: $\mathcal{P}$ can be a robot, a chemical reactor or whatever, while $\mathcal{C}$ is almost invariantly some software running on one or more CPUs, connected to $\mathcal{P}$ via convenient analogue/digital/analogue interfaces. As such, when addressing such 'classical' control-related problems, $\mathcal{P}$ obeys to physics in the most natural sense of the term, as its behaviour is ruled by equations that come from principles such as the conservation of mass and energy, and cannot be changed. The physics of $\mathcal{C}$, on the other hand, is actually 'created in the computer', and in principle has no universal law to obey, as highlighted – interestingly enough – in a famous quote by Linus Torvalds [36].

> 'I'm personally convinced that computer science has a lot in common with physics. Both are about how the world works at a rather fundamental level. The difference, of course, is that while in physics you're supposed to figure out how the world is made up, in computer science you create the world. Within the confines of the computer, you're the creator. You get to ultimately control everything that happens. If you're good enough, you can be God. On a small scale.'

Figure 3.1   Synthetic representation of a control system: $\mathcal{P}$ is the plant, $\mathcal{C}$ the controller

No doubt the quote is fascinating. However, from the control engineer's standpoint, it contains a little but very tricky flaw. It is not completely true that within a computer one 'creates the world'. One creates *most* of the world, but at the lowest level of this world there does exist some physics in the strict sense of the term. Therefore, we could say that trying to govern a computer system by directly figuring out an algorithm to do that, instead of starting from a model of it as a dynamic system, means attempting to 'create all the physics' from scratch, not accounting for the one that already exists, and *a priori* with no idea of the physical principles so created. We have already anticipated this idea in the book introduction. Let us now reason on it a bit further.

3.1   The quest for a computer physics

To establish some useful parallelisms, consider a control problem not in the computer domain, for example that of regulating the temperature in a room. At first, the engineer identifies the relevant phenomena: to keep the discussion simple, since we do not really need to solve this problem, let us limit the set of phenomena to the generation of thermal power in a heater, the thermal exchanges between heater, air, walls and the outside, and the storage of thermal energy in the walls and the contained air.

Since storage has been brought in, the resulting model will be dynamic—recall Section 2.1. Also, the nature of the storage dictates two important things:

- the type of dynamic equations to write, that is, energy balance ones,
- and that of the state variables, that simplifying for convenience can be one temperature for the air and one for the walls, assumed uniform (recall that we do not want to be realistic, just to understand the problem structure and the model creation process).

Then, the engineer has to figure out what to measure, and how to act on the system. In this simple case it is quite intuitive that the measured quantity needs to be the air temperature, while the means of influencing the system is by commanding the heater power.

As can be seen, in such classical problems, one has to specify the inputs, outputs and states for the object to describe, at the desired level of modelling detail, i.e., having decided which phenomena are relevant for the problem. Given that, the model equations come either from some conservation principle, or from some sufficiently established empirical correlation. Note that in so doing we are sticking to *first-principle*[1] models, leaving out (for the moment) those identified from measured data. The basic reason for doing so is that design problems inherently involve objects that do not yet exist.

In any case, we have to notice that in problems of practically any domain but computing systems, the mentioned principles are (dynamic) balances of mass, energy, momentum and so on, while empirical correlations are used, e.g., to relate flow rates to pressure drops, heat rates to temperature differences, forces to positions and/or velocities, and so forth. In other words, when tackling classical problems such as process or motion control ones, the physics is out there to use.

Better still, in classical contexts, physical quantities are rigorously defined that allow to summarise, in a limited number of 'macroscopic' equations, phenomena that in fact occur at a 'microscopic' scale. For example, sticking to the temperature control case, thermal phenomena depend on (microscopic) molecular motion, but temperature is a viable macroscopic entity to ground energy conservation upon.

Computing systems are in this respect radically different. Also in that domain, everything ultimately depends on extremely fine-grained facts, down to the detailed behaviour of a single assembler instruction, or even the electronic transients in a gate. However, thinking of molecular motion as the analogous of such microscopic facts, no macroscopic entities analogous to temperature have yet been defined.

To date, the problem of establishing a first-principle physics in computers stands thus open, and it is not the purpose of this book to solve it. Nonetheless, two intertwined considerations can be made. First, the discussion just carried out gives a somehow new flavour to the quote by Linus Torvalds above: it is good that 'within the confines the computer' one can create physics, provided that care is taken not to create one that is too difficult to model as dynamic systems. Second, and most important, in many cases it is in fact possible to identify within the same confines some 'first-principle' phenomena, and in such cases it is highly advised that the modelling activity stops at their level: the rest is control.

An instructive example is here too that of task scheduling already used in Section 2.1.1. No matter how the scheduler operates (the scheduler is control, not plant) a task receives the CPU, and releases it after the allotted time plus some disturbance[2] accounting for voluntary yields, interrupt delays, resource contention, or whatever. Extending (2.3), this is described by the dynamic model

$$T_{\text{CPU}}(k) = T_{\text{CPU}}(k-1) + b(k-1) + \delta b(k-1) \tag{3.1}$$

where δb is the mentioned disturbance.

In Chapter 5 it will be shown how so simple a model can be used to build a complete 'control-theoretical' scheduler. For the purpose of this section, however, the example serves to further evidence the radical novelty of the proposed approach with respect to common practices in the computer science domain. In fact, given that traditionally no first principles are brought into play, the scheduler actions – or policies – are typically defined by rules such as 'give the CPU to the task with the earliest deadline'. Such a policy, called the Earliest Deadline First (EDF) one, can

---

[1] First-principle models is another name for models based on (dynamic) conservation equations.

[2] The word 'disturbance' has in the control theory a specific meaning, see Chapter 4.

be proven to achieve some desired property, but only when the system is in some nominal conditions: specifically, EDF scheduling guarantees that there will be no deadline misses if the task pool is schedulable, i.e., if the total CPU need does not exceed the maximum available. If this is not true, or if any other unforeseen condition is encountered, no guarantees can be given.

More in general, in the computer domain, there is in the literature hardly any distinction among the behaviour of the system in the absence of control actions, the desired behaviour of the same system, and the way actions are to be determined based on the above two sets. In other words, in operating system design, the fundamental rules of control-oriented modelling are hardly ever (if ever) enforced.

If a control layer is then to be added on top of a system already designed this way – which is what we meant in Section 1.2 for 'already functional system', one has to face the problem of modelling the phenomenon of interest *plus all the 'created physics' around it*. In the case of a computer program, one could in principle model all the memory accesses done by the code and by all the other running tasks, their latencies and cache occupation. However, such an approach would result in adding unnecessary physics to the model, and would make a control-related use of it very impractical.

This should therefore further convince that one has in the first place to evidence the core phenomena of interest, i.e., those parts of the system behaviour that are really ruled by physical laws, and cannot be altered. Most often, modelling those phenomenon is enough to describe the system in a view to suitably control it.

In several cases, in addition, the so-obtained models will be not only very simple, see (3.1) above, but natively (almost) uncertainty-free,[3] making control design and assessment very straightforward. In other cases, there may be relevant uncertainty, or – in other words – some aspects of the computing system behaviour will not admit a clear physical interpretation. In such cases, treated later on in the book to a depth compatible with its scope, the best way to deal with the problem is to figure out some convenient 'grey box'[4] description based on qualitative considerations on input-output relationships. As will be shown, this approach generally leads to more complex but still tractable models: control design may be correspondingly harder, but still there will be the possibility of a rigorous assessment.

In Section 3.3, some examples are shown of how the proposed approach leads to dynamic models of computing system components that can successfully serve the evidenced needs, while being very simple and thus suitable for simulation, analysis and control result assessment.

3.2   Modelling and simulation

Before going into the details of the proposed modelling examples, some words are worth spending on what is meant by *simulation* in this book.

---

[3] In the control theory, the presence of disturbances does *not* imply model uncertainty, see again Chapter 4.
[4] The term 'grey box' will be explained in Chapter 8, see page 129.

In classical control domains – think about a physical phenomenon – simulation is the numerical integration of the differential (or difference) equations of the model under a prescribed *scenario*, i.e., an initial condition, some inputs (generally varying over time) and a simulation horizon, or duration. The result of the simulation is the trajectory with respect to time of the output (and of the states) of the dynamical system. There is a huge literature on continuous time simulation (see, e.g., Reference 37). However, since almost the totality of the models presented in this book are in the discrete-time domain, those results are not of interest here, and the numerical integration directly comes from the model itself, see some of the examples in Section 4.7.

Conversely, in the computing systems community, simulation is not related to the concept of modelling as intended here. Rather, simulation is generally viewed as connected to the idea of Instruction Set Architecture (ISA) of a specific hardware, and is usually denoted as Instruction Set Simulator (ISS). In fact, the ISS mimics the behaviour of a mainframe or microprocessor by 'reading' instructions and maintaining internal variables which represent the processor's registers.

Sticking to the temperature control example presented in the previous section, the ISS is closer to the simulator of molecular motion, rather than of temperature as conversely suggested in this section, and as a consequence is not suited for control purposes. Moreover, having a mathematical model allows the designer to study additional properties (both static and dynamical) of the system, without bringing simulation into play, as presented in Chapter 2. In synthesis, and to repeat once again for maximum clarity, here 'model' substantially means 'dynamic system', and 'simulation' is the computation of dynamic systems' motions.

3.3 Examples

3.3.1 Core allocation

Suppose that we want to control the useful work done by an application by assigning to it more or less CPU cores. Assume that a measurement of said work is available (e.g., if the application were a video encoder, the system could maintain a counter of the processed frames per second) and primitives are provided by the lower levels of the operating systems to assign the application the desired number of cores.

If a fine-grained (microscopic) model is sought, it must be considered for example that when a newly assigned core requests some data, these will not be available in its cache: this will then result in the necessity of loading those data from memory, thus *de facto* in additional work for that core, which from the application point of view is essentially an overhead. The consequence is that the response of the useful work done to the number of cores, will exhibit an initial undershoot, and then settle to higher a value than in the beginning, since when the initial haul of cache misses has exhausted, the new core will only do useful work. A similar phenomenon may occur when a core is subtracted, as in that case the others will need to take care of its data, but this may not be true if the subtracted core was in fact carrying no load, and in any case the involved dynamics will be potentially different. Also, both situations will most likely call for nonlinear models.

As such, the model seems to involve inverse response (when a new core is assigned, the useful work initially decreases and only later on increases) and possibly asymmetries between the assignment and subtraction operations. From a control-theoretical viewpoint, not a success at all.

However, if one notices that the time scale of the dynamics just described is invariantly much faster than that of the application, and in any case than the scale on which it is sensible to measure the useful work done, one can simply disregard the cache-related phenomena by treating them as instantaneous. If this is done, the model is significantly simpler, deliberately neglecting fine-grained phenomena with a sound justification for that, yet sufficient for the intended control purpose.

3.3.2 *Producer and consumer*

The producer-consumer problem, also known as the bounded-buffer problem, is a classical one in computer science. It refers to two entities – a producer and a consumer – that share a common buffer, possibly limited in size. The producer can only add elements to the buffer, while the consumer can only remove these elements, if present.

To model the situation, define a state variable x to represent the number of elements that the buffer contains at time k. Let then $p(k)$ be the amount of objects that the producer adds to the buffer between time $k - 1$ and time k, and let $c(k)$ be the amount of entities consumed within the same time span. A simple model is thus created as

$$\begin{cases} x(k) = x(k - 1) + p(k - 1) - c(k - 1) \\ y(k) = x(k) \end{cases} \qquad (3.2)$$

The inputs of this system are $p(k)$ and $c(k)$, while the output is the measured quantity $x(k)$, or the buffer level. This example clearly evidences the shift between 'modelling' in a general sense, and *equation-based* modelling. Once one gets accustomed to the use of equations, it is immediate to realise that the inputs of the system are both the amount of elements produced and the amount of requests consumed. Note that since the amount of consumed requests is a product of the system, a mistake easily committed if a systemic view is not taken, would be using that entity as the output of the system, and the amount of produced requests as the input. One may object that (3.2) can give rise to non physical situations, like a negative buffer occupation. Representing such phenomena would, however, complicate the model and, above all, the synthesis of its control. As will emerge in the following, it is sometimes convenient to allow the model of the uncontrolled system to exhibit non physical behaviours and then to prevent said behaviours by imposing suitable constraints in the control.

Indeed, (3.2) represents the easiest model that one can imagine for the producer-consumer problem, and with the proposed-approach, it is sufficient for control purposes.

3.3.3 Transmission over wireless sensor networks

Suppose to create a network, with a set of different nodes, each one reading information from a sensor, and transmitting the data over a wireless link to a central processing node. An important problem is to limit the amount of power consumed by each sensor node, as these are frequently battery powered. It is possible to write a model for the power consumption of each specific node, supposing that three components contribute to it.

A first component is the idle power, or to better say, the fact that the node consumes power even if it is not performing any action. This idle power can be identified with P_i, and most often can be considered constant. The second component is the reading power, i.e., the power that is consumed while reading the sensor data. This power can be identified with P_s, and is here considered constant while the sensor is in the reading state. A third component is the transmission power, that depends on the amount of to be are transmitted over the network, and also exhibits some connection startup offset. In this respect, define as P_t the power consumed to transmit one bit.

Suppose that the network has m nodes; the power consumed by the ith node in the time span between $k - 1$ and k is defined as $P_i(k)$, and is equal to

$$P_i(k) = \sigma_{s,i}(k - 1)\Delta_t P_s + \beta_t(k - 1)P_t + \Delta_t P_i \tag{3.3}$$

where Δ_t represents the amount of time between the instant $k - 1$ and k, the input variable $\sigma_{s,i}(k - 1)$ models the percentage of time that was spent in sensing in the same time span, while $\beta_t(k - 1)$ stands for the number of bits that are transmitted in the interval, accounting also for the data needed to setup a connection if required. The output variable is the consumed power.

3.3.4 Communication bandwidth partitioning

Bandwidth partitioning (or allocation) is the ability to specify how much of an available data connection is used by a set of programs. To exemplify, suppose that a pool of applications running on a single machine are requesting to send and receive data over the network. If this situation is not governed somehow, some of the applications could load the communication link so that other ones would experience failures and stalls. A typical case is provided by peer to peer clients, that if not properly limited, can saturate the link and thus slow down connectivity for all other applications and users.

Imagine that an operating system mechanism is available to decide exactly how much bandwidth is to be allocated to any specific application. Then, it is possible to describe the situation with the model

$$\begin{cases} \mu_i(k) = \mu_i(k - 1) + \psi_i(k - 1) + \delta\psi_i(k - 1) \\ \rho_i(k) = \rho_i(k - 1) + \eta_i(k - 1) + \delta\eta_i(k - 1) \end{cases} \tag{3.4}$$

where $\mu_i(k)$ is the total amount of data sent by the ith application from its starting time to time k, and $\psi_i(k)$ is the amount of data that the ith application is allowed to transmit in the interval between time k and time $k + 1$. Simultaneously, $\rho_i(k)$ is the amount of data received by the ith application over the link, and $\eta_i(k)$ is the amount of data that the ith application is allowed to receive in the time span from k to $k + 1$.

Intuitively, it is not possible to impose the amount of data that the application is allowed to send and receive. In fact, one can say that an application is allowed to transmit a certain amount of data, but the same application can ignore this value and avoid sending data at all, or use a different amount of bandwidth. Therefore, the disturbances $\delta\psi_i(k)$ and $\delta\eta_i(k)$ account respectively for any difference between the actual amount of sent data and the prescribed one, and for the actual amount of received data and the chosen one. Notice that some of the currently used applications are said to be 'auto-regulating' in the sense that they can limit the amount of requests sent through the link, typically based on hard bounds. From the modelling point of view, this is, however, nothing else than a possible behaviour of the application, thus irrelevant once disturbances are introduced as part of the model.

Hence, also bandwidth allocation shows its nature of a control problem. Indeed, the model presented above is totally invariant with respect to the particular desires, and thus to the resulting strategies used to allocate the bandwidth to each process. This is, in general, a different perspective with respect to what is usually done in the literature, as here we are completely separating the 'physical entity' to be controlled from the control policy. In fact, for example, a controller built on (3.4) would handle both auto-regulating and non-auto-regulating applications, and enforce bandwidth usage conditions at the system level, which apparently no single application can do.

To help the reader perceive the potential of the proposed approach, we push the treatise of this example a bit further, completing the core equations (3.4) so as to obtain a complete model for a specific case, and then turning that model into a simulation program, based on which some additional conceptual considerations will be carried out.

To this end, let N_a be the number of applications requiring the communication channel. For simplicity we assume N_a constant: extending the model would not be a problem but it is not advisable for the purpose of this chapter.

Figure 3.2 shows the simulation results of the upload bandwidth (the percentage of which is denoted by $b_{\%,i}$). The simulation is performed using model (3.4), where $N_a = 3$, and using a heuristic bandwidth allocation policy (which decides the values of ψ_i). Apparently, the policy achieves to keep the allocated bandwidth constant (see the top graph) for each application. However, sometimes it happens that an application does not manage to send all the data to be transmitted (see the graph in the middle), while the others are idle (see bottom graph), therefore wasting possible transmission time. As can be easily understood, this is not an optimal usage of the available bandwidth, and a more efficient solution can be found if a system-level viewpoint is taken, which in turn requires a control-theoretical approach. The simulation of the download bandwidth is analogous, and is left to the reader as an exercise. To accomplish said task, the reader can take as a reference the code used for the simulation that produced Figure 3.2, available in Appendix A.

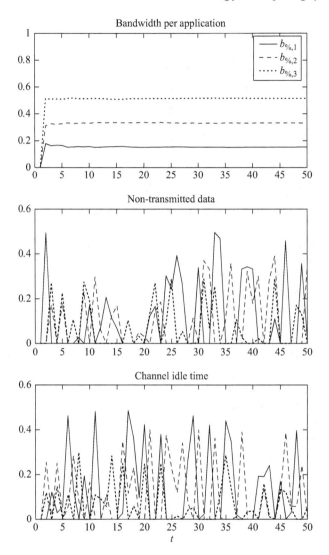

Figure 3.2   Simulation result of a bandwidth allocation policy

3.4   Concluding remarks

In this chapter, some quite simple but fundamental concepts were presented. In particular, three of them are in the authors' opinion very relevant in the context of the book.

First, when the aim is control, modelling a computing system component should only capture the main dynamics of the phenomena of interest, and not low-level details of their behaviour. This leads, in general, to simple models. To obtain such models, only the 'physical' part of the phenomenon to be controlled is to be taken into account; the rest is control.

Second, and connected to the last statement above, said models must refrain – to the maximum possible extent – from attempting to represent any policy already installed to control the behaviour of the mentioned phenomena. In other words, the models are not 'functional' themselves, but need something else that accounts for the desires on the system behaviour, and possibly for disturbances.

Finally, working with dynamic models is quite useful, as it allows engineers to perform simulations (in the sense clarified herein). The advantage is twofold. In the modelling phase, it is possible to better understand the dynamic behaviour and properties of the phenomenon of interest. In the control design phase, one can validate the controller. The use of simulation is of crucial importance in classical control domains, as it avoids to perform expensive and possibly dangerous experiments on real plants. This holds true also in the computing system domain. Dynamic simulations are generally faster than experiments on operating systems components and also than using ISSs, and do not require intrusive interventions on the addressed system to even obtain preliminary results. Furthermore, as will be shown in the rest of the book, simulation results are quite close to what is obtained with experiments.

The chapter presented some examples coming from the computing systems domain, showing the effectiveness of the modelling approach, also thanks to a simulation example. In the next chapter, a minimal treatise of the necessary discrete-time control theory is given, opening the possibility to design, starting from the presented models, control-theoretical components that can prescribe a desired behaviour to the phenomena of interest.

Chapter 4

A byte of basic control theory

This chapter provides knowledge of the basic control-related concepts required in the following. Needless to say, the scope and structure of this chapter reflect the same considerations reported at the outset of Chapter 2.

Given a dynamic system, one may want its output to evolve over time in a certain manner. Most frequently this means desiring that a prescribed *trajectory* be followed, or that the system motion minimise some *cost function* depending on output and/or state and possibly input, or any combination thereof, although here we shall restrict the scope to cases in which a reference output trajectory needs following.

To achieve the desired goal, the system to be controlled must be conveniently coupled to some other system, devoted to suitably determining its input. The former system is termed the *controlled system* or – for traditional reasons – the *plant*, the latter the *controller*, and the compound of the two the *control system*. The most typical control problem is to determine the controller given the controlled system and the specifications, which we now come to examine.

4.1 Specifications

Except for some particular cases that will be discussed specifically, we shall conduct our treatise in the LTI (and in general SISO) context. The controlled system is thus in the form (2.7) – or (2.27) – while requirements stem from typical desires expressed in the same terms as the controlled system's physics. For our purposes, said requirements are substantially a combination of the following:

- *Asymptotic stability.* The control system has to be asymptotically stable, thus forget its initial state and 'from some time on' behave in a manner dictated only by the specifications, which is definitely an intuitive desire.
- *Set point tracking.* Assuming there is some prescribed trajectory for the controlled variable, which is represented by a *reference signal* also called the *set point*, then said variable has to follow it with some precision properties, typically further divided into
    - *static precision*, the controlled variable must asymptotically approach the set point if this is kept constant for a sufficiently long period, or at least asymptotically lie or move "close enough" to the set point;
    - *dynamic precision*, when the set point is changed, the controlled variable must regain it (in the sense above) as quickly as possible and without too undesired behaviours, like, e.g., excessive oscillations.

It is worth noticing that some texts use the term 'set point' only when the desired trajectory is constant, which happens when the system is to be kept in a certain condition despite disturbances. If the desired trajectory is conversely time-varying, as, for example, in motion control systems, the term 'reference signal' is sometimes preferred. For our purposes we can, however, ignore this distinction.

- *Disturbance rejection.* Any quantity influencing the system without being manipulable like the control, is called a *disturbance*. The effects of disturbances has to be limited, so that tracking be preserved also in the presence of them – in other words, disturbances have to be *rejected*.

It is worth noticing that the requirements above, except for the stability one, must be intended to apply under 'reasonably expectable' behaviours of the set point and the disturbances. In other words, no matter how well a controller is designed, there surely exists some stimulation (be it a set point or a disturbance, or any combination thereof) that can drive the control system so far from the assumed operating conditions to cause set point tracking and/or disturbance rejection requirements not to be attained. The most intuitive reason for that resides in the unavoidable physical limitations of the controlled objects, but sometimes the control requirements too come into play, e.g., preventing too fast a response if the attempt to achieve it would result in a system too close to instability.[1]

To maintain as light a treatise as possible, some other relevant issues will be addressed in the next chapters, taking, however, a problem-specific attitude since a general discussion on them is not the purpose of this work. Others that are very relevant in different contexts (e.g., the idea of stability degree just mentioned in the footnote) will conversely not be treated at all, since they do not come into play in the problems considered in this book.

4.2 Main control schemes

Denoting by u the control signal, by y the controlled variable and by d a disturbance, and adopting the LTI formalism, the most natural way to describe the plant for the purposes of this book is

$$Y(z) = P(z)U(z) + H(z)D(z) \qquad (4.1)$$

where $P(z)$ and $H(z)$ are convenient transfer functions, and without any significant loss of generality for this work, $H(z)$ – not necessarily $P(z)$ – is supposed asymptotically stable. Also the controller is naturally expressed as a transfer function, $R(z)$ to name it, and a first point to address is how to connect the two.

There are many ways to do so, but for our purposes we can restrict the scope to two basic schemes, called *open-loop* and *closed-loop* (or *feedback*) control, both

---

[1] There is the possibility to quantify the 'stability degree' of a system, i.e.,'how close' it is to the loose asymptotic stability, with concepts like the *gain* or the *phase margin*.

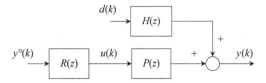

Figure 4.1 Open-loop control scheme

directly related to the typical block diagram structures discussed in Section 2.3.3. In all the schemes considered here, the output of $R(z)$ is the control signal u; the difference is in its input, or in other words, in the information available to the controller.

In open-loop control, the input of $R(z)$ is the set point, denoted from now on by y°. This leads to the scheme of Figure 4.1, and to write

$$Y(z) = P(z)U(z) + H(z)D(z) = P(z)R(z)Y^\circ(z) + H(z)D(z) \tag{4.2}$$

Evidencing the rational nature of the transfer functions we deal with, and using the subscripts N and D to denote their numerator and denominator polynomials, respectively, we thus have

$$Y(z) = \frac{P_N(z)R_N(z)}{P_D(z)R_D(z)}Y^\circ(z) + \frac{H_N(z)}{H_D(z)}D(z) \tag{4.3}$$

Assuming that no individual block has hidden parts, as we must apparently do when expressing a system directly in transfer function form, this means that the eigenvalues of the control system will be the union of those of $P(z)$, $R(z)$ and $H(z)$. However, this is not necessarily true for the poles, as some zero (pole) of $R(z)$ may cancel some pole (zero) of $P(z)$. It is always necessary to check for cancellations, and avoid critical ones, that would lead to non-asymptotically stable hidden parts. Finally, if the real $P(z)$ is different from that assumed in (4.2) and/or d is present, the action exerted by $R(z)$ in response to a certain y° will not be influenced by either fact. Summing up,

- open-loop control cannot produce a control system with stability characteristics different from those of $P(z)$, and in particular one cannot obtain a stable control system from an unstable plant,
- there is the possibility of generating hidden parts,
- and modelling errors, as disturbances, are not counteracted at all.

4.3 Feedback and its power

The simplest closed-loop control scheme is shown in Figure 4.2. Its key feature is that $R(z)$ is aware of the controlled variable's behaviour via that of the *error*, defined as $e(k) = y^\circ(k) - y(k)$. Figure 4.2 is analogous to Figure 2.4, is called *negative unity feedback* scheme, and is by far the most common case of feedback in control systems.

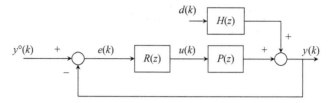

Figure 4.2   Closed-loop control scheme

Balancing along the loop yields

$$Y(z) = H(z)D(z) + P(z)U(z)$$

$$= H(z)D(z) + P(z)R(z)(Y^\circ(z) - Y(z)) \tag{4.4}$$

thus, solving for $Y(z)$,

$$Y(z) = T(z)Y^\circ(z) + H(z)S(z)D(z) \tag{4.5}$$

where

$$T(z) = \frac{L(z)}{1 + L(z)}, \quad S(z) = \frac{1}{1 + L(z)} \tag{4.6}$$

with

$$L(z) = R(z)P(z) \tag{4.7}$$

Functions $L(z)$, $S(z)$ and $T(z)$ are called respectively the *(open) loop transfer function*, the *sensitivity function* and the *complementary sensitivity function* (since $S(z) + T(z) = 1$).

Consider now the frequency responses of $T(z)$ and $S(z)$: for frequencies θ, where $|L(e^{j\theta})|$ is very large, $T(e^{j\theta})$ and $S(e^{j\theta})$ are close to one and zero, respectively. In force of Theorem 2.1, thus, set point components at those frequencies will be transmitted almost unaltered to the controlled variable. In other words, those signal components will be 'well tracked'. On the other hand, thanks to the same theorem, disturbance components at the same frequencies will be almost completely rejected. If one thus possesses a frequency domain characterisation of the set point and the expectable disturbances, functions $T(z)$ and $S(z)$ provide a synthetic and meaningful frequency domain description of the control system, and can be used to quantitatively assess its quality.

Example 4.1. Consider the scheme of Figure 4.2 and let

$$P(z) = \frac{1 + \delta}{z - 0.4}, \quad R(z) = \frac{z - 0.4}{z - 1} \tag{4.8}$$

as in this example we are not concerned with disturbances, thus with $H(z)$.

- Determine the range of δ – interpreted here as a plant gain uncertainty – for which the closed-loop system is asymptotically stable.

- Assuming $\delta = 0$, determine the magnitude $M_{0.1}$ and phase $\phi_{0.1}$ of the closed-loop frequency response from y° to y at the angular frequency $\theta = 0.1$.
- Quantify the variations of M and ϕ when δ goes from -0.5 to $+0.5$.

Solution. We have immediately (the cancellation in 0.4 is not critical)

$$L(z) = \frac{1+\delta}{z-1} \Rightarrow T(z) = \frac{1+\delta}{z+\delta} \tag{4.9}$$

hence the closed-loop system is asymptotically stable for $|\delta| < 1$. As for the frequency response $Y(e^{j\theta})/Y^\circ(e^{j\theta})$, its magnitude and phase are respectively

$$M(\theta,\delta) = \frac{1+\delta}{\sqrt{1+\delta^2+2\delta\cos\theta}}, \quad \phi(\theta,\delta) = -\text{atan}\,\frac{\sin\theta}{\delta+\cos\theta} \tag{4.10}$$

that for $\delta = 0$, $\theta = 0.1$ give respectively $M_{0.1} = 1$ and $\phi_{0.1} = -0.1\,rad$. Finally, studying M and ϕ for $\theta = 0.1$ and $\delta \in [-0.5, 0.5]$ show that M goes from 0.99 to 1.001, and ϕ from -0.19 to 0.06 approximately. Note, in particular, that a $\mp 50\%$ variation of the plant gain $G(1)$ results in a practically negligible variation of M at the considered frequency (where, as can be guessed, the magnitude of L is well greater than one). □

Coming back to the mainstream treatise, and assuming again that no individual block has hidden parts, the control system's eigenvalues are the solutions of $R_N(z)P_N(z) + R_D(z)P_D(z) = 0$, thus not the union of those of $R(z)$ and $P(z)$, while those of $H(z)$ still remain. Also, here too hidden parts may be generated, and critical cancellations must be avoided. Summing up again,

- closed-loop control can produce a control system with stability characteristics different from those of $P(z)$, and in particular one can obtain a stable control system from an unstable plant (and also vice versa if care is not taken),
- there is the possibility of generating hidden parts,
- and both set point tracking and disturbance rejection can be ensured (recall the role of $T(z)$ and $S(z)$ in providing a frequency domain control system's characterisation) also in the presence of 'reasonable' uncertainties on $P(z)$.

Feedback is thus an extremely powerful tool, and the backbone of most control strategies. The following sections put the concept to work, to the extent that is necessary for this book.

4.4   Feedback control synthesis

4.4.1   Synthesis by transfer function assignment (set point tracking)

Given the plant (4.1), let the control desires be expressed in the form of a required response to a given set point signal. This corresponds to requiring that the transfer function from $y°$ to y is a desired one, of course asymptotically stable, denoted in the following by $T°(z)$. As such, based on (4.5) and (4.6), a controller can be found as

$$\frac{R(z)P(z)}{1 + R(z)P(z)} = T°(z) \quad \Rightarrow \quad R(z) = \frac{1}{P(z)} \frac{T°(z)}{1 - T°(z)} \tag{4.11}$$

However, using (4.11) is possible only under two conditions. First, the plant must be asymptotically stable, and also its zeroes must all lie inside the unit circle,[2] as in the opposite case there would be a critical cancellation, and thus the control system would have a non-asymptotically stable hidden part (we have to notice that the ideas here described can be extended to the case of a plant with zeroes outside the circle, basically by having $T°(z)$ contain the same zeroes; however, this matter is not relevant for our purposes). Second, the relative degree of $T°(z)$ cannot be lower than that of $P(z)$, otherwise $R(z)$ would have more zeroes than poles, thus would not be realisable. Let us now see a couple of example problems.

Example 4.2. Given a plant with transfer function $P(z) = 0.5/(z - 0.3)$ and the set point signal $y°(k) = 2 \, \text{step}\,(k)$, we want the control system's output to reach the set point in two steps, 75% of the required motion occurring in the first step. Design the feedback controller.

Solution. The required response, from $k = 0$, is the sequence 0, 1.5, 2, 2,..., which means $y(k) = 1.5 \, \text{step}\,(k - 1) + 0.5 \, \text{step}\,(k - 2)$. Recalling (2.24) and (2.45), then,

$$Y(z) = \frac{1.5z}{z - 1} z^{-1} + \frac{0.5z}{z - 1} z^{-2} = \frac{3z + 1}{2z(z - 1)} \tag{4.12}$$

and from $w(k) = 2 \, \text{step}\,(k)$ we also have $Y°(z) = 2z/(z - 1)$, thus

$$T°(z) = \frac{Y(z)}{Y°(z)} = \frac{3z + 1}{4z^2} \tag{4.13}$$

Note that all the poles of $T°(z)$ are in the origin, consistently with the FIR nature we desire for the closed-loop system.[3] Since $P(z)$ has no zeroes and a single pole inside the unit circle, and the relative degree of $T°(z)$ is not lower than that of $P(z)$, we can apply (4.11) and obtain

$$R(z) = 0.75 \frac{(z + 1/3)(z - 0.3)}{(z - 1)(z + 1/4)} \tag{4.14}$$

that produces the required sequence 0, 1.5, 2, 2,... as the $y(k)$ response. Note that one zero of $R(z)$ cancels the pole of $P(z)$, and also that $R(z)$ has a pole in $z = 1$,

---

[2] Such systems are called *minimum-phase* ones, but in this work we do not have the space for discussing the matter.

[3] For completeness, requiring a closed-loop transfer function with all the poles in the origin is called in the literature *deadbeat* control.

i.e., contains an integrator – a concept on which we shall return later on, as already anticipated.   □

Example 4.3. Same as Problem 4.2 but with $P(z) = 0.5/(z - 0.3)^2$.

Solution. With this new plant and the same T° we would obtain an unrealisable controller, since the relative degree of $P(z)$ is two. Thus we need a $T^\circ(z)$ of (at least) the same relative degree. A way to obtain this is to accept a response duration of three steps instead of two and introduce a z^{-1} term, i.e.,

$$T^\circ(z) = \frac{3z + 1}{4z^3} \tag{4.15}$$

which gives the realisable regulator

$$R(z) = 0.75\frac{(z + 1/3)(z - 3/10)^2}{(z - 1)(z + 1/2)^2} \tag{4.16}$$

and the $y(k)$ response given by the sequence 0, 0, 1.5, 2, 2, . . .; note again that $R(z)$ cancels the poles of $P(z)$, and contains an integrator.   □

4.4.2 Synthesis by transfer function assignment (disturbance rejection)

The same reasoning of the section above can be applied to require a desired response to d instead of y°, thus constraining the transfer function $Y(z)/D(z)$ to be a desired one, $F^\circ(z)$ to name it. This means, based again on (4.5) and (4.6),

$$\frac{H(z)}{1 + R(z)P(z)} = F^\circ(z) \quad \Rightarrow \quad R(z) = \frac{1}{P(z)}\frac{H(z) - F^\circ(z)}{F^\circ(z)} \tag{4.17}$$

The same considerations about cancellations made in the previous section apply, while the matter of controller realisability is here a bit more tricky. To see why, rewrite (4.17) as

$$R(z) = \frac{1}{P(z)}\frac{H_N(z)F_D^\circ(z) - H_D(z)F_N^\circ(z)}{H_D(z)F_N^\circ(z)} \tag{4.18}$$

where the N and D subscripts denote the numerator and denominator polynomials of the involved transfer functions. For $R(z)$ to be realisable, the relative degree of the second fraction factor in (4.18) must be equal to that of $P(z)$, or greater. This means that the coefficients of $F_N^\circ(z)$ and $F_D^\circ(z)$ must be chosen so as to eliminate some of the highest powers of z in the polynomial $H_N(z)F_D^\circ(z) - H_D(z)F_N^\circ(z)$, subject to maintaining the roots of $F_D^\circ(z)$ inside the unit circle. This is cumbersome and may not be possible, depending on conditions on $H(z)$ that are not easy to manage intuitively. More precisely, the resulting problem may not admit a solution for *any* $T^\circ(z)$, hence in some cases the choice of that reference transfer function may be constrained (another matter on which we do not go into further details for space reasons).

We shall now see an example problem, but in general transfer function assignment is not the most natural way to cope with disturbance rejection requirements.

Example 4.4. Given a plant with transfer functions $P(z) = 2/(z - 0.5)$, $H(z) = 1/(z - 0.1)$, design a feedback controller so that a unit step disturbance be rejected completely in as few steps as possible.

Solution. Requiring complete step disturbance rejection means requiring that $F^\circ(z)$ has zero gain, i.e., $F^\circ(1) = 0$, while a finite response duration d calls for $F_D^\circ(z) = z^d$ – which by the way ensures closed-loop stability. As such, we can set

$$F^\circ(z) = \frac{(z - 1)\widetilde{F}_N^\circ(z)}{z^d} \tag{4.19}$$

We then write

$$R(z) = \frac{z - 0.5}{2} \frac{z^d - (z - 0.1)(z - 1)\widetilde{F}_N^\circ(z)}{(z - 0.1)(z - 1)\widetilde{F}_N^\circ(z)} \tag{4.20}$$

and look for d and $\widetilde{F}_N^\circ(z)$ to fulfil the realisability condition. In this very simple case we find that $d = 2$ and $\widetilde{F}_N^\circ(z) = 1$ can do the job, yielding

$$R(z) = 0.55\frac{(z - 1/2)(z - 1/11)}{(z - 1)(z - 1/10)} \tag{4.21}$$

but as anticipated, things may not be so easy with more complex transfer functions.   □

4.4.3 Synthesis by dominant pole assignment

The difficulties experienced in the previous section come essentially from the attempt of assigning the closed-loop transfer function *completely*. An intuitive idea is to relax expectations a bit, limiting for example the goal to assign the dominant pole of that transfer function. Once this is done, and of course under the stability condition, the obtained response will only transiently differ from the ideal one, which is in most cases acceptable in practice.

For brevity here we just mention the technique, but give no examples. More interesting for our purposes is the use of standard controller structures, dealt with in the following.

4.5 Some typical feedback controllers

So far, the structure of the controller was dictated by the problem. There are, however, some typical or *standard* controller structures that exhibit a particular flexibility, thereby allowing to address a variety of problems with quite small a set of parameters. Three of these structures, relevant for the book, are now examined. For each of them, three main aspects are touched:

- closed-loop stability;
- static precision, quantified as the steady-state error magnitude

$$e_\infty = \lim_{k \to \infty} |e(k)| \tag{4.22}$$

for a unit set point step, and expressed – under the closed-loop asymptotic stability condition – as $\lim_{z \to 1} |1 - T(z)|$, see (4.5);
- asymptotic disturbance rejection, quantified as e_∞ produced by a unit disturbance step, and expressed – under the same condition as above – in the form $\lim_{z \to 1} |H(z)S(z)|$.

Then, the examined controllers are applied to simple plant transfer functions, to see how easy it can be to parameterise them in cases that are quite frequently encountered in the context of this book, as the subsequent chapters will show. In such simple cases, also some response speed considerations will be carried out.

4.5.1 Proportional control

The simplest possible controller is the *proportional* one, that makes the control linearly proportional to the error, i.e., $u(k) = K_p e(k)$, and therefore $R(z) = K_p$. Applied to the plant (4.1), this produces

$$\begin{aligned}
\frac{Y(z)}{Y^\circ(z)} &= T(z) &&= \frac{K_p P(z)}{1 + K_p P(z)} = \frac{K_p P_N(z)}{P_D(z) + K_p P_N(z)} \\
\frac{Y(z)}{D(z)} &= H(z)S(z) &&= \frac{H(z)}{1 + K_p P(z)} = \frac{H_N(z)P_D(z)}{H_D(z)(P_D(z) + K_p P_N(z))}
\end{aligned} \tag{4.23}$$

Closed-loop stability is ensured if the roots of $P_D(z) + K_p P_N(z)$ lie inside the unit circle. Static precision quantification leads to

$$\begin{aligned}
\lim_{z \to 1} |1 - T(z)| &= \lim_{z \to 1} \left| 1 - \frac{K_p P_N(z)}{P_D(z) + K_p P_N(z)} \right| \\
&= \lim_{z \to 1} \left| \frac{P_D(z)}{P_D(z) + K_p P_N(z)} \right|
\end{aligned} \tag{4.24}$$

while for asymptotic disturbance rejection (recall that $H(z)$ is assumed asymptotically stable), we have

$$\lim_{z \to 1} |H(z)S(z)| = \lim_{z \to 1} \left| \frac{H_N(z)P_D(z)}{H_D(z)(P_D(z) + K_p P_N(z))} \right| \tag{4.25}$$

Thus, a larger K_p improves both static precision and asymptotic disturbance rejection, the limit being provided by the stability condition. However, in the quite frequent case of an asymptotically stable plant, neither $\lim_{z \to 1} |1 - T(z)|$ nor $\lim_{z \to 1} |H(z)S(z)|$ can be zero, meaning that in both cases some steady-state error has to be accepted.

4.5.2 Integral control

Another common controller structure is the *integral* one, that makes the control proportional to the (discrete) integral of the error, i.e., $u(k) = u(k-1) + K_i e(k)$, and therefore $R(z) = K_i z/(z-1)$. Applied to the plant (4.1), this produces

$$
\begin{aligned}
\frac{Y(z)}{Y^\circ(z)} = T(z) \quad &= \frac{\frac{K_i z}{z-1} P(z)}{1 + \frac{K_i z}{z-1} P(z)} \\[2mm]
&= \frac{K_i z P_N(z)}{(z-1) P_D(z) + K_i z P_N(z)}
\end{aligned}
\tag{4.26}
$$

$$
\begin{aligned}
\frac{Y(z)}{D(z)} = H(z) S(z) &= \frac{H(z)}{1 + \frac{K_i z}{z-1} P(z)} \\[2mm]
&= \frac{(z-1) H_N(z) P_D(z)}{H_D(z)((z-1) P_D(z) + K_i z P_N(z))}
\end{aligned}
$$

Closed-loop stability requires the roots of $(z-1) P_D(z) + K_i z P_N(z)$ to lie inside the unit circle. Static precision is quantified as

$$
\begin{aligned}
\lim_{z \to 1} |1 - T(z)| = \lim_{z \to 1} \left| 1 - \frac{\frac{K_i z}{z-1} P_N(z)}{P_D(z) + \frac{K_i z}{z-1} P_N(z)} \right| \\[2mm]
= \lim_{z \to 1} \left| \frac{(z-1) P_D(z)}{(z-1) P_D(z) + K_i z P_N(z)} \right| = 0
\end{aligned}
\tag{4.27}
$$

and asymptotic disturbance rejection as

$$
\begin{aligned}
\lim_{z \to 1} |H(z) S(z)| = \lim_{z \to 1} \left| \frac{H_N(z) P_D(z)}{H_D(z) \left(P_D(z) + \frac{K_i z}{z-1} P_N(z) \right)} \right| \\[2mm]
= \lim_{z \to 1} \left| \frac{(z-1) H_N(z) P_D(z)}{H_D(z)((z-1) P_D(z) + K_i z P_N(z))} \right| = 0
\end{aligned}
\tag{4.28}
$$

Integral control hence guarantees zero steady-state error and perfect asymptotic disturbance rejection for step-like set point and disturbance variations. This is why the presence of an integrator is in general desired in a control loop, and if perfect tracking is required, it emerges naturally as we have already noticed in a couple of examples before. However, in general the presence of an integrator tends to have a price in terms of a slower system response.

4.5.3 Proportional-integral (PI) control

Joining the two controllers just mentioned, the PI one is written as

$$
R(z) = K_p + \frac{K_i z}{z-1}
\tag{4.29}
$$

or equivalently as

$$R(z) = K \frac{z - \dfrac{Ni - 1}{Ni}}{z - 1} \tag{4.30}$$

with

$$K = K_p + K_i, \quad N_i = 1 + \frac{K_p}{Ki} \tag{4.31}$$

that may seem less immediate to recognise than (4.29) but has (at least) two advantages. First, omitting lengthy but trivial computations based on (2.12)–(2.14), it can be shown that its response to a unit error step takes the form $u(k) = K + k/N_i$, thus K is the amplitude of the instantaneous control response and N_i the number of steps (not necessarily integer) required for that response to reach $2K$; in other words, K quantifies the 'prompt' control response to an error step, and N_i the slope with which the control signal increases with k if the error does not decrease. Second, (4.30) evidences both the integrator and the controller's zero, which can be useful for selecting 'good' PI parameters – again, the following examples with simple processes will clarify.

For compactness, the PI controller can also be represented as

$$R(z) = \kappa \frac{z - \zeta}{z - 1} \tag{4.32}$$

that is less informative than (4.30) and (4.31) in the sense just suggested, but undoubtedly simpler from the implementation standpoint.

4.6   Standard controllers on simple plants

In several problems of interest for us, the plant can be satisfactorily modelled by a first-order asymptotically stable $P(z)$, while the disturbance can instantaneously affect the controlled variable without further dynamics, i.e., without loss of generality, $H(z) = 1$, or in fact exert its action at the input of $P(z)$, i.e., $H(z) = P(z)$. In some other cases the above assumption on $P(z)$ is not true, but the plant model exhibits a dominant pole that makes the envisaged situation approximate reality well enough. We shall thus now apply PI control (P and I are sub-cases left to the reader as an exercise) to the described context, and comment on the results.

Let p, $|p| < 1$, be the single pole of $P(z)$, and write

$$P(z) = \frac{\mu(1 - p)}{z - p} \tag{4.33}$$

so that μ be its gain. Taking (4.30) as controller and using its zero to cancel the plant pole – i.e., setting $N_i = 1/(1 - p)$ – produces the open-loop transfer function

$$L(z) = R(z)P(z) = \frac{K\mu(1 - p)}{z - 1} \tag{4.34}$$

and thus

$$T(z) = \frac{K\mu(1-p)}{z - 1 + K\mu(1-p)}, \quad S(z) = \frac{z - 1}{z - 1 + K\mu(1-p)} \tag{4.35}$$

This achieves zero steady-state error for a set point and a disturbance step, while the closed-loop pole is $1 - K\mu(1-p)$. Assuming for simplicity $\mu > 0$ (generalising is straightforward) and recalling that $|p| < 1$ implies $0 < 1 - p < 2$, asymptotic stability is thus guaranteed by

$$K < \frac{2}{\mu(1-p)} \tag{4.36}$$

while the response speed of the system – measured, e.g., as its settling time, see (2.56) – is easily governed with K under the constraint above. Note that if one also desires to avoid oscillatory system behaviour, the stability condition could be replaced by the more restrictive one of having the closed-loop pole lie on the segment $(0,1)$ of the real axis. Analysing and comparing the two cases is left as an exercise to the interested reader.

4.7 From controller model to control law

Once a suitable $R(z)$ is determined, one needs to turn into a time domain control law, i.e., to express the present control $u(k)$ as a function of its past values, and of the present and past values of the error.

To do so, it is enough to recall that $R(z) = U(z)/E(z)$, and to exploit the one-step advance property of the $\mathcal{Z}$ transform. An example is the best and quickest way to illustrate the procedure.

Example 4.5. Obtain the time domain control law for

$$R(z) = \frac{z - 0.2}{(z - 1)(z - 0.9)} \tag{4.37}$$

Solution. First write

$$(z^2 - 1.9z + 0.9)U(z) = (z - 0.2)E(z) \tag{4.38}$$

Then, in force of the mentioned property,

$$u(k + 2) - 1.9u(k + 1) + 0.9u(k) = e(k + 1) - 0.2e(k) \tag{4.39}$$

Finally, solve for the most recent u and shift all time indices, which is legal given the time invariant nature of the system, so that said most recent u be $u(k)$. This provides

$$u(k) = 1.9u(k - 1) - 0.9u(k - 2) + e(k - 1) - 0.2e(k - 2) \tag{4.40}$$

□

It is now easy to obtain the control algorithm. Sticking to Example 4.5, the pseudocode presented in Algorithm 4.1 (not dealing with initialisations for brevity) is readily written.

Algorithm 4.1 Control law of Example 4.5.

---

procedure CONTROLLAW(e)
    $u \leftarrow 1.9 * u1 - 0.9 * u2 + e1 - 0.2 * e2$
    $u2 \leftarrow u1;$ // $u1$ stands for $u(k - 1)$, and so forth
    $u1 \leftarrow u;$ // Note that $u1, u2, e1, e2$ need to be preserved
    $e2 \leftarrow e1;$ // among subsequent function calls
    $e1 \leftarrow e;$
    return $u;$
end procedure

4.7.1 Managing control saturations

In any real world case, the control signal has some physical limits: let us say that it is constrained to lie within a closed interval, that is, $u(k) \in [U_{min}, U_{max}] \, \forall k$.

In the presence of a dynamic controller, this may cause significant inconveniences if not dealt with correctly. Here too, an example is the best way to explain.

Suppose that the set point of a feedback control loop is set to so high a value that even setting $u = U_{max}$ cannot attain it (we consider all gains positive for simplicity and without loss of generality). Of course the controller will eventually compute values of u greater than U_{max}, in an attempt to recover the set point, but the physical limit will intervene, and whatever the computed control is, the plant will not see anything greater than U_{max}.

At some time, the set point is modified to a value that can be attained. The controller will then start reducing u, but since the past control values remembered are greater than U_{max}, according to the control law it will take some steps before the computed control re-enters the admissible interval. Until this time, the plant has been continuing to receive U_{max}, the result being a delay in the response of the controlled variable with respect to the time when the set point was modified.

The problem is known as the *windup* one, and there are several solutions to it. The most straightforward one is to avoid remembering infeasible control values, thus modifying the previous algorithm as presented in Algorithm 4.2.

Such an *antiwindup* functionality, like any other of the same type, is apparently nonlinear, as by the way is the saturation phenomenon. As such, antiwindup is typically not considered in the controller synthesis, and just applied *a posteriori* to the control *algorithm* as a safety measure. There are in the literature numerous works that conversely treat control synthesis and saturation management jointly, but discussing them is not necessary in our context (see Reference 75 for details on the matter).

Algorithm 4.2 Control law of Example 4.5 with saturation management.

```
procedure CONTROLLAWANTIWINDUP(e)
    u ← 1.9 * u1 − 0.9 * u2 + e1 − 0.2 * e2
    if u > U_max then
        u ← U_max;
    end if
    if u < U_min then
        u ← U_min;
    end if
    u2 ← u1;
    u1 ← u;
    e2 ← e1;
    e1 ← e;
    return u;
end procedure
```

4.8   Problems

Problem 4.1. *Consider the scheme of Figure 4.1 with*

$$P(z) = \frac{0.2}{(z - 0.5)}, \quad H(z) = 1 \tag{4.41}$$

- *Determine $R(z)$ so that the response of $y(k)$ to a unit step of $y°(k)$ settle to zero error in four steps, at each of which 25% of the total motion has to occur.*
- *With the so obtained $R(z)$, evaluate the asymptotic amplitude of the effect on $y(k)$ of a disturbance in the form $d(k) = 0.2 \sin(0.01k)$.*

Problem 4.2. *Consider this time the scheme of Figure 4.2, again with*

$$P(z) = \frac{0.2}{(z - 0.5)}, \quad H(z) = 1 \tag{4.42}$$

- *Answer the same two questions of Problem 4.1.*
- *Compare the asymptotic disturbance response in the two cases.*

Problem 4.3. *Complete the discussion of Section 4.6 by analysing the P and I sub-cases.*

Problem 4.4. *Consider the controller*

$$R(z) = \frac{0.4z}{(z - 1)} \tag{4.43}$$

and write the corresponding time domain control law, assuming 0 and 1 as the control variable's saturation values.

Chapter 5

Scheduling

One of the key activities of an operating system is 'scheduling' applications so that they appear to execute 'in parallel' on a single processing unit.[1] In fact the main resource that the applications need to share is the processing unit itself, that is executing both the applications and the operating system.

Roughly speaking, a scheduler needs to choose a specific task to be executed from a task pool, and to decide for how much time the processing unit is assigned to this task. In operating systems, applications are typically packaged in processes and threads. In the rest of the chapter, we will use the term "task" to refer to both a process or a thread, since the considerations that follow apply to both.

The generic task pool to be scheduled contains tasks having each its own characteristics. For example, a task can have a deadline, which means that its code has to be executed before a specific amount of time elapses. Also, a task has requirements in terms of the resources – for example disk space and memory – that it needs. However, the scheduler is generally not aware of such task characteristics, and from a design point of view it is sane to assume this, since one can install on the system applications with virtually any combination of characteristics, and the scheduler cannot be reprogrammed.

A vast *corpus* of scheduling techniques do exist [38]. In specific cases, a schedule is produced offline, and the online scheduler has only to enforce the validity of the provided schedule by switching the active task with the following one. However, this is not true when general-purpose applications have to be scheduled, and a general-purpose operating system is analysed. In this case, the number of scheduling policies is still very large, spanning from simple to more complex ones. A simple one can be the execution of the first task entering the pool until this task terminates its computation. A more complex one can determine the next task to be executed, and a processing time to allot it, based on some measured quantities, e.g., how much time the task has spent waiting for the processing unit.

The purpose of this chapter is to address the scheduling problem as a control one, and more in general, to ease the introduction of some new ideas in the scheduling

---

[1] The extension of the proposed approach to multiple processing units is at present in progress, thus not treated here, see Section 11.3.1 for a sketch of work to be done in the near future.

paradigm. In fact, a general need is to devise an 'adaptive' scheduling policy, or in other words, a policy that is able to modify itself when different conditions are experienced. For example, an adaptive policy can behave differently when the system is overloaded – i.e., it needs more processing capability than the available one – or underloaded. At the same time, an adaptive policy can allow to change some of its parameters, for example the round robin *quantum*,[2] again to enforce some properties. However, all this changing and tweaking tends to complicate the scheduler's code (recall the remark of page 2, and the quote from Reference 28 in Section 1.2).

This chapter presents the development of a model and a control policy for the scheduling problem. To simplify the treatise, as anticipated, in the following only a single-processor case is taken into account; however, the considerations introduced herein hold also in the case of multi-core computing systems. In this chapter, the scheduling problem is entirely treated using the class of discrete-time dynamic systems as the main modelling instrument. The general model obtained can be seen as a switching system [39]; however, one of the main take-outs of this chapter is that simplifying the model and representing only the necessary involved quantities, allows to exploit even simpler modelling frameworks like the one of linear time-invariant systems. This is herein used to develop an entirely new scheduler, based on the concepts introduced in the previous chapters. The devised scheduler is implemented on a microcontroller kernel, and some benchmark are shown to validate the design approach. Also, the problem is considered of providing the scheduler with a configuration interface that is 'friendly' for the typical system administrator, who in general has little (if any) knowledge of the control theory.

5.1   Modelling

Consider a single-processor multitasking system with a preemptive scheduler – 'preemptive' meaning that the scheduler can block the execution of the current task and substitute it with another one – at a certain time instant, counted by the integer k (said instants, recall Chapter 2, in general are not equally spaced in time). Suppose that N tasks are running in the system. The scheduler decides which task should run next among the N present in the pool, and for how much time. However, one can also assume that the scheduler programs a certain number of tasks to be run for some time, up to selecting a time for all the tasks in the pool. Without loss of generality, one can say that the scheduler decides upon a time, in the following called *burst*, for each of the N tasks. This time can possibly be zero for some of them, or even for all of them but one. The word *round*, contrary to its meaning in the simplest round robin case, is thus here used to refer to the time between two subsequent scheduler interventions.

---

[2] Round robin scheduling, in its simplest form, means executing the scheduled tasks circularly, each one for a time quantum.

Formally, the following quantities can be defined:

Quantity	Description
$\tau_t(k) \in \mathbb{R}^N$	the CPU (processing unit) times *actually* used by the tasks in the kth round, which can be measured after their execution;
$\tau_r(k) \in \mathbb{R}$	the time duration of the kth round;
$\rho_t(k) \in \mathbb{R}^N$	the *times to completion*, or the remaining CPU time needed by the tasks to end their job at the beginning of the kth round for the tasks that have a duration assigned, $+\infty$ otherwise;
$b(k) \in \mathbb{R}^{n(k)}$	the *bursts*, i.e., the CPU times allotted by the scheduler to the tasks at the beginning of the kth round;
$\delta b(k) \in \mathbb{R}^{n(k)}$	the disturbances possibly acting on the scheduling action during the kth round;
$n(k) \in \mathbb{N}$	the number of tasks that the scheduler considers at each round.

where the disturbances $\delta b(k)$ are due, e.g., to the fact that one of the tasks can *yield* (i.e., release) the CPU before its burst has expired, or to the necessity of managing an interrupt amidst the task operation. Furthermore, notice that in the traditional scheduling policies $n(k)$ is constant and equal to one, but if one redesigns the scheduler, this constraint is not necessarily to be enforced anymore.

Denoting by t the total time actually elapsed from the system initialisation, a model for the phenomenon of interest is then

$$\begin{cases} \tau_t(k) = S_\sigma(k-1) \cdot b(k-1) + \delta b(k-1) \\ \tau_r(k) = \mathbf{1}_{1 \times N} \cdot \tau_t(k-1) \\ \rho_t(k) = \max\left(\rho_t(k-1) - S_\sigma(k-1)b(k-1) - \delta b(k-1), 0\right) \\ t(k) = t(k-1) + \tau_r(k) \end{cases} \tag{5.1}$$

where $S_\sigma(k) \in \Sigma$ a $N \times n(k)$ switching matrix. The elements of S_σ are zero or one, and each column contains at most one element equal to one. Matrix S_σ determines which tasks are considered in each round, to the advantage of generality (and possibly for future extensions to multiple processing units). Notice that, since $n(k)$ is bounded, the set Σ is finite for any N.

Several scheduling policies can be described with the presented formalism, by merely choosing $n(k)$ and/or $S_\sigma(k)$. For example,

- $n = 1$ and an N-periodic $S_\sigma(\cdot)$ with

$$S_\sigma(k) \neq S_\sigma(k-1), \quad 2 \leq k \leq N \tag{5.2}$$

produce all the possible Round Robin (RR) policies having the (scalar) $b(k)$ as the only control input, and obviously the pure RR if $b(k)$ is kept constant,

- generalisations of the RR policy are obtained if the period of $S_\sigma(\cdot)$ is *greater* than N, and (5.2) is obviously released,
- $n = 1$ and an $S_\sigma(\cdot)$ chosen so as to assign the CPU to the task with the minimum row index and a ρ_t greater than zero produces the First Come First Served (FCFS) policy,
- $n = 1$ and an $S_\sigma(\cdot)$ that switches according to the increasing order of the initial ρ_t vector produces the Shortest Job First (SJF) policy (notice that this is the same as SRTF if no change to the task pool occurs),
- $n = 1$ and an $S_\sigma(\cdot)$ selecting the task with the minimum ρ_t yields the Shortest Remaining Time First (SRTF) policy.

The capability of model (5.1) to reproduce the mentioned policies is shown in Figure 5.1, in the case of $n(k) = 1$, $N = 5$ and $S_\sigma(k)$ chosen as described above.

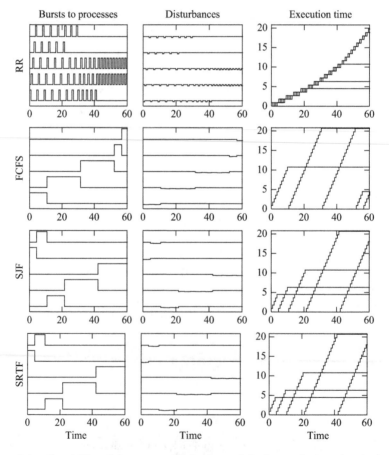

Figure 5.1   Capability of the presented single *model of reproducing classical scheduling policies such as RR, FCFS, SJF and SRTF*

5.1.1 The core phenomenon

In all these policies, it can be noticed that the *core phenomenon*, i.e., the part of the system that cannot be changed in any way since it represents the underlying 'physics' of the scheduled pool, has for each task the simple form

$$\tau_{t,i}(k) = b_i(k-1) + \delta b_i(k-1), \quad i = 1, \ldots, N \tag{5.3}$$

where k counts the scheduler interventions, $\tau_{t,i}$ is the actually used CPU time, and b_i the burst. The disturbance δb_i accounts for any action on the phenomenon other than that of allotting b_i, such as, e.g., anticipated CPU yields, delays in returning the CPU whatever the cause is, and so forth.

On the other hand, the *added physics*, i.e., what can be changed by the designer in order to control the behaviour of the system, can be noticed to be the algorithm used to select $n(k)$ and/or $S_\sigma(k)$.

If one attempts to model both things together, to close the loop around the existing scheduler, then switching systems must be brought into play, complicating the model and making it difficult to devise a controller for it. If, on the contrary, one models the core phenomenon only, and treats all the rest as control (recall the concluding remarks of Chapter 3), the single (5.3) is enough to model the plant to be controlled. Notice that here in modelling the core phenomenon no uncertainty is present, nor is there any measurement error, since the only required operation is to read the system time whenever a task starts and terminates its execution in the current round.

Extending (5.3) to the entire pool, one obtains the model

$$\begin{cases} \tau_t(k) = b(k-1) + \delta b(k-1) \\[2mm] t(k) = t(k-1) + \sum_{i=1}^{N} b_i(k-1) + \sum_{i=1}^{N} \delta b(k-1) \\[2mm] \tau_r(k) = \sum_{i=1}^{N} \tau_{t,i}(k) \end{cases} \tag{5.4}$$

where summations are over the pool, τ_r is the time between two subsequent scheduler interventions (no matter how many tasks were allotted a non-zero burst nor in which order), and t is the system time.

Notice that (5.4) looks very similar to (5.1), but there is an important difference. Model (5.4) respects the rules set out in Chapter 3, in that it is entirely physical, accounts for all the entities acting on the phenomenon, and exposes both the actually used CPU times and the time between two subsequent instants when the scheduler regains control. Based on those quantities, desires on fairness, responsiveness, and so forth (i.e., on the most typical metrics used to evaluate schedulers' behaviour) can be reformulated in control-theoretical terms.

Figure 5.2 gives a visual representation of the meaning of the involved quantities and their behaviour in time, introducing also the presence of the scheduler operations and context switches; vector τ_t represents the actually elapsed task times. In the figure, the time spent executing the first task, $\tau_{t,1}$ is greater than the one assigned

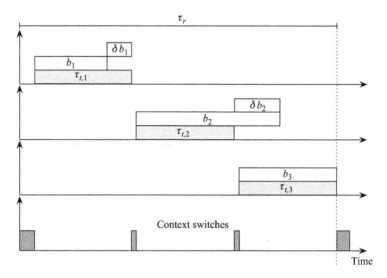

Figure 5.2   Meaning and behaviour over time of the involved quantities. This figure is adapted with permission from ACM article 'Task scheduling: a control-theoretical viewpoint for a general and flexible solution' [40], to appear in ACM Transactions on Embedded Computer Systems © 2013 ACM

by the scheduler (corresponding to b_1), e.g., because the task was not correctly preempted when its burst expired. In this case the value of the corresponding disturbance δb_1 is greater than zero. On the contrary, the second task executed for less time than planned, for example because it executed a yield, or stopped while waiting for an I/O operation to complete. In this case δb_2 is a negative value that accounts for the difference. The third tasks just used its burst. The fourth line represents scheduling time and context switches duration. Also, the round time τ_r is depicted.

5.2   Control synthesis

In this section, a new scheduling policy termed I+PI (the motivation follows in due course) is devised. The I+PI scheduler and the controlled task pool are completely represented by the block diagram of Figure 5.3, which was used to synthesise and assess the policy, and also for verification-oriented simulations prior to the actual implementation. In that scheme, $P(z)$ – plus the input summation node – is the 'controlled plant', i.e., the first equation in (5.4) with control input b, disturbance input δb, and output τ_t; the block denoted by Σ realises the third equation in (5.4), producing the round duration τ_r; the other blocks compose the controller, and will be dealt with in the next sections.

The scheme is of the so-called *cascade* type, as two nested loops can be recognised. The inner loop is devoted to ensuring the prescribed distribution of the CPU

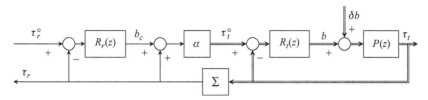

Figure 5.3   The proposed scheduler as a feedback control block diagram. This
figure is adapted with permission from ACM article 'Task scheduling:
a control-theoretical viewpoint for a general and flexible solution' [40],
to appear in ACM Transactions on Embedded Computer Systems ©
2013 ACM

time, acting on the bursts. The outer loop introduces an additive burst correction so
as to keep the round time to the desired value.

5.2.1   Inner loop

The inner loop is composed of the task pool and a diagonal integral (I) regulator,
realised by block $R_t(z)$, whence the first part of 'I+PI'. Since also model (5.4) is
diagonal as for the $b \mapsto \tau_t$ relationship, the result is a diagonal (or 'decoupled')
closed-loop system, that can be studied by simply considering one of its scalar elements. Also, the choice of the (diagonal) I structure stems from the pure delay nature
of said elements – evidenced by the first equation in (5.4) – as a typical control design
procedure, see Reference 41. In view of this, for each burst b_i an integral discrete-time
controller with gain k_I is adopted, i.e.,

$$b_i(k) = b_i(k-1) + k_I \left(\tau_{t,i}^{\circ}(k-1) - \tau_{t,i}(k-1) \right) \tag{5.5}$$

where $\tau_{t,i}^{\circ}$ is the set point for the ith component $\tau_{t,i}$ of τ_t. The inner closed loop's
element (referring to one task) is thus represented in state space form by

$$\begin{bmatrix} \tau_{t,i}(k) \\ b_i(k) \end{bmatrix} = \begin{bmatrix} 0 & 1 \\ -k_I & 1 \end{bmatrix} \begin{bmatrix} \tau_{t,i}(k-1) \\ b_i(k-1) \end{bmatrix} + \begin{bmatrix} 0 \\ k_I \end{bmatrix} \tau_{t,i}^{\circ}(k-1) + \begin{bmatrix} 1 \\ 0 \end{bmatrix} \delta b_i(k-1) \tag{5.6}$$

Observing system (5.6) with inputs $\tau_{t,i}^{\circ}$, δb_i and output $\tau_{t,i}$, it can be concluded that the disturbance is asymptotically rejected and the set point followed with
a response time (in rounds) dictated by k_I, provided that the eigenvalues magni-
tude is less than the unity, i.e., $\left| 1 \pm \sqrt{1 - 4k_I} \right| < 2$. A good default choice is to
have two coincident eigenvalues in 0.5, hence $k_I = 0.25$. Higher values of k_I make
the controller respond 'more strongly' to the difference between the desired and
achieved $\tau_{t,i}$, thus making the system faster at rejecting disturbances (owing to a
prompt action) but easily producing oscillatory responses to set point variations
(owing to a possibly transiently excessive action); lower values of k_I, intuitively,
cause the reverse to happen. Figure 5.4 illustrates the matter, and shows why 0.25
could be used as default for a scheduler with no real-time requirements, and 0.5 could
be used for a soft real-time one.

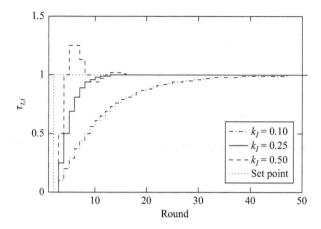

*Figure 5.4   Inner loop set point responses for different values of k_I. This figure
is adapted, with permission, from ACM article 'Task scheduling:
a control-theoretical viewpoint for a general and flexible solution' [40],
to appear in ACM Transactions on Embedded Computer Systems ©
2013 ACM*

Trivial computations lead to write from (5.6) the iterative law describing the
MIMO closed inner loop's behaviour in time, which takes the form

$$\begin{cases} \tau_t(k) = \tau_t(k-1) - k_I I \tau_t(k-2) + k_I I \tau_t^\circ(k-2) + \delta b(k-1) - \delta b(k-2) \\ b(k) = b(k-1) - k_I I \tau_t(k-1) + k_I I \tau_t^\circ(k-1) \end{cases}$$

$$(5.7)$$

where I is the identity matrix of dimension equal to the number of tasks. This
realises $R_t(z)$, as the second equation of (5.7) is the required control algorithm for
the inner loop.

5.2.2   Outer loop

Once the inner loop is closed, the convergence of the actual CPU times to the required
ones is ensured, since choosing eigenvalues with magnitude lower than the unity
ensures asymptotic stability, and the regulator contains an integral action, see again
Reference 41. To determine the set point τ_t°, an outer loop is used that provides an
additive correction (b_c in Figure 5.3) so as to maintain the round duration τ_r to a
prescribed value τ_r°; the computation of b_c is accomplished by block $R_r(z)$. It can be
verified that choosing a single k_I for the inner loop results in a $b_c \mapsto \tau_r$ relationship
independent of α, i.e.,

$$\frac{T_r(z)}{B_c(z)} = \frac{k_I}{z(z-1)}$$

A suitable controller structure for the outer loop, along considerations analogous to
those that led to the I one for the inner loop, is then the Proportional plus Integral

one (PI), whence the rest of 'I+PI'. Reasoning in the same way as for (5.6) this leads to determine the closed outer loop's behaviour, in transfer function form, as

$$\frac{T_r(z)}{T_r^\circ(z)} = \frac{k_I k_R (z - z_R)}{z^3 - 2z^2 + (1 + k_I k_R) z - k_I k_R z_R} \tag{5.8}$$

which corresponds in the time domain to

$$\tau_r(k) = 2\tau_r(k-1) - (1 + k_I k_R)\tau_r(k-2) + k_I k_R z_R \tau_r(k-3)$$
$$+ k_I k_R \tau_r^\circ(k-2) - k_I k_R z_R \tau_r^\circ(k-3) \tag{5.9}$$

while the controller dynamics are

$$\begin{cases} x_R(k) = x_R(k-1) + k_R(1 - z_R)\left(\tau_r^\circ(k-1) - \tau_r(k-1)\right) \\ b_c(k) = x_R(k) + k_R\left(\tau_r^\circ(k) - \tau_r(k)\right) \end{cases} \tag{5.10}$$

where (5.10) provides the control algorithm for $R_r(z)$ (x_R is the PI state variable), and the role of block α should now be self-evident. The PI parameters k_R and z_R can be set in various ways, and are both connected to the response speed.

Stability is ensured if the roots of the denominator of the transfer function (5.8)

$$\lambda^3 - 2\lambda^2 + (1 + k_I k_R)\lambda - k_I k_R z_R = 0 \tag{5.11}$$

in the unknown λ, have magnitude less than the unity, i.e.,

$$\begin{cases} k_I \neq 0 \\ k_R \neq 0 \\ z_R < 1 \\ \sqrt{\dfrac{1 - k_I k_R}{k_I^2 k_R^2}} + z_R > \dfrac{1}{k_I k_R} \end{cases}$$

This readily provides parameter bounds, while disturbance rejection is still guaranteed by the contained closed inner loop. The absence of α in the synthesis of the outer loop may suggest that possible variations of that vector in time do not affect the overall system's stability, although its time-invariant character is lost. It is possible to formally prove the statement above, but doing so would stray from the scope of this work. As a result of the synthesis process just sketched, the I+PI algorithm is unambiguously defined in Algorithm 5.1.

5.2.3 Complexity comparison with existing policies

Given the novel structure of the proposed policy, it is not immediate to establish a comparison metric to prove its advantages over existing ones. In fact, the metrics available in the literature are not designed for the evaluation of a control system, thus (no criticism intended) they are quite unfit here. As such, in the following Section 5.4, some experimental examples of schedulers' behaviour (including I+PI) will be shown, and relevant enforced properties (not the most used metrics, for the reason just given) will be highlighted.

For a complete evaluation, it is, however, advisable to address also the implementation complexity. This section thus compares the I+PI scheme to two well known

---

Algorithm 5.1 I+PI algorithm (the complete C++ implementation can be found in Appendix A.2).

Initialise the I and the PI state variables
for each scheduling round k **do**
    Read the measured CPU times used by the N tasks
    in the previous round into vector $\tau_t(k-1)$
    Compute the measured duration of the last round:
    $\tau_r(k-1) = \sum_{i=1}^{N} \tau_{t,i}(k-1)$
    Read the required round duration $\tau_r^\circ(k-1)$
    if the task pool cardinality or parameters have changed **then**
        Re-initialise $b_i(k)$ to the default values
    else
        Compute the burst correction $b_c(k)$ for this round by the PI algorithm:
        $b_c(k) = b_c(k-1)$
            $+ k_R\left(\tau_r^\circ(k-1) - \tau_r(k-1)\right) - k_{RZR}\left(\tau_r^\circ(k-2) - \tau_r(k-2)\right)$
        Apply saturations to $b_c(k)$
        Compute the vector $\alpha(k)$ of required CPU time fractions
        for each task i **do**
            Compute the burst vector $b(k)$ for this round
            by the I algorithm:
            $\tau_{t,i}^\circ(k) = \alpha_i(k)\left(\tau_r(k) + b_c(k)\right)$
            $b_i(k) = b_i(k-1) + k_I(\tau_{t,i}^\circ(k-1) - \tau_{t,i}(k-1))$
            Apply saturations to $b_i(k)$
        end for
    end if
    Activate the N tasks in sequence
    preempting each of them when its burst is elapsed
end for

---

policies from the time complexity point of view. The two considered policies are an open-loop one, the Round Robin (RR), and a closed-loop one, the Selfish Round Robin (SRR).

The RR policy simply consists of having the scheduler scan the pool of processes sequentially and periodically, assigning the CPU to each of them in turn for a burst that in the simplest implementation is fixed. More complex realisation may adapt said burst, typically in open loop, and based, e.g., on some priority mechanism. The SRR policy is similar to the RR one, but attempts to solve the so-called 'starvation' problem, that occurs when a low-priority process is steadily prevented from gaining the CPU. In SRR, newly arrived processes are not placed in the round (the 'waiting queue' in the SRR terminology) directly, but wait in a 'holding queue' until they have been 'starving' for the CPU long enough to gain a sufficient priority, thus to be accepted in the waiting queue. The waiting queue is managed as a round robin one, while priorities in the holding queue increase linearly in time with a prescribed rate – a parameter of the SRR together with the queues' cardinalities.

In the following, denote as t_Σ, t_S, t_Π, and $t_\rightarrow$ the (average) duration of a sum, subtraction, multiplication and bit-shift operation, respectively. Assume (for a fair comparison) that all the mathematical operations in the compared policies are performed at the same machine precision. Also, denote as t_c the (average) duration of a context switch. The time σ_{POL} spent in the scheduling task within one round (i.e., to schedule *all* the N processes *once*, possibly giving zero time to some of them) by the policy POL (where for this study POL can be RR, SRR, or I+PI) is therefore

$$\sigma_{\text{RR}} = N \cdot t_\rightarrow + N \cdot t_c$$

$$\sigma_{\text{SRR}} = N \cdot t_\rightarrow + N \cdot t_c + N^2 \cdot (t_S + t_\Pi) \tag{5.12}$$

$$\sigma_{\text{I+PI}} = N \cdot t_\rightarrow + N \cdot t_c + (N+1) \cdot t_s + (2N+1) \cdot t_\Sigma + (2N+2) \cdot t_\Pi$$

To derive the expressions above it is enough to count the arithmetic operations necessary to execute the various schedulers' code. Denoting by q the quantum where applicable, it is possible to compute the total duration of one round as

$$\tau_{r,\text{RR}} = N \cdot q, \quad \tau_{r,\text{SRR}} = N_w \cdot q, \quad \tau_{r,\text{I+PI}} = \tau_r^\circ \tag{5.13}$$

where $N_w \leq N$ is the number of processes in the waiting queue in the SRR case. Note that for simplicity 'ideal control' is assumed: in I+PI scheme this means that the round duration is exactly τ_r°, while in the RR and SRR cases this means that all the processes use their burst completely. The ratio η between the time spent in scheduling and the round duration is then

$$\eta_{\text{RR}} = \frac{t_\rightarrow + t_c}{q}$$

$$\eta_{\text{SRR}} = \frac{N^2 (t_S + t_\Pi)}{N_w q} + \frac{N}{N_w} \eta_{\text{RR}} \geq \eta_{\text{RR}} + N \frac{t_s + t_\Pi}{q} \tag{5.14}$$

$$\eta_{\text{I+PI}} = \frac{N t_\rightarrow + N t_c + (N+1)t_s + (2N+1)t_\Sigma + (2N+2)t_\Pi}{\tau_r^\circ}$$

where, again, the subscripts identify the policies.

Suppose now to express τ_r° in the form $N \cdot q$, i.e., to require the same round duration for the two proposed policies and for the RR (the computationally lightest one, apparently). In this case, the I+PI leads for $N \to \infty$ to an increase of η, with respect to the RR, quantified as $(t_s + 2t_\Sigma + 2t_\Pi)/q$.

Therefore, the asymptotic *time* complexity of the proposed policies is constant, and (as expected) can be reduced by increasing the round duration. Moreover, said policies are computationally (slightly) more complex than the RR, but can enforce properties that the (open-loop) RR policy cannot. On the other hand, the proposed policies are definitely *less* complex than the SRR, and although the SRR can somehow address the same issues as said policies, its parameters do not have a clear interpretation, nor can they be selected based on a system-theoretical analysis.

5.2.4   Simulation example

Equations (5.7), (5.9) and (5.10) also allow to simulate the control system. An example is shown in Figure 5.5 to illustrate the set point following and disturbance rejection characteristics.

A pool of three tasks is considered, and both the required CPU distribution (vector α) and the desired round duration (τ_r°) are varied. When the set point is modified, the behaviour of the system changes accordingly, therefore resulting in different curves. Also, step-like disturbances are periodically introduced in the actual CPU time consumed by the tasks. In the same conditions, the system reacts to disturbances exactly in the same way. When the set point changes, the reaction is different. However, as can be seen, both characteristics (CPU distribution, i.e., weighted fairness, and round time, i.e., responsiveness) can be prescribed as set points, and the system achieves them also in the presence of disturbances. Note, in this respect, how fast the CPU times and the round duration converge to their set points, and how quickly the effect of disturbances vanishes. Also, note the smooth behaviour of the allotted bursts.

Once the control system is assessed as dynamic system, and simulated to get further insight on the aspect of the obtained transients, the code-abstracted part of the design is completed. From now on, in other words, it is *proven* that the solution matches the problem, and the only issue is to check that the code, that comes unambiguously from the scheduler-related equations, matches the solution.

5.3   Set point generation for (soft) real-time systems

This section delves a bit further into the actual implementation of the I+PI scheme inside a kernel, and treats for the first time the matter of how the I+PI set points can be produced based on application needs, in the specific case of (soft) real-time systems.

The complete scheduler implementation is outlined in Figure 5.6, and the C++ code of the I+PI part can be found in Appendix A.2. The scheduler can be divided into two parts:

- The *I+PI controller algorithm*, which computes the burst values. It should be stressed that I+PI runs once per round, *not once per task activation*. At the beginning of each round I+PI computes the values $b(k)$ for all the units present in the task pool. Tasks can be then run one after the other without any further scheduler intervention, except for very simple context switches.
- The *set point generator*, that needs running only when changes occur in the task pool, the required CPU distribution, the required round duration, or any combination thereof. Its aim is to compute the reference signals for the I+PI algorithm. Set point generation can be further divided into 'overload detection and rescaling' and 'reinitialisation and Feed Forward (FF)'.

It is worth evidencing that the correct behaviour of the scheduler in terms of stability and performance depends inherently on the correct realisation of the I+PI algorithm only, and thus can be checked formally. The rest is, in control-theoretical

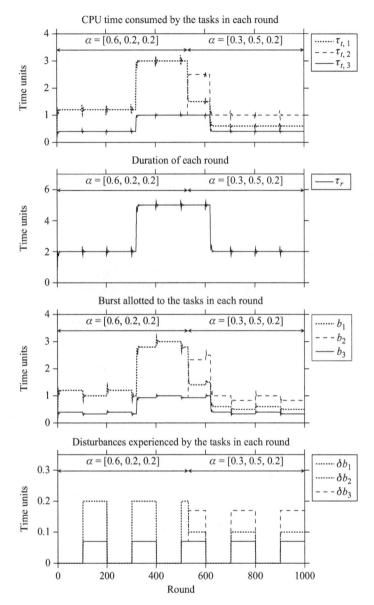

Figure 5.5   Simulation results to demonstrate set point following and disturbance rejection. This figure is adapted with permission from ACM article 'Task scheduling: a control-theoretical viewpoint for a general and flexible solution' [40], to appear in ACM Transactions on Embedded Computer Systems © 2013 ACM

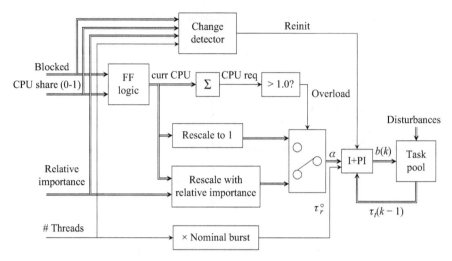

Figure 5.6   Implementation scheme, containing the I+PI regulator and the set point generator. This figure is adapted with permission from ACM article 'Task scheduling: a control-theoretical viewpoint for a general and flexible solution' [40], to appear in ACM Transactions on Embedded Computer Systems © 2013 ACM

terms, 'outside the loop', and cannot alter the system stability as assessed on the model. This is very important to streamline the design process, as once the core algorithm is written, parameterised and checked, the rest of the code *structurally cannot* have unexpected or disruptive impacts on the system. Needless to say, also the code structuring and modularisation takes profit from the concepts just recalled.

Since I+PI is a closed-loop scheduler, it requires measurements of the actual CPU times consumed by the individual tasks in the previous scheduling period $\tau_i(k-1)$. To achieve that, the implementation makes use of a hardware timer that can also be configured for scheduling preemption. The timer is started at the end of the context switch code, and its value is read at the beginning of the next switch. This allows to measure execution times with a fine-grained resolution.

Set point generation is ruled by two input parameters. One is an estimate of the *CPU percentage* that each task requires, for example not to miss deadlines. The second is the *relative importance* of each task, which is used to handle CPU overload situations. These parameters can be set by the task itself through an API provided by the used kernel, and can be changed during the lifetime of the task to reflect changes in its behaviour. In addition, the scheduler needs to know which tasks are blocked, for example sleeping or waiting for I/O operations.

Further details on how to generate set points for general purpose systems are provided in Section 5.5.

5.3.1   Overload detection and rescaling

From time to time, especially in soft real-time systems, the CPU utilisation may exceed the unity. This means that the sum of the required CPU shares (for all non-blocked tasks) exceeds one. This situation is used in the proposed solution to detect a CPU overload situation, signalling that the task pool is not schedulable. This overload indicator is used to select the rescaling policy to be used.

If the task pool is schedulable the 'rescale to one' policy is used to produce vector α, by rescaling the required CPU percentage vector so that its sum equals to one (of course, one task can be the "idle task", to seamlessly account for CPU underloading). For example, consider a task pool with four tasks, of which three require a 0.2 CPU share, and the fourth one is blocked and therefore requires zero CPU share. The policy will result in an α array of $[0.33, 0.33, 0.33, 0]$. This policy will, by design, give a CPU share greater or equal than the one requested by the tasks, ensuring that the tasks have enough CPU to carry out their job successfully. It is particularly significant that this policy ensures good real-time performance – the following benchmarks should evidence it – even without the scheduler having any knowledge of deadlines whatsoever. In other words, deadlines are *implicitly* enforced by ensuring that the involved tasks receive enough CPU share on time.

In the presence of CPU overload, conversely, this policy is not adequate. Consider an example with three tasks, all of which require a 0.5 CPU share. The rescaling would give a CPU share of 0.33 to all three tasks, so if deadlines are present, all tasks will eventually start missing them. In this case the 'rescale with relative importance' policy is thus used (see Figure 5.6). This policy first weights the CPU share using the relative importance parameter, and then rescales the resulting α vector to have unitary sum as before. As a result, two tasks that require the same CPU share will receive a burst proportional to their relative importance parameter. This significantly differs from classical approaches to tackle similar issues, that are typically based on *task priorities*, in that the proposed policy allows to *predict* the CPU share that will be received by all tasks even in the case of overload. Also, and again differing from priority-based techniques, the relative importance parameter is only taken into account when CPU overload occurs, therefore having no influence when the pool is schedulable. Notice that the relative importance parameter can be set based on the task importance, but is a parameter of the control system, and does not influence its formal assessment.

Once again, recall that both these techniques for rescaling simply produce the set points for the same regulator and control algorithm just described, that stays untouched and cannot experience instability.

5.3.2 Reinitialisation and feedforward

Regulator reinitialisation and feedforward can be introduced to improve the scheduling dynamic performance in the presence of task blockings. A task is said to 'block' if it stops being able to accept the CPU for a period of time. Blocking causes include for example voluntarily sleeping, waiting on a locked mutex or other synchronisation primitives, or waiting for an I/O operation to complete.

The I+PI algorithm is intrinsically capable of responding to task blockings due to its closed-loop nature – in other words, due to past behaviour measurements – without any external intervention. However, reinitialisation and feedforward control were introduced to improve its *dynamic* performance. To show the advantages of

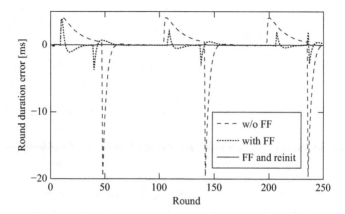

Figure 5.7   Effects of task blockings, in terms of round duration error, with
$\tau_r^\circ = 8$ ms (data from hardware implementation). This figure is
adapted with permission from ACM article 'Task scheduling:
a control-theoretical viewpoint for a general and flexible solution' [40],
to appear in ACM Transactions on Embedded Computer Systems ©
2013 ACM

using these two features, a simple example of what happens if reinitialisation and
feedforward are not present is presented. Consider a case with two tasks, of which
one repeatedly blocks. In this case, the external PI regulator is able to quickly regain
control of the round time duration, but in the meantime, the integral regulator of
the blocked task is subject to a constant error and, as such, diverges till saturation
occurs. When the blocked task becomes ready again, the scheduler assigns to it a very
long burst, equal to the saturation value – a typical case of integral windup. While
this situation is recovered after a short number of rounds, these spikes in the round
duration may cause deadline misses. A simulation experiment showing how this can
actually happen is depicted in Figure 5.7.

The I+PI scheduler is a dynamic system, and as such has an internal state. The
reinitialisation policy works by resetting this state to its default value whenever the
task pool parameters change. This includes resetting the saturated integral regulator
of a blocked task, therefore improving the dynamic response to task blockings.

The feedforward policy is instead grounded on the fact that task blocking is a
measurable disturbance. A task, to sleep or wait, has to call some kernel API and
as such, the scheduler is informed of this fact. This allows to further improve the
dynamic response by changing the I+PI set points, namely by setting to zero the α
elements corresponding to blocked tasks, and distributing the round time among non-
blocked tasks only. All the following benchmarks results have been obtained with
both features enabled.

It is worth evidencing that the proposed scheme can be thought as a hybrid system,
with a single discrete state, where the reinitialisation request is viewed as a switching
signal that resets the system state to a default value. As such, a stability analysis of
the hybrid system under arbitrary switch is required, but not reported here for the sake

of brevity. Anyway, it can be conjectured, and is proven by experience, that the reset mechanism does not lead to unstable behaviours.

5.4 Experimental results and comparisons

The I+PI algorithm, together with RR and EDF for comparisons, has been implemented in the Miosix kernel, see Chapter 10 for further details. All the tests were made with a `stm3210e-eval` board, equipped with a 72 MHz ARM microcontroller and a 1-MB external RAM, from which the code executes.

Some test sets are now presented. The first demonstrates the ability of the I+PI implementation to effectively distribute the CPU to the running tasks and the correctness of the tasks execution, comparing their output with the reference one proposed in the benchmark suite. The second compares I+PI to RR and EDF with a benchmark conceived for periodic tasks, limiting the scope to feasible CPU utilisations, and shows that I+PI closely approaches the EDF (optimal) results although not being tied to the concept of deadlines. Also, in this case some numbers concerning the scheduling overhead are presented. The third set considers the apparently off-design condition of a non schedulable task pool owing to CPU over-utilisation, where the approach behind I+PI makes it inherently superior to non-control-theoretic ones.

5.4.1 MiBench benchmark

The open source MiBench suite [42] is used here to assess the correctness of the Miosix scheduler implementation. The suite contains applications that span from mathematical computation to image encoding, network routing, cryptography and GSM audio encoding/decoding, thereby representing a variety of workloads. There are two tests per benchmark, a 'small-' and a 'large-input' one. Owing to the available hardware limitations, only the small-input one is here used (apparently, with no generality loss). Table 5.1 reports some execution time and memory occupation results. There are no significant differences between the results of Miosix and the reference ones provided with the suite.

In addition to the above test, that consider one application at a time, a further experiment was done by simultaneously running several applications, one per category, each in a thread of its own, with I+PI and RR scheduling (using EDF would imply setting fictitious deadlines, to the detriment of test significance). The used applications are `basicmath`, `jpeg`, `stringsearch`, `dijkstra`, `sha`, and `gsm`. With both schedulers each output correctly matches its reference.

In Table 5.2, column T_{ind} and T_{sim} respectively report the sum of the *individual* applications' execution times, and the duration of their *simultaneous* execution. As can be seen, both schedulers are capable of re-assigning CPU time when one or more thread gets stuck (in this case, owing to I/O operations). However, I+PI is more effective, as witnessed by both the pure parallel execution times and the differences between the sequential and parallel times. This suggests that the I+PI scheduling overhead tends to be of modest entity with respect to improvements in CPU time management.

Table 5.1   Summary of relevant MiBench [42] execution data

c[1]	benchmark	time [s]	.text [B]	.data [B]	.bss [B]	stack [B]	heap [B]
A	basicmath	61.431	75600	1288	348	1472	4684
A	bitcount	8.531	63848	1288	348	1416	4148
A	qsort	3.545	90420	1328	140604	1336	5212
A	susan[2]	8.711	97008	1328	604	370312	179588
C	jpeg[3]	14.812	231016	1336	660	3440	246228
C	tiff2bw	67.359	259200	1728	780	2408	45492
C	tiffdither	85.801	259040	1624	788	3036	41652
C	tiffmedian	113.334	253136	1600	133428	1344	160700
O	ispell	5.206	134668	1736	31436	4460	732252
O	stringsearch	0.023	64116	1280	1380	1664	6948
N	dijkstra	14.290	90384	1328	41436	1356	14308
N	patricia	10.628	57516	1328	604	1556	14308
N, S	sha	3.354	70596	1280	348	2976	5596
S	pgpsign	6.969	262980	5288	230140	14376	13588
S	pgpverify	1.088	263076	5288	230140	15964	25780
S	rijndael[4]	44.913	104128	1296	356	1416	8908
N, T	crc32	162.554	68708	1280	348	1336	7484
T	fft/ifft	94.993	71184	1288	348	1504	160652
T	adpcm[3]	52.983	69636	1280	2852	1360	8148
T	gsm[3]	12.145	135972	1576	604	1832	9300

[1] Categories are: Automotive/industrial, Consumer, Office, Network, Security, Telecommunications.
[2] Execution time includes all the three phases (edge detection, corner detection, and smoothing).
[3] Execution time includes both encoding and decoding.
[4] Source code was flawed, thus it was fixed and output correctness was compared under Linux with the fixed version instead of the reference.

Table 5.2   Summary of simultaneous MiBench [42] execution times (expressed in seconds)

Scheduler	basicmath	jpeg	stringsearch	dijkstra	sha	gsm	T_{ind}	T_{sim}
I+PI	61.641	14.812	0.023	14.290	3.354	12.145	**106.055**	**100.535**
RR	60.207	14.883	0.023	14.038	3.555	11.031	**103.737**	**101.504**

5.4.2   Hartstone benchmark

The Hartstone benchmark [43] is used here to compare I+PI to EDF and RR. Hartstone is composed of several series of tests; each consists of starting from a baseline system, verifying its correct behaviour, and then iteratively adding stress to that system and re-assessing its behaviour until said assessment fails. The amount of added (affordable) stress allows to measure the system capabilities.

This work concentrates on the Hartstone PH (Periodic tasks, Harmonic frequencies) series, that refers to periodic tasks, and stresses the system by adding tasks and/or modifying their period and/or workload. The baseline system is composed

Table 5.3   The Hartstone [43] baseline task set

Task	Frequency (hertz)	Workload (kilo-Whets)	Workload rate (workload/period) (kWIPS)
1	2	32	64
2	4	16	64
3	8	8	64
4	16	4	64
5	32	2	64

of five periodic tasks, that execute a specific number of Whetstones [43] within a period; the workload rate is thus expressed in kilo-Whets Instruction Per Second [kWIPS]. A kilo-Whet corresponds in our architecture to a CPU occupation of 1.25 ms, maintained constant through all the tests. As per the benchmark, all the tasks are independent: their execution does not involve synchronisation, they do not communicate with one another, and are all scheduled to start at the same time. The deadline for the workload completion of each task is the beginning of its next period. The used series might thus represent a program that monitors several banks of sensors at different rates, and displays the results with no user interventions or interrupt requirements.

Table 5.3 gives details on the baseline system. In the first test, the highest-frequency task (number 5) has the frequency increased by 8 Hz at each iteration, until a deadline is missed. This tests the system ability to switch rapidly among tasks. In the second test, all the frequencies are scaled by 1.1, 1.2, . . ., at each iteration, until a deadline is missed. This means testing the system's ability to handle an increased but still balanced workload. The third test starts from the baseline set and increases the workload of each task by 1, 2, . . ., kilo-Whets at each iteration. This increases the system overhead in a non-balanced way. In the last test, at each iteration a new task is added, with a workload of 8 kilo-Whets and a frequency of 8 Hz (as the third task of the baseline set). This test stresses the system's ability to handle a large number of tasks.

Figure 5.8 graphically shows the results for the four tests, presenting both the number of successful iterations (higher is better) and the number of context switches per second in the last successful iteration (lower is better). In most cases the number of successful iterations and context switches per second of I+PI are similar to those of EDF, which is notoriously optimal for a schedulable set of periodic tasks. In fact, EDF significantly outperforms I+PI only in the first test, which is apparently the most extreme as for asymmetry in the task periods. This is not to diminish the relevance of the fact, but for example, if in an embedded device a critical task needs to be executed at so higher a rate than the others, one would probably consider hooking said task to a timer interrupt. On the other hand, I+PI is definitely superior to RR in any sense.

An overhead analysis is also in order, and therefore we recorded the duration of a context switch for the baseline test with each of the implemented scheduling algorithms. The numbers are computed running the baseline task set, and using an oscilloscope to read a general purpose input/output (GPIO) signal raised whenever

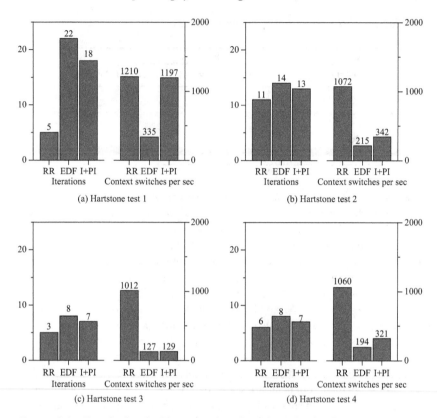

Figure 5.8   *Results for the Hartstone benchmark [43]. This figure is adapted with permission from ACM article 'Task scheduling: a control-theoretical viewpoint for a general and flexible solution' [40], to appear in ACM Transactions on Embedded Computer Systems © 2013 ACM*

Table 5.4   Context switch duration within the Hartstone [43] baseline task set

Scheduler	Average (μs)	Long (μs)	Short (μs)
I+PI	75.8	205.6	43.4
EDF	30.8		
RR	50.4		

the scheduler starts its execution, and cleared as it finishes. For the I+PI, the context switch in which the scheduler calculates the bursts is obviously longer than the other ones, as clearly shown in Table 5.4. It is worth recalling that this longer context switch happens just once per round. In fact, whenever I+PI has to apply a previously computed control signal, it results faster than RR, but intuitively slower than EDF.

Table 5.5   Relevant data on the schedulers' execution

Scheduler	.text [B]	.data [B]	.bss [B]
I+PI	1464	12	40
EDF	476	0	4
RR	600	0	20

However, on average, the overhead of the technique is in general heavier. A possible way to speed up the computation is to select an architecture with hardware support for floating point operations, or to use dedicated hardware. Also, data on the schedulers execution is here reported. Table 5.5 shows some relevant data about the schedulers' execution, retrieved with the size utility contained in the Miosix kernel.

5.4.3   Extended Hartstone benchmark

Benchmarks like Hartstone are useful to provide a simple and clear comparison testbed, but do not aim at representing 'real life' workloads. For example, any scheduler regularly encounters pools of tasks where each one has its own characteristics. Also, a scheduler may be requested to recover correct operation of (soft) real time tasks after a transient CPU over-utilisation, or even to withstand a long-lasting over-utilisation by maintaining the timely operation of certain tasks.

The general approach behind I+PI is well suited to address such issues. To witness that, I+PI is here compared to EDF and RR in an extension of the Hartstone benchmark. In the reported tests of Section 5.4.2, the way of increasing the system load is the same of the corresponding tests of Figure 5.8. However, the load is not increased gradually, but set so as to result in a 48% CPU utilisation from 0 to 30 seconds, then in a 120% utilisation from 30 to 45 seconds, and in 48% again till the end of the test, at 120 seconds. Figure 5.9(a), (b), (c) and (d) report respectively the total number of misses and of context switches per second in the four tests (lower is better for both). As can be seen, I+PI invariantly achieves the least miss rate, with a moderately higher number of context switches per second with respect to EDF; RR performances are definitely inferior.

5.4.4   Summary of results

From all the reported tests, it can be concluded that I+PI may in some cases be not optimal, but normally approaches optimal performance and above all does not require any assumption on the nature of the tasks (e.g., periodic or not). An interesting extension to I+PI, to witness the general nature of the approach, is presented in References 44, 45, but not discussed here for the sake of brevity. It is also worth noticing, as a final remark, that the I+PI implementation shown here was realised with floating point computations with an architecture that has no hardware support for them [40]. This was done for convenience reasons inessential to explain here, but could be safely replaced by a sufficiently precise fixed point arithmetic version. Needless to say, this would move the experimental evaluation balance further towards I+PI.

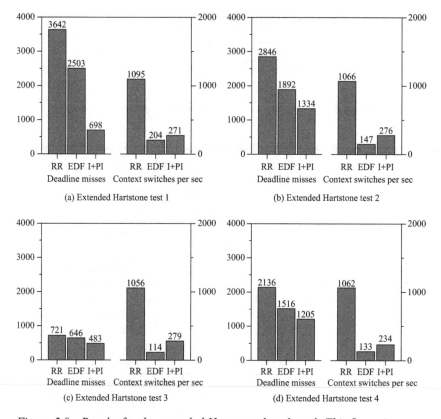

Figure 5.9   Results for the extended Hartstone benchmark. This figure is adapted with permission from ACM article 'Task scheduling: a control-theoretical viewpoint for a general and flexible solution' [40], to appear in ACM Transactions on Embedded Computer Systems © 2013 ACM

5.5   Set point generation for general purpose systems

As the reader may have noticed, the flexibility of the proposed scheduling solution comes from its separation into two components. One is the I+PI scheduler, and the other is the set point generation logic. A set point generator was already presented, particularly suited for (soft) real-time systems. This, however, is not the only possible choice. This section thus presents a different option, primarily targeted to general purpose systems. The key idea is to consider four models of execution that cover the vast majority of application workloads, and provide suitable tuning parameters to let a system administrator optimise the scheduler for the specific characteristics of the system at hand. It is worth stressing, once again, that the set point generation does not affect the stability properties of the controlled system.

System administrators are used to classify tasks and select for them a management policy *a priori*, knowing (on an essentially heuristic basis) that said policy is likely to produce the desired system's behaviour. For example, periodic tasks are distinguished into batch and interactive ones, the two types being assigned respectively a sequence of periodic deadlines or a single terminal one. A third type of task can be the 'continuously running' one without specific deadlines (think for example of an interactive application). For such tasks one typically relies on the idea of 'priority', to make it capable of interrupting the others 'frequently enough' to appear sufficiently responsive to the operator. There can finally be then event-triggered tasks, which are typically awakened by an interrupt (consider as an example the mouse driver) and then set back to sleep. All the above can be replicated at different priority levels, involving multiple queues, and transitions of a task from one to another in the case, e.g., of excessive observed starving. Finally, other heuristics may alter priorities over time, act on entities like the nice number, and so forth.

Apparently, hardly anything can be farther from a control-centric viewpoint than the mentality induced by the above *modus operandi*. Again, this is no criticism for alternatives to our approach, rather just noticing how difficult it can be to find a common framework to represent said alternatives. However, although the proposed scheme was already proven to be capable of consistently managing all the task types above, the way of structuring and parameterising the scheme has proven to date virtually impossible to explain to administrators unless they possess a control background, which in general is not (and must not required to be) the case.

To address this important acceptance-related problem, it is useful to split it in three parts. First, one should think of the controllers' structuring. Second, a convenient set point and α generation mechanism needs devising. Last, the parameterisation of the two entities just mentioned has to be addressed. In the authors' opinion, said subproblems are quite naturally related – and naturally attributed – to the *three* involved professionals, namely the control engineer, the computer engineer, and the system administrator *stricto sensu*.

With reference to the control structure of Figure 5.3, it was stated that by governing τ_r° and α, any requisite of fairness, timeliness, and so forth, can be enforced [46]. Further details on the matter are here provided, leading to show how the computer engineer acts as a *trait d'union* towards the system administrator's culture, once the correct control functioning is guaranteed by the control engineer, who may also set parameter bounds when necessary.

Premising that the contents of this section is still partial as research is underway, it can, however, be shown how the computer engineer can 'pre-configure' a system for its administrator, referring – for the moment – to the four basic task types just introduced.

5.5.1 Tasks with periodic deadlines

Let T_i be the period of a task, and W_i its workload in the period (i.e., every T_i time units, the task must receive the CPU for W_i time units). The *accumulated* CPU time in the period needs thus following the trapezoidal profile of Figure 5.10, the start

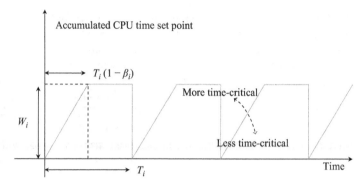

Figure 5.10   Accumulated CPU time set point for periodic tasks

of which is triggered by a periodic interrupt, while the end can be required by the task once its per-period workload is accomplished (all the major operating systems already provide primitives for such a signalling).

This means that at the beginning of each period the task will be allotted a *tentative* α component, denoted by $\widehat{\alpha}_i$, given by

$$\widehat{\alpha}_i(k) = \frac{W_i}{(1 - \beta_i)T_i\tau_r^\circ(k)}, \quad 0 \le \beta_i < 1$$

while the meaning of 'tentative' has to do with preserving the unity sum of α, as already explained in Section 5.3.1. The same $\widehat{\alpha}_i$ will be reset to zero by the task itself, to which – correctly, for the scheduler's generality – any decision is devoted on what to do if T_i expires before W_i is accomplished. Note that $\widehat{\alpha}_i$ remains constant unless τ_r° is changed. Note also that a β_i close to one requests the CPU time 'as soon as possible', which diminishes in general the probability of missing a deadline. Building on such an idea, one can probably hope in the future to have some tuning knob to pass with continuity to non-real-time through soft, and maybe even up to hard real-time constraints.

5.5.2   Tasks with a single deadline

Such tasks (e.g., batch ones) are managed in the same way as those with periodic deadlines, except that only one period, of length equal to the desired task duration, is triggered at its arrival. Also the meaning of W and β are the same as in Section 5.5.1.

5.5.3   Tasks without deadlines

This is the typical situation for interactive tasks, such as desktop applications. Since the proposed scheduling framework uses neither deadlines nor priorities, and in some sense Sections 5.5.1 and 5.5.2 lead to emulate a deadline mechanism, relying for its enforcement on the feedback action, the same idea can be used to emulate priorities for tasks that do not have deadlines. As such, one can define *for these only* a *real* – i.e., not integer nor quantised if not by the machine's nature – priority range, say from zero (lowest) to one (highest), and obtain the corresponding tentative α elements as

$$\widehat{\alpha}_i(k) = \alpha_{\min,i} + p_i(\alpha_{\max,i} - \alpha_{\min,i}), \quad 0 \le p_i \le 1$$

where $\alpha_{\max,i}$ and $\alpha_{\min,i}$ are, respectively, the maximum and the minimum α that can be assigned to the process i, while p_i is the mentioned 'priority' – the quotes indicating that its effect on the actually allotted CPU time is definitely more direct and interpretable than it would be if the term was given the traditional meaning.

5.5.4 *Event-triggered tasks*

This is the case of many services, think, e.g., of the mentioned mouse driver. The idea is that when awakened, the task gets a certain tentative α element, which then decays to zero at a given rate, i.e., as

$$\widehat{\alpha}_i(k) = \alpha_i(k-1) \cdot a_i^{-(k-k_{0,i})}, \quad 0 < a_i < 1$$

and is reset to the initial value ($\widehat{\alpha}_{i0}$ in the following) when a new awakening event is triggered, typically via an interrupt, that simply has to reset $k_{0,i}$ to the current time index. Note that this is the only case in which $\widehat{\alpha}_i$ can in general undergo variations over each round. If this is not acceptable for any reason, one could for example allot a 'small' fixed CPU share to the task, and consider it blocked when not awakened. It was already shown that the proposed scheduler manages blockings correctly (see Section 5.3.2), so the only price to pay for such a choice is a potentially (slightly) increased overhead. Of course the computer engineer could prevent one or the other choice from being taken by the administrator on a given system.

Once all the tentative components $\widehat{\alpha}_i$ are available, α is simply obtained by rescaling so that its sum be one, as described in Section 5.3.1. In the case of particularly critical periodic tasks, a flag can be introduced to prevent their components from being rescaled. The computer engineer in charge of pre-configuring a system has essentially to set limits on the admissible values for parameters $\alpha_{\min,i}$ and $\alpha_{\max,i}$ and possibly narrow those for β_i, p_i and a_i, either for system-wide or for some classes of tasks. Also, he/she has to decide how many tasks can be excluded from rescaling, and so forth. The idea is to set – if necessary – 'safe' limits for the choices of the system administrator, and the interesting feature is that said limits can be clearly interpreted in terms of the used control scheme.

5.5.5 *Parameter setting*

Parameter setting is the role of the system administrator, and once confined as per the choices above, there should not be the possibility of provoking undesired behaviours, while a graceful degradation is expected (thanks to rescaling) in the case of overloading. To further ease the administrator's work, the computer engineer could also prepare some pre-defined parameter settings, suitable for certain task types, and by means of profiling, those settings could be refined on the field. Here too, the advantages of a direct control-theoretical meaning should be apparent.

5.5.6 Simulation examples

The presented results are obtained from a PC-based simulator of the scheduler as implemented in Miosix (see Chapter 10). The simulation code is available in Appendix A.1.4. Given the nature of the problem, and in particular the absence of any significant measurement error, simulation results are in this case practically equivalent to real-hardware ones.

The scheduler used for the example is the I+PI designed as described in Section 5.3, i.e.,

$$R_t(z) = \text{diag}\left\{\left\{\frac{0.5}{z-1}\right\}_i\right\}, \quad R_r(z) = 2.5\frac{z-0.5}{z-1} \quad (5.15)$$

The task pool characteristics are summarised in Table 5.6. There are tasks of all the four defined types: for the two periodic ones the period, the workload and the value of β are given; the two batch ones are specified in the same way, except for the replacement of 'period' with 'duration' and the presence of an arrival time; the three prioritised ones are specified by the corresponding values of priority p; finally, the two event-based ones have an initial CPU share and a decay rate as parameters, and are triggered at prespecified times. During the simulation, some priority

Table 5.6   *Task pool for the simulation example*

ID	Periodic	Period	Workload	β
1	Tpe1	50	0.5	0.5
2	Tpe2	120	0.8	0.7

	Batch	Arrival	Workload	Duration	β
3	Tba1	125	60	300	0.1
4	Tba2	150	70	450	0.1

	Prior.	Priority
5	Tpr1	0.1 for $\tau < 250$ and $\tau > 375$, else 0.25
6	Tpr2	0.5
7	Tpr3	0.18

	Ev.-based	In. share	Dec. rate	Trig. times
8	Teb1	0.02	0.6	10, 20, 100, 280, 300
9	Teb2	0.03	0.7	5, 15, 50, 80, 150, 400

modifications are impressed, to investigate the system's response. No other actions on the pool are shown to avoid too confusing a presentation, and since the purpose here is to illustrate the effects of the proposed parameterisation scheme, care is taken in this example to avoid over-utilisation.

Figures 5.11–5.13, with vertical axes graduated in time units, report the results of a simulation run spanning 500 time units. In detail, Figure 5.11 shows the round duration, that apparently keeps its set point of 0.5 time units despite all the underlying pool-generated events and the δb disturbance, chosen so as to generate on average a 10% deviation of the actual from the allotted CPU use for all the tasks. Figure 5.12 shows the accumulated CPU times for the periodic tasks, evidencing the effect of β. In this example no task is excluded from α rescaling, whence the observed (and desired if rescaling is not used) slope modifications. Finally, Figure 5.13 reports the CPU shares for all the tasks in the pool, evidencing how the desired set points are met, and mutual influences are dealt with thanks to the control-based approach.

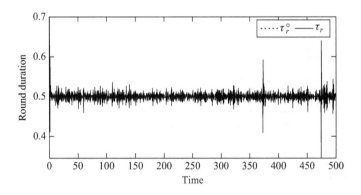

Figure 5.11   Simulation example – round duration control

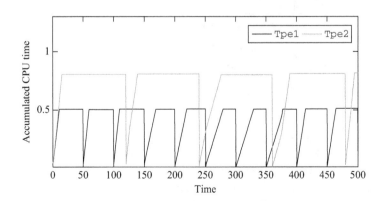

Figure 5.12   Simulation example – accumulated CPU time for periodic tasks

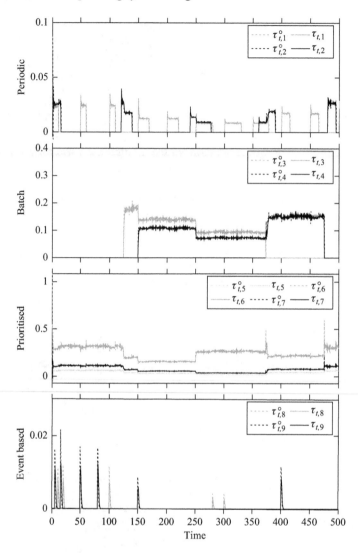

Figure 5.13   Simulation example – CPU distribution

5.5.7   Concluding remarks

In synthesis, the presented example should have evidenced that the proposed control structure can be parameterised by a system administrator in a comprehensible manner, see Table 5.6. Other phenomena, such as over-utilisation or other actions on the pool, are dealt with correctly by the scheduler *as already proved* in previous sections, and the proposed parameterisation actually seems to serve the envisaged purpose satisfactorily.

Chapter 6

Memory management

Besides CPU time, a very important resource to be managed by an operating system is memory, as for an effective operation it is necessary that each process, and the operating system itself, have the required memory available at any given time.

No doubt the remark just made is quite trivial, but it evidences two points that make memory management a problem worth addressing in this book. First, despite technology improvements are providing an increasing memory capacity to virtually any device, applications have over time become more and more memory-hungry, and thus memory is very often a limited resource. Second, the memory required by processes is not constant from the time they are started till they terminate. Instead, memory is requested and relinquished by processes over time, either explicitly, through system calls, or implicitly, for example when a function call causes a stack growth. As such, the time scale of memory usage – and therefore management – is quite fast.

Modern general-purpose operating systems manage memory through a *paging* mechanism, and reserve a swap space on disk to allow the pool of running processes to collectively access more memory than the available RAM, creating a *virtual memory* system. Therefore, the general term 'memory' actually refers to two entities, namely physical memory (RAM) and swap space.

The memory management activity is generally devoted to a software *kernel allocator*, that interacts on one side with the running processes, and on the other with a hardware *Memory Management Unit* (MMU), with the overall goal of satisfying the systems' memory needs by means of RAM and swap space.

Focusing on general purpose operating systems, one can notice an interesting fact: despite they differ significantly in the way scheduling is dealt with, the same is not true as for memory management. A reason may be that scheduling is still considered an open problem, and many solutions are being proposed, targeting both general-purpose systems and specific (e.g., real-time) ones. As a result, hardly any two operating system kernels have a similar scheduler, and in some cases the scheduler is even completely different between two versions of the same kernel.[1]

On the other hand, it seems that the initial research effort on virtual memory, carried out in the early days of multitasking computers, has nowadays almost faded

---

[1] A notable case concerns the Linux scheduler, that changed very significantly in kernel version 2.6.23, when the $O(1)$ scheduler was replaced with another one called the 'Completely Fair Scheduler'.

out, and that at present operating systems essentially manage memory all (more or less) in the same way. New research directions hardly include anything but implementing swap on more modern memory technologies than disks, or studies on distributed virtual memory. In one word, at least to the best of the authors' experience and knowledge, the foundations of the design of memory management – except for the distributed case, on which however we do not concentrate here – are practically not questioned.

To support this claim, it is interesting to briefly outline how the typical (hereinafter, 'traditional') memory management systems work, and then review some of the milestones of the consolidation of such a design.

At the depth required in this chapter, traditional memory management can be represented as in Figure 6.1. At the highest level there is the set of processes that allocate and deallocate memory. Memory allocation can occur explicitly, such as through the brk() and mmap() system calls, which are used, e.g., by the malloc() and free() C library functions, and the C++'s new and delete operators. Memory allocation can however also occur implicitly, when a stack growth causes a *page fault*, and requires the allocator to provide the process with one or more additional memory pages.

Memory *requests* are served by the kernel allocator, which is a software component that has also the task of moving memory pages from RAM to swap space if no available RAM is found. Memory *accesses* on the part of processes, are instead served by the MMU, a hardware component that performs the translation between virtual and physical addresses (details on how this happens are inessential here). If a memory access falls in a page that has been swapped out, the MMU causes a *page fault*, i.e., an event that triggers the kernel allocator to load that page into RAM. The need for a hardware component is due to the fact that memory accesses occur at such

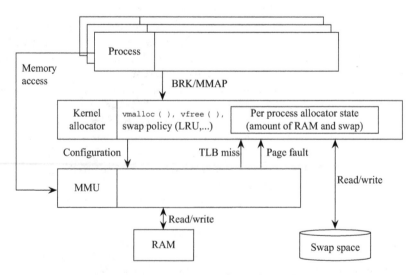

Figure 6.1   A schematic representation of a traditional memory management

a high frequency (every CPU instruction implies at least one memory access) that the address translation functionality cannot be implemented in software, for efficiency reasons.

Traditionally, the kernel allocator is thus a purely event-triggered component, called as the result of a memory-related system call or page fault. Therefore, every performed action – including swapping memory pages out to disk, or vice versa from disk into RAM – is dictated solely by the memory access patterns of the processes. When RAM is available, the kernel allocator performs the operations that the processes requested, including swapping in pages where a page fault occurred. On the other hand, when the RAM is full, the allocator needs to swap out some pages. To choose which ones, many algorithms have been proposed. The Least Recently Used (LRU) is probably the most frequent choice, and a very common (not to say, virtually general) fact concerning said algorithms, is that the decision on which page(s) to swap out is taken system-wide, not on a per-process basis.

The idea of virtual memory dates back to the first multitasking systems. The reasons for its introduction were to provide the same address space to all processes, to enforce memory protection, to allow sharing of common code among multiple running instances of the same program, and – in the case of shared libraries – among multiple programs, and finally to allow processes to allocate more memory than the amount of RAM available in the system. The last feature introduces the disk as the last level of the memory hierarchy. Due to the large difference between RAM and disk access times, diverse replacement strategies were tested for swapping process data to disk. One of the first works on the subject [47], proposed an on-demand page swapping scheme that is triggered when a page fault occurs to swap the required page into memory. In this occasion, and when memory allocation occurs, if the physical memory is exhausted, one or more pages are swapped out to disk. That work proposes different algorithms to select which page(s) to swap out, including a round robin one. Despite the publication dates back to 1969, this scheme is surprisingly similar to what is used nowadays.

A different approach was adopted in the VAX/VMS virtual memory implementation [48]. The VAX/VMS design is centred around the idea of the *resident set*, which can be thought of as a hard limit on the amount of memory that a process can allocate in RAM. If this limit is reached, every new allocation will cause the swap-out of pages taken from the same process. This solution introduces the concept of *memory access temporal isolation*, since a process making an excessive use of memory cannot swap out pages from other ones, causing unpredictable system-wide slowdowns. A major advantage of this design is that of addressing responsiveness on a per-process basis, thus providing a notable exception to the remark above, but a disadvantage is a sub-optimal RAM utilisation. In fact, analogously to Example 3.3.4, a process above its memory limit is forced to swap out even if there is plenty of available RAM, and thus the mentioned swap-out is in fact not necessary.

Virtual memory implementations significantly different from the mainstream type just sketched, were only proposed for specific applications, such as swapping out entire processes when memory is exhausted, and swapping them back in when memory becomes sufficient again, to optimise throughput for batch jobs [49].

As anticipated, anyway, after this first research effort, the design of a virtual memory system was practically consolidated to be on-demand paging with LRU-based page replacement, and the literature became virtually silent on this subject.

6.1   Problem statement

It is nowadays taken for established that swapping in and out needs to be triggered by application events only, such as memory requests and page faults. In this case, the only decision to be taken is *what* to swap out when RAM is not sufficient, with LRU being the most common means to decide.

However, this scheme has two major issues. One is related to the system-wide nature of the LRU scheme currently adopted, the other to the purely demand-based (or in other terms, event-triggered) activation of the memory manager. As a result, its behaviour is not optimal in many significant use cases.

A typical example is when a memory-intensive background task is run concurrently to some interactive ones, which can easily happen when using the same machine for running both heavy batch jobs and a window manager to provide a graphical user interface. When the background task's memory allocations cause the exhaustion of the available RAM, the LRU scheme will swap out pages from arbitrary processes, most probably including the interactive ones, thus causing a significant reduction in their responsiveness. This is caused by the lack of a memory manager that can act on a per-process basis, so as to control *which* are the processes that have exceeded their memory limit, and have to be selected as targets for swap-outs.

The negative impact of swapping out pages onto application responsiveness is a widely known fact, however at present (at least, to the best of the authors' knowledge) no systematic attempts to model the problem have emerged, and only *ad hoc* solution have been introduced. One such solution is the *swappiness* parameter of the Linux kernel, that allows to choose whether the kernel should prefer to swap out processes or to reduce disk buffers when running out of memory. However, this solution is still far from being comprehensive, as witnessed by the quote from Reference 50 below, that incidentally explicitly questions the system-wide approach to swap-outs.

> 'The swappiness parameter should do what a lot of users want, but it does not solve the whole problem. Swappiness is a global parameter; it affects every process on the system in the same way. What a number of people would like to see, however, is a way to single out individual applications for special treatment.'

Another limitation of current memory management systems is their purely event-triggered nature. A typical example that exacerbates this limitation is when a process transiently allocates a large amount of memory, as it frequently happens for the linking phase at the end of the compilation of large software projects. In this case part of that process will be swapped out, and due to the system-wide LRU scheme, also part of other processes will. When the complex task ends, the memory occupation drops sharply, resulting in a large amount of free RAM. If in this situation the system is left idle, it will not recover as fast as it could, due to swap-in being only triggered by application page faults. Therefore, it may happen that memory pages remain swapped out for a long time even if RAM is available. Then, when a process requests those pages, a disk access will be triggered, stalling that process and decreasing its responsiveness. Moreover, the swap-in of those pages may occur when the CPU is highly loaded, while from the swap-out instant till the page faults there may have been plenty of time with a low load.

Among the community of Linux system administrators, it is not uncommon to use the workaround of disabling and immediately re-enabling the swap, using the commands swapoff -a; swapon -a, to force the operating system to perform a full swap-in, and recover from a transient memory over-utilisation. This is a result of the lack of control about *when* to perform swap-in. If an active swap-in mechanism were available to gradually free the swap space when there is room in RAM and the CPU load is low, a benefit for the overall system responsiveness would be gained.

Summarising, in the opinion of the authors, there are two fundamental questions that current memory management schemes fail to address, which are *what* and *when*. The first question addresses per-process memory limits, and could be used to achieve *memory access temporal isolation*, in more structured a manner than the early VAX/VMS ideas did. The second question opens the door to transfers between swap and RAM that are time-triggered, instead of event-triggered by process page faults.

This chapter shows how an integrated solution can be devised with the adopted control-theoretical approach. The solution takes the form of a feedback controller, and as usual allows for a formal assessment of the obtained control system as for performance and robustness (in the sense those terms are given in the systems theory).

The proposed solution exhibits some resemblance with the VMS one, but a significant difference is that the hard limit of the VMS approach is here substituted with a soft limit, therefore allowing to fully utilise the available RAM, avoiding sub-optimal swap-outs. In the proposed scheme, a process can exceed its memory use limit as long as there is enough memory in the system, i.e., other applications are using less memory than their limit. If the applications below their own limit subsequently allocate more memory, and the available total is exceeded, only the applications above their limit will experience swap-outs. Therefore, unlike in the VMS solution, it is not true that memory allocations cause swap-outs only from the same process that originated them. On the contrary, memory allocations cause swap-outs only from processes that are exceeding their use limit. Finally, the proposed solution performs an automatic swap-in, which is not present in the VMS approach.

6.2   The plant model

In order to design a per-process basis memory manager, a model of the processes behaviour needs to be sought, analogously to what has been done for the scheduling problem in the previous chapter. In particular, from the memory manager's point of view, a process can perform the following actions:

- Allocate a quantity of memory. Since it is reasonable that the allocated memory will be used almost immediately, the memory manager will directly allocate it in RAM.
- Deallocate a memory area, that can be either in RAM, or entirely or partially swapped out. The allocator can obviously free swap memory without intermediately moving it to RAM.
- Generate page faults.

Accounting for those remarks, a generic (*i*th) process can be represented for the purpose of this chapter by the discrete-time, LTI model

$$\begin{cases} m_i(k+1) = m_i(k) + a_i(k) - dm_i(k) + pf_i(k) + u_i(k) \\ s_i(k+1) = s_i(k) - ds_i(k) - pf_i(k) - u_i(k) \end{cases} \tag{6.1}$$

where the state variables m_i and s_i are, respectively, the quantity of allocated RAM and swap memory. The index k counts the memory-affecting operations, making (6.1) discrete-time but not sampled-signals. The other quantities are either process-generated requests – i.e., a_i, dm_i, pf_i, ds_i, treated here as disturbances – or memory-manager decisions – i.e., u_i, that is the input of the model (explained below).

In detail, a_i and dm_i are respectively the allocated and deallocated quantity of memory in RAM, and ds_i is the deallocated memory from swap. The term pf_i represents the page faults that a process can generate (in a highly unpredictable manner, depending on its memory use pattern) and acts symmetrically on RAM and swap.

Note that all the quantities mentioned so far (except for u_i) are physically bound to be nonnegative. Also note that all are known by the memory manager, therefore measured without error.

As for u_i, this is the only variable on which the memory manager can act, and represents the amount of memory that is moved from RAM to swap or vice versa; u_i is thus the only quantity that can take both positive and negative values. The resulting model is composed of two discrete integrators per process, subject to physical constraints, which are

$$\begin{cases} m_i(k) \geq 0 \qquad \forall i = 1, \ldots, N \\ \sum_{i=1}^{N} m_i(k) \leq \beta \overline{M} \\ s_i(k) \geq 0 \qquad \forall i = 1, \ldots, N \\ \sum_{i=1}^{N} s_i(k) \leq \overline{S} \end{cases} \tag{6.2}$$

where N is the number of processes, $\overline{M}$ and $\overline{S}$ are, respectively, the maximum amount of memory and swap in the system, and β takes into account that some of the physical memory may be reserved, for example by the kernel itself. The $\beta \overline{M}$ term is here called *global maximum memory occupation*, and is considered a configuration parameter.

Some of the physical constraints in (6.2) are naturally enforced by the system. For example, if a process has no swap, it cannot generate page faults that would cause the swap state variable to become negative. Analogously, a process cannot deallocate memory that it does not have. Actually it could *attempt* to do so, owing, e.g., to a programming error, but in this case the kernel would detect the error and terminate the process before the memory system is set to an inconsistent state. In designing the controller we are not concerned with such an event, that we can consider not to be a 'reasonably expectable' disturbance behaviour, recall Section 4.1.

Some other constraints, conversely, are not naturally enforced in the same way. For example, memory *allocations* are in principle not limited, as a process can hog up as much memory as it desires. Here too, thus, we have to assume some 'sanity' in the memory use on the part of the processes, as from a systemic point of view said use must be irrelevant for the memory manager (like the reasons for not releasing the CPU on time had to be for the scheduler, recall). In some sense, we are here too grounding the design on some idea of reasonableness, which is aligned to the used approach (see above).

Incidentally, however, the possibility for processes to allocate memory in an arbitrary manner indicates that the system cannot be guaranteed to work (well) in the total absence of control. In this respect, e.g., traditional management system normally include only last-resort components such as the Linux *out of memory killer*, with quite obvious meaning. Apparently, in the presence of a process that ran amok, sooner or later termination will eventually be the only action to take, but before that, control can at least avoid the whole system to be excessively upset.

Coming back to the main problem, control is here represented by $u_i(k)$, that is constrained by

$$\begin{cases} u_i(k) \geq -m_i(k) - a_i(k) + dm_i(k) - pf_i(k) \\ u_i(k) \leq s_i(k) - ds_i(k) - pf_i(k) \\ \sum_{i=1}^{N} u_i(k) \leq \beta \overline{M} - \sum_{i=1}^{N} (m_i(k) + a_i(k) - dm_i(k) + pf_i(k)) \end{cases} \tag{6.3}$$

It is interesting to further stress that since an intervention of the out of memory killer is a pathological condition, it *de facto* indicates a malfunction of some process – that should occur very sporadically – or an erratic swap space configuration on the part of the system administrator, and neither case is to be dealt with by the memory manager. Translating in terms of the model just written, this means that from the point of view of the memory manager the swap space can be considered infinite, and the only constraint is to guarantee (by means of convenient swap-outs) that the physical memory is not exhausted.

Therefore, just as in the scheduler case, the model provided so far is the true *uncontrolled system model*, and not a model of an existing memory manager. In fact, as existing memory managers have to guarantee that the total RAM memory allocated by processes is below the available one, they are already closing a loop. Starting from a model encompassing only the underlying physical phenomenon that cannot be changed, as usual but worth repeating, puts us in the best position to redesign a memory manager from scratch as a controller.

Interestingly enough, however, in this particular problem the proposed model *can* also represent existing solutions, i.e., memory managers. It suffices to assume $m_i(k)$, $a_i(k)$, $dm_i(k)$, $ds_i(k)$ and $pf_i(k)$ as disturbances – as they *de facto* are from the memory manager's standpoint – and add some logic to represent, e.g., the LRU policy.

A last note regards the fact that the kernel handles memory in terms of pages, which are a set of contiguous memory locations, with a typical size being 4 KB. Therefore, all quantities in the model are expressed in memory pages.

6.2.1   Requirements

The currently available memory managers are not designed as controllers, and simply act in response to process-originated requests, having the sole purpose of fulfilling (6.3). However, it has already been shown that such managers perform sub-optimally in some relevant cases. The idea is here to act on $u_i(k)$ on a per-process basis, and to introduce an additional input u_s (see Figure 6.2) to cause the system to proactively free the swap space when possible.

As will be shown, this can be done with a very simple control structure, ultimately determining *how much* memory to swap in or out for each process. Within the process memory space, one can clearly continue using LRU-like policies, or alternative ones, to decide *what* to swap-out.

To design the mentioned layer, the following requirements, in addition to (6.3), need fulfilling:

- if there is not enough RAM for all the processes, pages will be swapped out only from those that are exceeding a given limit (that can be different for each process);
- if there is available RAM and occupied swap, the latter has to be reloaded in RAM at a system-wide minimum specified rate (another configuration parameter), and that rate can be increased if swapping in is explicitly required by some process by means of page faults.

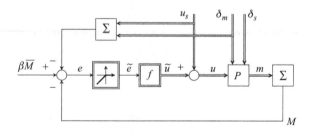

Figure 6.2   The proposed control scheme; each element of P has the form (6.1)

6.3　Control synthesis

The requirements just expressed can be summarised by saying that when there is RAM available, the system has to behave like an open-loop (vector) integrator, with divergence (and in particular the violation of the $m_i(k), s_i(k) \geq 0$ constraint) being avoided by the behavioural properties of processes, in the sense discussed above when talking about 'sanity'. In addition, active swap-in has to occur if possible. On the contrary, when the required RAM is not available, swap-out has to occur in such a way to recover the required RAM distribution, i.e., not penalising processes that are not exceeding their memory limit.

A control scheme that can fulfil these requirements is presented in Figure 6.2. The first component is a block predicting the memory status at the next $(k + 1)$ step, which is $M(k)$ plus the sum of RAM disturbances $\delta m(k)$ (which collects $a(k) - dm(k) + pf(k)$), plus an input vector u_s that is the input added to perform active swap-in. This, of course, is the prediction of the total memory occupation at the next step *in the absence of control*. That predicted value is compared to $\beta \overline{M}$, and passed through a saturation having zero as the upper limit.

This results in a control loop that closes only if the memory state at the next step would exceed the limit, as in the opposite case the output of the saturation block is zero whatever the input is (thus, the loop is open). When the loop is closed, the saturation block passes over its negative input, which amounts to the RAM that needs to be swapped out, to a nonlinear function. This function, denoted here by f, has the purpose of distributing that amount of memory among processes, considering per-process limits. Function f – crucial to achieve per-process control action – will be discussed a bit later on; for now, it is only important to note that for the control scheme to work, the sum of the elements of its output vector $\tilde{u}$ should be equal to its input $\tilde{e}$, which contains by construction an integer number of pages. The active swap-in vector u_s can be normally zero and periodically set to have all positive elements, therefore introducing a time-triggered memory manager activation, in addition to the event-triggered one already present.

To analyse this control scheme, it is convenient to focus on the system with input $\tilde{e}$ and output M, which makes sense assuming that no process saturation is active.

$$
\begin{cases}
m(k + 1) = m(k) + \delta m(k) + u_s(k) + f\ (sp(k), m(k), \tilde{e}(k)) \\
M(k) = \mathbf{1}_{1 \times N} m(k)
\end{cases}
$$

Starting from this system, one can perform a coordinate change in the state space, using the nonsingular matrix

$$
T = \begin{bmatrix}
1 & 1 & \cdots & 1 & 1 \\
0 & 1 & \cdots & 0 & 0 \\
\vdots & \vdots & \ddots & \vdots & \vdots \\
0 & 0 & \cdots & 1 & 0 \\
0 & 0 & \cdots & 0 & 1
\end{bmatrix}
$$

As a result, the new state vector becomes

$$\underline{m}(k) = T \cdot m(k) = \begin{bmatrix} \sum_{i=1}^{N} m_i(k) \\ m_2(k) \\ \vdots \\ m_N(k) \end{bmatrix}$$

and the system can be rewritten as

$$\begin{cases} \underline{m}(k+1) = \underline{m}(k) + \begin{bmatrix} \sum_{i=1}^{N} \left(\delta m_i(k) + u_{si}(k) + f_i\left(sp_i(k), m(k), \widetilde{e}(k)\right) \right) \\ \delta m_2(k) + u_{s2}(k) + f_2(sp_2(k), m(k), \widetilde{e}(k)) \\ \vdots \\ \delta m_N(k) + u_{sN}(k) + f_N(sp_N(k), m(k), \widetilde{e}(k)) \end{bmatrix} \\ M(k) = [1\ 0 \cdots\ 0]\ \underline{m}(k) \end{cases}$$

Noticing that

$$\sum_{i=1}^{N} f_i\left(\alpha_i(k), m(k), \widetilde{e}(k)\right) = \widetilde{e}(k)$$

and letting $\delta = \sum_{i=1}^{N} (\delta m_i(k) + u_{si}(k))$, the system can be rewritten as

$$\begin{cases} \underline{m}(k+1) = \underline{m}(k) + \begin{bmatrix} \delta + \widetilde{e}(k) \\ \delta m_2(k) + u_{s2}(k) + f_2(sp_2(k), m(k), \widetilde{e}(k)) \\ \vdots \\ \delta m_N(k) + u_{sN}(k) + f_N(sp_N(k), m(k), \widetilde{e}(k)) \end{bmatrix} \\ M(k) = [1\ 0 \cdots 0]\ \underline{m}(k) \end{cases}$$

In this model only the first state variable, which represents the sum of the RAM memory allocated by all processes, affects the output, and it is not influenced by the nonlinear function, whose only purpose is to partition the swap-out signal among processes. This allows to employ, for the purpose of this section, the simplified model of Figure 6.3.

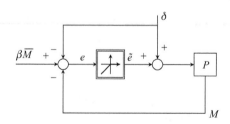

Figure 6.3　The reduced control scheme

This model has only one state variable, namely $M(k)$, which is the total RAM in use by processes, and its state equation reads

$$M(k+1) = M(k) + d(k) + \min\left(0, \beta\overline{M} - \delta(k) - M(k)\right) \tag{6.4}$$

To understand how the system works, it is possible to consider separately its two modes of operation, depending on the saturation, which leads to write

$$\begin{cases} M(k+1) = M(k) + d(k) : M(k) + d(k) < \beta\overline{M} \\ M(k+1) = \beta\overline{M} \qquad\quad : M(k) + d(k) \geq \beta\overline{M} \end{cases} \tag{6.5}$$

As can be seen, the controller can ensure that the global RAM limit is never exceeded, as long as no saturations in the processes occur. Function f has then to prevent such saturations, and once this is guaranteed, its presence is irrelevant for the control loop.

Coming specifically to function f, its purpose is to partition the swap-out request that is dictated by the control loop among processes, considering their memory state and memory limit, while at the same time avoiding saturations (e.g., swapping more memory than a process has). It also has to produce integer output values, since memory is managed by pages and should guarantee that the sum of the elements of its output vector is equal to the input signal. A way to do so is to first try to swap out only the processes that are above their memory limit. If this is not sufficient (e.g., if at the previous k all processes were below their limit, and this is the first allocation that causes RAM to be exhausted) the processes which are allocating memory are chosen as targets for swap-outs. The function can thus be implemented as Algorithm 6.1.

Algorithm 6.1 The swap-out partitioning function.

```
function F(sp, m, ẽ, δ_m)
    totalover ← ∑_{i=1}^{N} max (0, m_i − sp_i);
    if totalover > 0 then
        swapshare ← max (0, m − sp)/totalover;              // So that ∑ swapshare = 1
        result ← integerShare(min (ẽ, totalover), swapshare);
    else
        result ← 0;
    end if
    if ẽ > totalover then
        allocating ← max (0, δ_m);
        totalAllocating ← ∑_{i=1}^{N} allocating_i;
        result ← result + integerShare(ẽ − totalover, allocating/totalAllocating);
    end if
    return result;
end function
```

In the presented algorithm, the *integerShare*(a, b) function takes a scalar a and a vector b, and returns a vector containing $a \cdot b$ rounded so that the elements are all integers and their sum is again a. A Scilab implementation of both f and *integerShare* is reported in Appendix A.1.2. Recall once more that once function f fulfils the specifications, details on its internal behaviour are irrelevant for the control scheme.

6.4   Simulation results

The proposed memory manager has been simulated to assess its properties. The full simulator code is available in Appendix A.1.3.

Figure 6.4 shows an example of the simulation results. At the beginning of the simulation there are three processes, each with 100 RAM pages allocated and no swap. The processes start allocating memory, and the first two exceed their RAM limit around $k = 40$ and $k = 90$, respectively. However, since there is still RAM available in the system, no control action is taken. Then, around $k = 100$, the global memory limit is reached, and the first two processes start swapping. The third process does not swap, and is even allowed to continue allocating RAM, as it is still below its limit: the memory needed by the third process is obtained by swapping the processes with a memory usage above their limits.

Around $k = 200$ the processes stop allocating memory. The third process is still below its limit and has no swap. The remaining RAM is partitioned among the other two processes, which are left with as much RAM above their limit as the available one allows. As can be seen from the bottom plot, the RAM is fully utilised.

At $k = 500$ the RAM allocation limits are changed, but no page faults occur. In this situation the presence of the active swap-in vector causes a slow but sustained change of the processes' RAM towards the new limit. In the presence of page faults, the mentioned change rate would be faster, thereby quickly accommodating for the applications' desires.

At $k = 700$ the third process terminates. This causes the immediate deallocation of both RAM and swap. The availability of additional RAM, coupled with the existence of used swap, triggers the active swap-in activity, which causes a swap-in of the two remaining processes, again in the absence of page faults. Around $k = 880$ all the swapped-out pages have been brought back into RAM, so that when the processes will access their memory pages, no page faults will occur, significantly increasing responsiveness.

6.5   Implementation-related considerations

From an implementation point of view, the modifications that need to be done to an existing kernel allocator to implement the proposed scheme are outlined in Figure 6.5 as 'new elements'.

The feedback manager is the newly introduced component, and needs to be called every time memory allocations, deallocations or page faults occur, augmenting the

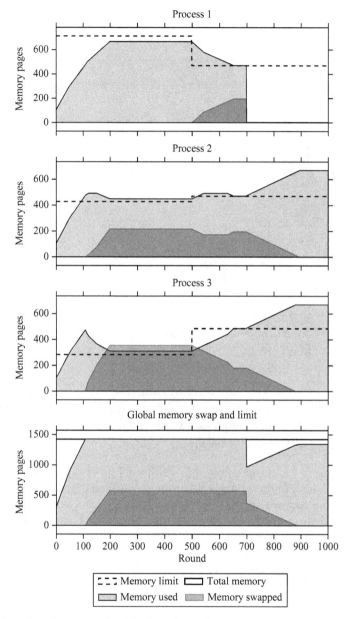

Figure 6.4   Simulation results. The first three plots show RAM occupation, RAM limit and swap space of each process. The bottom plot shows system-wide RAM, limit and swap usage

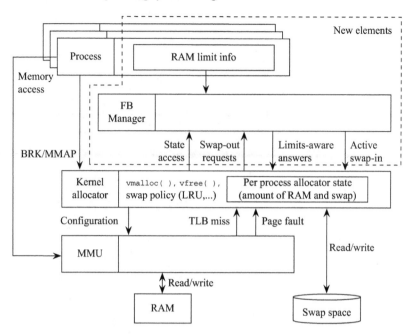

Figure 6.5   The additional memory management layer and its integration with the kernel allocator

pre-existing decision-making logic. In particular, when swap-outs are needed, the existing LRU policy needs to be reorganised by letting the feedback manager decide how many pages to swap out from each process; after that, LRU is used to decide which pages of each process to swap out.

To realise the active swap-in functionality, the feedback manager needs to be periodically called – at a convenient rate, which can be a configuration parameter – also in the absence of process-triggered memory operations. Note that when a page fault occurs, this happens on a specific swapped page, so the kernel allocator has no degree of freedom regarding which page to swap in; on the contrary, for what concerns active swap-in, the problem of deciding which pages to move arises. A possible solution, substantially analogous to the LRU policy, is to introduce a mechanism that we might call Least Recently Swapped (LRS) policy, with obvious meaning. Once again, recall that the internals of such a mechanism are irrelevant for the controller.

6.6   Concluding remarks

This chapter addressed the problem of memory management from quite a novel perspective. Current memory managers employed in general purpose operating systems care most about *what* to swap out, and *how much* can be viewed essentially as just a consequence of that decision. In addition, memory managers are thought of as purely event-triggered systems, and therefore do not swap pages in unless explicitly requested to, as a result of page faults. In this case, the word *management* is interpreted as doing the least amount of actions, therefore operating only upon process requests.

Despite it has been shown that such traditional solutions suffer from some limitations, the literature appears to be practically silent on this topic, and the current issues seem to be almost considered as unavoidable. In this chapter it has been shown how, by formulating the problem as a control one, an entirely different solution can be devised, mitigating the issues of current ones while still fulfilling physical constraints.

The content of this chapter is new, and unfortunately at the time of writing no implementation of a so described memory management has been performed yet in a real kernel, to assess its performance. In this respect, however, it is noteworthy to underline how a control-theoretical approach has the advantage of allowing easy simulations to test a control scheme, even in the (temporary) absence of a real implementation.

Chapter 7

A byte of advanced control techniques

This chapter presents more advanced control techniques with respect to those of Chapter 4, that will be used in the following. In particular, Section 7.1 presents the main results on Model Predictive Control (MPC) that are relevant for this book. The main concepts related to model identification and adaptive control are presented in Sections 7.2 and 7.3 respectively. The purpose of this chapter is to introduce the reader to the basic concepts and terminology related to those control techniques, with the same attitude of Chapters 2 and 4. More details on the matter can be found in the cited literature, and particularly in References 51–54.

7.1 Model Predictive Control

In this section, we introduce the basic ideas and terminology about MPC. In Section 7.1.3, a SISO state-space model with an embedded integrator is introduced, which is used in the design of predictive controllers with integral action. In Section 7.1.4, we describe the design of predictive control within an optimisation window. With the results obtained from said optimisation, in Section 7.1.5, we discuss the ideas of Receding Horizon Predictive Control (RHPC), of state feedback gain matrices, and of the closed-loop configuration of predictive control systems. The results can be easily extended to MIMO systems, although the matter is omitted given the introductory tutorial purpose of this chapter.

7.1.1 Predictive control

The objective of MPC is to compute the future trajectory of the control variable u so as to optimise the future behaviour of the controlled variable y. The optimisation is performed within a limited time window, based on plant information gathered at the beginning of that window.

Before going into the mathematical details of MPC, some basic terminology and concepts need to be presented.

Generally, in MPC there exists a *moving horizon window*, which is a time-dependent window from an arbitrary time k to $k + H_p$, where H_p is the length of the window, and usually remains constant. This parameter is also known as the *prediction horizon*, and dictates 'how far' we wish the future to be predicted.

The *receding horizon control* is a typical control policy adopted in MPC. Although an optimal trajectory of the future control signal u is computed for the whole moving horizon window, the actual control input to the plant takes only the first value of the computed control signal, neglecting the rest of the future trajectory—this concept will be further explained in Section 7.1.5.

In planning the optimal trajectory of u, the state information $x(k)$ is needed in order to predict the future; the state of the system can be either *measured* or *estimated*.

A *model* that describes the dynamics of the system is thus of high importance. A good dynamic model will give a consistent and accurate prediction of the future, hence a more effective control.

In order to take the best decision, a criterion is needed to reflect the objective. This is typically based on an *objective function* depending on the difference between the desired and the actual behaviour of the system, and/or on other involved quantities, e.g., the entity or the variation of the control signal. This objective function is here called J, and the optimal control action is found by minimising it within the optimisation window, possibly with some constraints. In this chapter, however, we are focusing only on the unconstrained case.

7.1.2   Review on predictive control techniques

Predictive control is one of the most effective and studied control techniques, due to its simplicity and flexibility. In the literature, three main approaches to predictive control design can be found. In the earlier formulation of MPC, Finite Impulse Response (FIR) models and step response ones were preferred. FIR model (or step response model–based) design algorithms include Dynamic Matrix Control (DMC) [55] and in particular its quadratic formulation [56]. FIR models are appealing to process engineers, because their structure gives a transparent description of process time delay, response time and gain. However, they are limited to stable plants, and often require large orders. This structure typically requires 30 to 60 impulse response coefficients, depending on the process dynamics, and the choice of the sampling interval.

Transfer function models give a simpler description of process dynamics, and are applicable to both stable and unstable plants. Representatives of transfer function model–based predictive control include predictor-based self-tuning control [57] and the Generalised Predictive Control (GPC) algorithm [58,59]. Transfer function model–based predictive control is, however, often considered to be less effective in handling multivariable plants, and as a consequence, a state-space formulation of GPC has been presented in Reference 60. Recent years have seen the growing popularity of predictive control design using state-space design methods [61,62]. In this work, we concentrate on state-space models.

7.1.3   State-space models

An MPC-type controller is designed starting from a mathematical description of the object to be controlled. The model to be used in the control system design is a state-space form.

For simplicity, we focus on a SISO LTI system (see Chapter 2, for basic definitions), which reads as

$$\begin{cases} x_m(k+1) = A_m x_m(k) + B_m u(k) \\ y(k) = C_m x_m(k) \end{cases} \tag{7.1}$$

of dimension n_m. Note that we have implicitly assumed $D_m = 0$.

Applying the difference operation to both sides of the state equation of (7.1), we obtain

$$x_m(k+1) - x_m(k) = A_m(x_m(k) - x_m(k-1)) + B_m(u(k) - u(k-1)) \tag{7.2}$$

Denoting the difference of the state variable by

$$\Delta x_m(k+1) = x_m(k+1) - x_m(k) \tag{7.3}$$

and the difference of the control variable by

$$\Delta u(k) = u(k) - u(k-1) \tag{7.4}$$

the difference version of the state-space equation is

$$\Delta x_m(k+1) = A_m \Delta x_m(k) + B_m \Delta u(k) \tag{7.5}$$

The next step is to introduce the new state variable vector

$$x(k) = \begin{bmatrix} \Delta x(k) \\ y(k) \end{bmatrix} \tag{7.6}$$

Note that

$$\begin{aligned} y(k+1) - y(k) &= C_m(x_m(k+1) - x_m(k)) = C_m \Delta x_m(k+1) \\ &= C_m A_m \Delta x_m(k) + C_m B_m \Delta u(k) \end{aligned} \tag{7.7}$$

Putting together (7.5) with (7.7), and defining the matrices

$$A = \begin{bmatrix} A_m & 0_{1 \times n_m} \\ C_m A_m & 1 \end{bmatrix}, \quad B = \begin{bmatrix} B_m \\ C_m B_m \end{bmatrix}, \quad C = \begin{bmatrix} 0_{n_m \times 1} & 1 \end{bmatrix}$$

leads to the state-space model

$$\begin{aligned} x(k+1) &= Ax(k) + B\Delta u(k) \\ y(k) &= Cx(k) \end{aligned} \tag{7.8}$$

Notice that the input of this system is not the control signal $u(k)$, but its increment $\Delta u(k)$ with respect to the previously applied value. The system (7.8) is called the *augmented model*, and is the basis for the predictive control methods used herein.

7.1.4 *Predictive control within a single optimisation window*

After formulating the mathematical model, the next step in the design of a predictive control system is to calculate the predicted plant output, with the future control signals as the adjustable variables. This prediction is carried out within an optimisation window, and is the subject of this section. Here, we assume that the current time is k and the length of the optimisation window is H_p, and we use the augmented model (7.8).

7.1.4.1   Prediction of state and output variables

Assuming that at the sampling instant k, $k > 0$, the state variable vector $x(k)$ is available through measurement or estimated, the state $x(k)$ provides the current plant information. The future control trajectory is denoted by

$$\Delta \mathcal{U} = \begin{bmatrix} \Delta u(k) \\ \Delta u(k+1) \\ \vdots \\ \Delta u(k+H_c-1) \end{bmatrix}$$

where H_c is called the *control horizon*, and dictates the number of parameters used to capture the future control trajectory. From $x(k)$, the future state variables are predicted for H_p samples, where H_p is called the prediction horizon. We denote the future state variables as

$$x(k+1|k), \; x(k+2|k), \ldots, x(k+m|k), \ldots, x(k+H_p|k)$$

where $x(k+m|k)$ is the predicted state variable at $k+m$ based on the current state $x(k)$. Notice that the control horizon H_c must be chosen to be less than (or equal to) the prediction horizon H_p.

From the augmented model (7.8), the future state can be computed using the set of future control parameters

$$x(k+1|k) = Ax(k) + B\Delta u(k)$$
$$x(k+2|k) = Ax(k+1|k) + B\Delta u(k+1)$$
$$= A^2 x(k) + AB\Delta u(k) + B\Delta u(k+1)$$

$$\vdots$$

$$x(k+H_p|k) = A^{H_p}x(k) + A^{H_p-1}B\Delta u(k) + A^{H_p-2}B\Delta u(k+1)$$
$$+ \cdots + A^{H_p-H_c}B\Delta u(k+H_c-1)$$

From the predicted state variables, the predicted output variables are, by substitution,

$$y(k+1|k) = CAx(k) + CB\Delta u(k)$$
$$y(k+2|k) = CA^2 x(k) + CAB\Delta u(k) + CB\Delta u(k+1)$$

$$\vdots \qquad\qquad\qquad\qquad\qquad\qquad (7.9)$$

$$y(k+H_p|k) = CA^{H_p}x(k) + CA^{H_p-1}B\Delta u(k) + CA^{H_p-2}B\Delta u(k+1)$$
$$+ \cdots + CA^{H_p-H_c}B\Delta u(k+H_c-1)$$

Note that all predicted variables are expressed in terms of current state variable information $x(k)$ and future control trajectory $u(k + j)$, where $j = 0, 1, \ldots, H_c - 1$.

Now, denoting with

$$
\mathcal{Y} = \begin{bmatrix} y(k + 1|k) \\ y(k + 2|k) \\ \vdots \\ y(k + H_p|k) \end{bmatrix}
$$

the future trajectory of the output over the prediction horizon H_p, we can collect the (7.9) together in a compact matrix form as

$$
\mathcal{Y} = Fx(k) + \Phi \Delta \mathcal{U} \tag{7.10}
$$

where

$$
F = \begin{bmatrix} CA \\ CA^2 \\ CA^3 \\ \vdots \\ CA^{H_p} \end{bmatrix} ;
$$

$$
\Phi = \begin{bmatrix} CB & 0 & 0 & \ldots & 0 \\ CAB & CB & 0 & \ldots & 0 \\ CA^2B & CAB & CB & \ldots & 0 \\ \vdots & \vdots & \vdots & \ddots & \vdots \\ CA^{H_p-1}B & CA^{H_p-2}B & CA^{H_p-3}B & \ldots & CA^{H_p-H_c}B \end{bmatrix} \tag{7.11}
$$

7.1.4.2 Optimisation

For a given set point signal $y^\circ(\cdot)$ at time k, within a prediction horizon, the objective of the predictive control system is to bring the predicted output as close as possible to the set point signal. It is reasonable to assume that the set point is constant within the prediction horizon. This objective is directly translated into finding the best control (future) trajectory $\Delta \mathcal{U}$ such that the cost function J be minimised.

Assuming that the vector containing the set point information within the optimisation window is

$$
\mathcal{Y}^\circ = \begin{bmatrix} 1 \\ 1 \\ \vdots \\ 1 \end{bmatrix} y^\circ(k) = \mathbf{1}_{H_p \times 1} \cdot y^\circ(k) \tag{7.12}
$$

where $\mathbf{1}_{H_p \times 1}$ is an all-ones vector of length H_p, the cost function J is written as

$$
J = (\mathcal{Y}^\circ - \mathcal{Y})' Q (\mathcal{Y}^\circ - \mathcal{Y}) + \Delta \mathcal{U}' R \Delta \mathcal{U} \tag{7.13}
$$

where the first term is connected to the objective of minimising the discrepancy between the predicted output and the set point signal, while the second term reflects the consideration given to the size of $\Delta\mathcal{U}$ when the objective function J is made as small as possible. $\mathcal{Q}$ and $\mathcal{R}$ are diagonal matrices containing weights for the future control signal. Weights can be considered as the tuning parameters for the desired closed-loop performance. Sometimes, the same cost function is also written as

$$J = \|\mathcal{Y}^\circ - \mathcal{Y}\|_\mathcal{Q} + \|\Delta\mathcal{U}\|_\mathcal{R}$$

For simplicity, in this part, we use the same weight for all future error and control signals, which allows the matrices to be expressed in the form $\mathcal{Q} = q \cdot I_{H_p \times H_p}(q \geq 0)$ and $\mathcal{R} = r \cdot I_{H_c \times H_c}(r \geq 0)$, where q and r are the only tuning parameter.

For the case $r = 0$, the cost function (7.13) is interpreted as a situation where no attention is paid to how large $\Delta\mathcal{U}$ might be, and the goal is solely to make the error $\|\mathcal{Y}^\circ - \mathcal{Y}\|$ as small as possible. For the case of large r, the cost function (7.13) is interpreted as the situation where one carefully considers how large $\Delta\mathcal{U}$ might be, and only cautiously reduces the error.

To find the optimal $\Delta\mathcal{U}$ that will minimise J, by using (7.10), J is expressed as

$$\begin{aligned} J = {} & (\mathcal{Y}^\circ - Fx(k))'\mathcal{Q}(\mathcal{Y}^\circ - Fx(k)) \\ & + -2\Delta\mathcal{U}'\Phi'\mathcal{Q}(\mathcal{Y}^\circ - Fx(k)) + \Delta\mathcal{U}'(\Phi'\mathcal{Q}\Phi + \mathcal{R})\Delta\mathcal{U} \end{aligned} \tag{7.14}$$

Notice that minimising this cost function is a convex problem, and can be easily handled by off-the-shelf optimisation solvers (also in the constrained case not treated here, incidentally). Anyway, it is interesting to solve the unconstrained problem in closed form, in order to find an explicit control law.

From the first derivative of the cost function J, i.e.,

$$\frac{\partial J}{\partial \Delta\mathcal{U}} = -2\Phi'\mathcal{Q}(\mathcal{Y}^\circ - Fx(k)) + 2(\Phi'\mathcal{Q}\Phi + \mathcal{R})\Delta\mathcal{U} \tag{7.15}$$

a necessary condition to find a minimum of J is obtained as

$$\frac{\partial J}{\partial \Delta\mathcal{U}} = 0 \tag{7.16}$$

from which we find the optimal solution for the control signal as

$$\Delta\mathcal{U} = (\Phi'\mathcal{Q}\Phi + \mathcal{R})^{-1}\Phi'\mathcal{Q}(\mathcal{Y}^\circ - Fx(k)) \tag{7.17}$$

with the assumption that $(\Phi'\mathcal{Q}\Phi + \mathcal{R})^{-1}$ exists; this matrix

$$\mathcal{H} = (\Phi'\mathcal{Q}\Phi + \mathcal{R})^{-1}$$

is also the Hessian matrix. Note that $\mathcal{Y}^\circ$ is a data vector that contains the set point information expressed as in (7.12). The optimal solution for the control signal is thus related to the set point signal $y^\circ(k)$ and the state variable $x(k)$ via

$$\Delta\mathcal{U} = \mathcal{H} \cdot \Phi'\mathcal{Q}(1_{H_p \times 1} \cdot y^\circ(k) - Fx(k)) \tag{7.18}$$

7.1.5 Receding-horizon predictive control

The control law (7.18) is the optimised trajectory of Δu within the control horizon H_c, i.e., $\Delta\mathcal{U}$ contains the controls $\Delta u(k), \Delta u(k+1), \ldots, \Delta u(k+H_c-1)$.

However, one should keep in mind that the model is never perfect, and some discrepancies between it and the plant may (and, in general, do) occur. The receding-horizon principle is based on this fact, and in order to be reactive to the model uncertainties and external disturbances, applies to the plant only the first value of ΔU, ignoring the rest. When the next sample period arrives, the more recent measurement is taken to form the state vector $x(k + 1)$ for the calculation of the new sequence of control signals (of which, again, only the first one is applied). This procedure is repeated at each step to give the RHPC control law.

7.1.5.1 Closed-loop control system

By examining the obtained control law (7.18), the optimal control vector ΔU can be written as

$$\Delta U = \mathcal{H}\Phi'Q\,1_{H_p \times 1} \cdot y^\circ(k) - \mathcal{H}\Phi'QFx(k) \tag{7.19}$$

where $(\Phi'Q\Phi + \mathcal{R})^{-1}\Phi'1_{H_p \times 1}$ depends on the set point change, while $-(\Phi'Q\Phi + \overline{R})^{-1}\Phi'F$ provides state feedback. Both terms depend on the system parameters, hence being constant matrices for a time-invariant system.

Because of the RHPC principle, we only take the first element of ΔU at time k as the incremental control, thus

$$\Delta u(k) = \begin{bmatrix} 1 & \mathbf{0}_{1 \times H_c - 1} \end{bmatrix} \cdot \left(\mathcal{H}\Phi'Q\,1_{H_p \times 1} \cdot y^\circ(k) - \mathcal{H}\Phi'QFx(k) \right)$$
$$= K_y y^\circ(k) - K_{fb} x(k) \tag{7.20}$$

where, clearly,

$$K_y = \begin{bmatrix} 1 & \mathbf{0}_{1 \times H_c - 1} \end{bmatrix} \cdot \mathcal{H}\Phi'Q\,1_{H_p \times 1}$$
$$K_{fb} = \begin{bmatrix} 1 & \mathbf{0}_{1 \times H_c - 1} \end{bmatrix} \cdot \mathcal{H}\Phi'QF \tag{7.21}$$

Equation (7.20) is in the standard form of linear time-invariant state feedback control. The state feedback control gain vector is K_{fb}. Therefore, with the augmented model, the closed-loop system is obtained by substituting (7.20) into the augmented equation (7.8), leading to the closed-loop one

$$x(k + 1) = Ax(k) - BK_{fb}x(k) + BK_y y^\circ(k)$$
$$= (A - BK_{fb})x(k) + BK_y y^\circ(k) \tag{7.22}$$

Thus, the closed-loop eigenvalues are the solutions of

$$\det \begin{bmatrix} \lambda I - (A - BK_{fb}) \end{bmatrix} = 0 \tag{7.23}$$

Because of the special structure of matrices C and A, the last column of F is identical to $1_{H_p \times 1}$, therefore K_y is identical to the last element of K_{fb}. Noting that the state variable vector $x(k)$ is defined in (7.6) as $[\Delta x_m(k)' \; y(k)]'$, and recalling the definition of K_y in (7.21), we can write

$$K_{fb} = \begin{bmatrix} K_x & K_y \end{bmatrix} \tag{7.24}$$

where K_x corresponds to the feedback gain vector related to $\Delta x_m(k)$, and K_y to that related to $y(k)$.

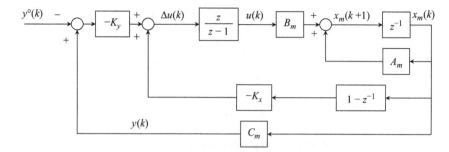

Figure 7.1   Block diagram of a predictive control system

The closed-loop block diagram for the predictive control system is depicted in Figure 7.1. The diagram shows the state feedback structure for MPC with integral action, in which the module $z/(z-1)$ denotes the discrete-time integrator.

7.2   Model identification and adaptive systems

In this section, we present the main results of model identification and adaptive systems that are relevant for this work. In particular, we present the Least Squares (LS) procedure for the identification of an AutoRegressive with eXogenous input (ARX) model (Section 7.2.1), and the persistent excitation problem typical of the identification theory (Section 7.2.2). Finally, in Section 7.2.3, we present the recursive version of LS, typically used in the context of adaptive[1] control systems.

7.2.1   Least squares

In the dynamic system context, the most used identification methods, among the Prediction Error Minimisation (PEM) ones, are LS and Maximum Likelihood. When the parameters of an ARX model need to be identified, and the chosen optimality criterion is the PEM, the LS method is the most suited. In the following, we will operate under these assumptions, since ARX models are adequate for the problems addressed herein.

The generic form of an ARX(n_a, n_b) model is

$$y(k) = \sum_{i=1}^{n_a} a_i y(k-i) + \sum_{j=1}^{n_b} b_j u(k-j) + \xi(k) \tag{7.25}$$

where $y(\cdot)$ are the values of the output, $u(\cdot)$ those of the input, and $\xi(\cdot)$ is an unmeasured noise that accounts for unmodelled dynamics as well as measurement errors. Almost invariantly, it is assumed that the noise has a fixed probability distribution (usually a Gaussian one) with constant expected value and variance.

---

[1] In control theory, a controller is said to be "adaptive" if it comprises some mechanism capable of changing the parameters of its control law during operation.

Denoting with ϑ the model parameter vector, i.e.,

$$\vartheta = [a_1 \ a_2 \ \cdots \ a_{n_a} \ b_1 \ b_2 \ \cdots \ b_{n_b}]' \tag{7.26}$$

and with $\varphi(k)$ the observations vector at time instant k

$$\varphi(k) = [y(k-1) \, y(k-2) \ \cdots \ y(k-n_a) \, u(k-1) \, u(k-2) \ \cdots \ u(k-n_b)]' \tag{7.27}$$

Equation (7.25) can be written in the more compact form

$$y(k) = \varphi(k)'\vartheta + \xi(k) \tag{7.28}$$

which leads to a very simple predictive model

$$\hat{y}(k) = \varphi(k)'\vartheta \tag{7.29}$$

The prediction error can be computed as

$$\varepsilon(k) = y(k) - \varphi(k)'\vartheta \tag{7.30}$$

The cost function used to estimate the parameter vector ϑ is the quadratic one

$$J = \frac{1}{N} \sum_{k=1}^{N} \varepsilon(k)^2 \tag{7.31}$$

where N is the cardinality of the data set used for the minimisation problem.

Substituting (7.30) in (7.31), one can easily conclude that all the minimum point of the cost function can be obtained solving the *Normal Equation* (7.32).

$$\left[\sum_{k=1}^{N} \varphi(k)\varphi(k)' \right] \cdot \vartheta = \sum_{k=1}^{N} \varphi(k)y(k) \tag{7.32}$$

If the matrix

$$S(N) = \sum_{k=1}^{N} \varphi(k)\varphi(k)' \tag{7.33}$$

is invertible, (7.32) admits a unique solution given by

$$\hat{\vartheta}_N = S(N)^{-1} \sum_{k=1}^{N} \varphi(k)y(k) \tag{7.34}$$

which is the LS formula.

7.2.2 Persistent excitation

As anticipated in Section 7.2.1, the uniqueness of the solution for the parameter estimation problem, requires the invertibility of $S(N)$, which is then the condition for the applicability of the LS identification method. It is now worth spending some words analysing the $S(N)$ matrix, as defined in (7.33).

Consider an ARX(1, 1) model with an observation vector defined as

$$\varphi(k) = \begin{bmatrix} y(k-1) \\ u(k-1) \end{bmatrix}$$

Thus

$$\varphi(k)\varphi(k)' = \begin{bmatrix} y(k-1)^2 & y(k-1)u(k-1) \\ u(k-1)y(k-1) & u(k-1)^2 \end{bmatrix}$$

and

$$S(N) = \begin{bmatrix} \sum_{k=1}^{N} y(k-1)^2 & \sum_{k=1}^{N} y(k-1)u(k-1) \\ \sum_{k=1}^{N} u(k-1)y(k-1) & \sum_{k=1}^{N} u(k-1)^2 \end{bmatrix}$$

Defining matrix $R(N) = 1/N \cdot S(N)$, always in the case of an ARX(1, 1), yields

$$R(N) = \begin{bmatrix} \dfrac{1}{N}\sum_{k=1}^{N} y(k-1)^2 & \dfrac{1}{N}\sum_{k=1}^{N} y(k-1)u(k-1) \\ \dfrac{1}{N}\sum_{k=1}^{N} u(k-1)y(k-1) & \dfrac{1}{N}\sum_{k=1}^{N} u(k-1)^2 \end{bmatrix}$$

If $u(\cdot)$ and $y(\cdot)$ are stationary processes,[2] matrix $R(N)$ – that expresses a sample mean over N data – asymptotically converges to the probabilistic average

$$\overline{R} = \begin{bmatrix} \gamma_{yy}(0) & \gamma_{uy}(0) \\ \gamma_{yu}(0) & \gamma_{uu}(0) \end{bmatrix}$$

where $\gamma_{yy}(\cdot)$ and $\gamma_{uu}(\cdot)$ are the $u(\cdot)$ and $y(\cdot)$ correlation functions.

In general, under this hypothesis, matrix $R(N)$ will converge to

$$\overline{R} = \mathbb{E}\left[\varphi(k)\varphi(k)'\right]$$

The same matrix can be partitioned into four blocks, namely

$$\overline{R}_{uu}^{(n)} = \mathbb{E}\left[\begin{bmatrix} u(k-1) \\ u(k-2) \\ \vdots \\ u(k-n) \end{bmatrix} \begin{bmatrix} u(k-1) & u(k-2) & \cdots & u(k-n) \end{bmatrix} \right] \tag{7.35}$$

$$\overline{R}_{yy}^{(n)} = \mathbb{E}\left[\begin{bmatrix} y(k-1) \\ y(k-2) \\ \vdots \\ y(k-n) \end{bmatrix} \begin{bmatrix} y(k-1) & y(k-2) & \cdots & y(k-n) \end{bmatrix} \right] \tag{7.36}$$

---

[2] This is a technical hypothesis impossible to discuss herein. We have reported it for correctness and completeness, but the reader can assume in our context that it holds true in all cases of practical interest.

Similarly, the reader can infer the $\overline{R}_{uy}$ and $\overline{R}_{yu}$ definition. Matrix $\overline{R}$ can be rewritten using (7.35) and (7.36), as

$$\overline{R} = \begin{bmatrix} \overline{R}_{yy}^{(na)} & \overline{R}_{yu} \\ \overline{R}_{uy} & \overline{R}_{uu}^{(nb)} \end{bmatrix} \tag{7.37}$$

As previously discussed, the invertibility of the $\overline{R}$ matrix is a necessary and sufficient condition for the parameter estimation problem's solution uniqueness. Matrix $\overline{R}$ is positive semi-definite for structural reasons, hence $\overline{R}$ is invertible only if it is positive definite (i.e., $\overline{R} > 0$).

According to the Schur's lemma, $\overline{R}$ is positive definite (i.e., in this context, it is invertible) only if $\overline{R}_{uu}^{(nb)}$ is invertible.

Notice that $\overline{R}_{uu}^{(nb)}$ is a *Toeplitz* matrix, i.e., the elements on the diagonals are coincident. Thus, on the main diagonal the elements represent the process variance $u(\cdot)$, while on the other diagonals the elements represent the one-step-ahead correlation, the two-steps-ahead correlation, and so on. This is expressed by writing

$$\overline{R}_{uu}^{n} = \begin{bmatrix} \gamma_{uu}(0) & \gamma_{uu}(1) & \cdots & \gamma_{uu}(n-1) \\ \gamma_{uu}(1) & \gamma_{uu}(0) & \cdots & \gamma_{uu}(n-2) \\ \vdots & \vdots & \ddots & \vdots \\ \gamma_{uu}(n-1) & \gamma_{uu}(n-2) & \cdots & \gamma_{uu}(0) \end{bmatrix} \tag{7.38}$$

and the input $u(\cdot)$ is said to be persistently exciting of order n if $\overline{R}_{uu}^{n}$ is invertible.

In conclusion, estimating the parameters of an ARX(n_a, n_b) model requires a persistently exciting input signal $u(\cdot)$ at least of order n_b. From a physical viewpoint, persistent excitation is a property of the input signal, which represents the 'richness' of its spectrum components as for their ability to stimulate the system dynamics, aimed at identifying the model parameters. It is obvious that if a signal is persistently exciting of order n, it is also persistently exciting of an order lower than n.

7.2.3 Recursive least squares

When LS is used to identify the parameters of an ARX model, the input/output data are processed all together. More precisely, data are considered only once from the first to the last. For that reason, LS identification is a *batch method*, in which data are collected *before* their elaboration, and such procedure is called *offline* identification.

In several applications, the parameter estimation cannot be done offline, and *online* identification is needed. In these cases, recursive identification algorithms are used. In such methods, the estimation of the parameters at the time k is obtained updating the one at the time $k-1$ on the basis of the last observed datum. The online identification procedure for ARX models is called Recursive Least Squares (RLS).

Considering the LS equation (7.34) at a generic instant k, one has

$$\hat{\vartheta}_k = S(k)^{-1} \sum_{i=1}^{k} \varphi(i) y(i) \tag{7.39}$$

where

$$S(k) = \sum_{i=1}^{k} \varphi(i)\varphi(i)' \tag{7.40}$$

By expanding

$$\sum_{i=1}^{k} \varphi(i)y(i) = \sum_{i=1}^{k-1} \varphi(i)y(i) + \varphi(k)y(k) \tag{7.41}$$

and writing (7.39) at time $k - 1$, (7.42) directly yields

$$\sum_{i=1}^{k-1} \varphi(i)y(i) = S(k-1)\hat{\vartheta}_{k-1} \tag{7.42}$$

Applying the definition of (7.40) in (7.41) provides

$$\sum_{i=1}^{k} \varphi(i)y(i) = S(k-1)\hat{\vartheta}_{k-1} + \varphi(k)y(k) \tag{7.43}$$

Moreover, it is apparent from (7.40) that

$$S(k) = S(k-1) + \varphi(k)\varphi(k)' \tag{7.44}$$

Hence, (7.43) can be equivalently expressed as

$$\sum_{i=1}^{k} \varphi(i)y(i) = \left(S(k) - \varphi(k)\varphi(k)' \right)\hat{\vartheta}_{k-1} + \varphi(k)y(k) \tag{7.45}$$

Substituting (7.45) in (7.39) we obtain the first form of the RLS as

$$\begin{aligned}
\hat{\vartheta}_k &= \hat{\vartheta}_{k-1} + K(t)\varepsilon(k) \\
K(k) &= S(k)^{-1}\varphi(k) \\
\varepsilon(k) &= y(k) - \varphi(k)'\hat{\vartheta}_{k-1} \\
S(k) &= S(k-1) + \varphi(k)\varphi(k)'
\end{aligned} \tag{7.46}$$

This is not the only form in which the RLS algorithm can be written. Two other forms can be obtained from the first one, with appropriate algebraic manipulations. Considering that $R(k) = 1/k \cdot S(k)$ and dividing both sides of (7.44) by k, we obtain

$$\begin{aligned}
\frac{1}{k}S(k) &= \frac{1}{k}S(k-1) + \frac{1}{k}\varphi(k)\varphi(k)' \\
&= \left(\frac{k-1}{k} \right)\left(\frac{1}{k-1} \right)S(k-1) + \frac{1}{k}\varphi(k)\varphi(k)'
\end{aligned} \tag{7.47}$$

Hence the recursive expression for $R(k)$ is

$$R(k) = \frac{k-1}{k}R(k-1) + \frac{1}{k}\varphi(k)\varphi(k)'$$ (7.48)

Now we can easily obtain the second form expression of the RLS as

$$\hat{\vartheta}_k = \hat{\vartheta}_{k-1} + K(k)\varepsilon(k)$$

$$K(k) = \frac{1}{k}R(k)^{-1}\varphi(k)$$

$$\varepsilon(k) = y(k) - \varphi(k)'\hat{\vartheta}_{k-1}$$ (7.49)

$$R(k) = R(k-1) + \frac{1}{k}(\varphi(k)\varphi(k)' - R(k-1))$$

The main disadvantage of using the first (7.46) and second (7.49) form of RLS, however, is that in both cases at each time instant a square matrix, of dimension equal to the number of parameters to estimate – $S(k)$ and $R(k)$, respectively – is to be inverted.

From a computational viewpoint, it is worth finding a third form which requires to invert only a scalar. To this end, the following lemma is needed:

Lemma 7.1 (Matrix inversion lemma). *Consider four matrices F, G, H and K with dimensions such that the quantity $F + GHK$ is well defined. Supposing that F, H and $(F + GHK)$ are invertible,*

$$(F + GHK)^{-1} = F^{-1} - F^{-1}G\left(H^{-1} + KF^{-1}G\right)^{-1} KF^{-1}$$

Applying Lemma 7.1 to $S(k)$, with $F = S(k-1)$, $G = \varphi(k)$, $H = 1$ and $K = \varphi(k)'$, leads to

$$S(k)^{-1} = S(k-1)^{-1}$$
$$+ S(k-1)^{-1}\varphi(k)\left(1 + \varphi(k)'S(k-1)^{-1}\varphi(k)\right)^{-1}\varphi(k)'S(k-1)^{-1} \quad (7.50)$$

Thus, from (7.46), denoting with $V(k) = S(k)^{-1}$, the third form of the RLS method

$$\hat{\vartheta}_k = \hat{\vartheta}_{k-1} + K(k)\varepsilon(k)$$

$$K(k) = V(k)\varphi(k)$$

$$\varepsilon(k) = y(k) - \varphi(k)'\hat{\vartheta}_{k-1}$$ (7.51)

$$V(k) = V(k-1) - \beta_{k-1}^{-1}V(k-1)\varphi(k)\varphi(k)'V(k-1)$$

$$\beta_{k-1} = 1 + \varphi(k)'V(k-1)\varphi(k)$$

is obtained, which requires only the inversion of the scalar β.

7.3   Adaptive control techniques

7.3.1   *Online identification and adaptive control*

In many prediction and control problems, the system may be subjected to several (e.g., parameteric) variations, sometimes hardly predictable. In order to face such situations, *adaptive* schemes are commonly used.

In an adaptive system, the predictor, filter or controller dynamics are not fixed, but they are periodically updated according to the observed behaviour of the system. An adaptive scheme can be applied to a variety of entities such as filters, predictors, controllers, and so forth, and *de facto* to any structure represented by a model with some parameters to be adapted.

Given the scope of this book, the treatise on adaptive systems is not deepened herein: the interested reader can find all the details in References 51, 53.

For reasons that will be clearly explained later, we focus in particular on adaptive control, where – owing to the time-variance of the (model of) the plant, in the sense of Definition 2.2 – the controller parameters have to be periodically updated online.

A general scheme of adaptive control is represented in Figure 7.2, where the device that adapts the controller parameters is called 'observer' or 'tuner'.

Usually, the adjustment mechanisms work as a feedback one. The typical adaptive control scheme is shown in Figure 7.3.

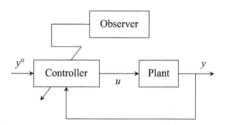

Figure 7.2   General scheme of adaptive control

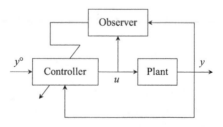

Figure 7.3   General scheme of feedback adaptive control

7.3.2 Adaptive identification

7.3.2.1 Adaptive identification algorithms with forgetting factor

Classical identification techniques, both offline and online (see Section 7.2), have the purpose of identifying *time-invariant* parameters. If the dynamic system under question is conversely time-varying, those methods are not so efficient, and may not be able to identify the model parameters, especially when the variations are not predictable. Hence, some classical methods have been modified to estimate also time-varying parameters.

In the LS identification method, the classical cost function is

$$J = \frac{1}{k} \sum_{i=1}^{k} \varepsilon(i)^2 \tag{7.52}$$

More recent data (at the time k) and older data (at time 1) have the same importance. To estimate time-varying parameters, giving progressively less importance to older data and more importance to more recent ones, the cost function is modified as

$$J = \frac{1}{k} \sum_{i=1}^{k} \mu^{k-i} \varepsilon(i)^2 \tag{7.53}$$

where $\mu \in (0, 1]$. In so doing, data have a variable weight: more precisely, while data at time k has weight 1, the one at time $k - 1$ has weight μ, the one at time $k - 2$ has weight μ^2, and so on. Older data have progressively lower weights, such that the estimation is more influenced by recent data. The smaller the μ, the faster the past is forgotten.

For such a reason the coefficient μ is called the 'forgetting factor', or more precisely the 'exponential forgetting factor'. The number of data that, owing to the weights, are actually considered by the algorithm is about $1/(1 - \mu)$, which is the value of the time constant of the discrete exponential μ^{k-i}.

The value $1/(1 - \mu)$ is thus the algorithm *window*; for example, if $\mu = 0.99$ the window contains about 100 data, if $\mu = 0.98$ the window contains about 50 data, if $\mu = 0.96$ the window contains about 25 data, and so forth.

Similarly, the RLS method can be modified to identify time-varying parameters. For our purpose, suffice to present the third form of the RLS method (refer to Reference 53 for the first and the second form, and the procedure to obtain the third form formulae).

The third form of the RLS method with forgetting factor is

$$\hat{\vartheta}_k = \hat{\vartheta}_{k-1} + K(k)\varepsilon(k)$$
$$K(k) = V(k)\varphi(k)$$
$$\varepsilon(k) = y(k) - \varphi(k)'\hat{\vartheta}_{k-1} \tag{7.54}$$
$$V(k) = \frac{1}{\mu}V(k-1) - \beta_{k-1}^{-1}V(k-1)\varphi(k)\varphi(k)'V(k-1)$$
$$\beta_{k-1} = \mu + \varphi(k)'V(k-1)\varphi(k)$$

where, by choosing $\mu = 1$ yields the classical RLS formulae of (7.51).

7.4 Problems

Problem 7.1. *Given the first-order system*

$$x_m(k+1) = 0.5x_m(k) + u(k)$$

$$y(k) = x_m(k)$$

- *Write the augmented state-space model.*
- *Assuming a prediction horizon $H_p = 5$ and control horizon $H_c = 2$ calculate the prediction of the future output $\mathcal{Y}$.*
- *Find the optimal solution $\Delta \mathcal{U}$.*
- *Compute the value of $\delta u(k)$ given that $x(k) = [0.1\ 0]'$, $\mathcal{Q} = I$, and $\mathcal{R} = I$. How the control signal changes if $\mathcal{R} = 0.1I$?*

Problem 7.2. *Given a state-space model of the form*

$$x_m(k+1) = A_m x_m(k) + B_m u(k)$$

$$y(k) = C_m x_m(k)$$

where

$$A_m = \begin{bmatrix} 0.5 & 0.5 & 1 \\ 0 & -0.9 & -0.1 \\ 0 & 0 & 0.8 \end{bmatrix}, \quad B_m = \begin{bmatrix} 0 \\ 0 \\ 1 \end{bmatrix}, \quad C_m = \begin{bmatrix} 1 & 0 & 0 \end{bmatrix}$$

- *Calculate the transfer function of the plant with input $u(k)$ to output $y(k)$, and the transfer function of the augmented state-space model that relates the input $\Delta u(k)$ to the output $y(k)$.*
- *Compare the poles and zeros of the two transfer functions.*
- *Design a model predictive control with a set point $y^\circ(k) = 1$. For the design of the controller use $H_c = 3$, $H_p = 5$, $\mathcal{Q} = I$ and $\mathcal{R} = 0.1I$.*

Problem 7.3. *Given the model ARX(1, 1)*

$$y(k+1) = 0.9y(k) + 0.01u(k)$$

1. *Compute the transfer function of the model.*
2. *Design a model predictive control with a set point $y^\circ(k) = 1$. For the design of the controller use $H_c = 5$, $H_p = 10$, $\mathcal{Q} = I$ and $\mathcal{R} = 0.5I$.*
3. *Calculate the gain matrices K_y and K_{fb} for the predictive control system and comment where the closed-loop eigenvalues are. Verify also that the K_{fb} can be written as (7.24).*
4. *Simulate the closed-loop predictive control system using the receding horizon principle, with initial condition of the augmented plant $x(0) = [1\ 0]$.*

Problem 7.4. *Given a process of the form ARX(1, 1)*

$$y(k+1) = ay(k) + bu(k) + \xi(k)$$

where $u(k) = 0$ and $\xi(\cdot)$ is a white noise, and given the following observations of the process

k	1	2	3	4	5	6	7	8	9	10
y(k)	1	0	−1	0	1	0	−1	0	1	0
k	11	12	13	14	15	16	17	18	19	20
y(k)	−1	0	1	0	−1	0	1	0	−1	1

find the parameter a that minimises the prediction error

$$J(a) = \sum_{k=1}^{20} \left(y(k) - \hat{y}(k|k - 1; a) \right)^2$$

assuming that for $k \leq 0 \; y(k) = 0$).

Problem 7.5. *Consider the model and the dataset of the previous problem. Using a Recursive Least Squares procedure of (7.54), find for each time instant the best estimate of the parameter a, considering an initial guess of the parameter is $a(0) = -0.5$, $V(0) = I$, $\beta(0) = 1$ and a forgetting factor $\mu = 1$. What happens if $\mu = 0.9$?*

Chapter 8

Resource allocation

Nowadays, the resource allocation problem is one of the most interesting and challenging ones in the computing systems domain. Since it is a quite general problem, it is not possible to cover every instance and formulation of it. As such, without loss of generality for our purposes, the rest of this chapter uses for the treatise a representative example, namely the allocation of computational resources – number of cores, core frequency, memory, disk quota, and so on – to running applications. Before going into the details of the specific example, however, some preliminary and general remarks are in order.

The word *resource* may assume different meanings. In a single device, an application may receive computational units or memory, while in a cloud infrastructure, a resource can be a server devoted to responding to some requests. Each manageable resource is here a *touchpoint* in the sense given to this term in Reference 63. Some proposals to address the management of a single resource were published in the literature. However, the management of multiple interacting resources is still an open research problem, and solutions are less frequent. Intuitively, the number of ways the system capabilities can be assigned to different applications grows exponentially with the number of resources under control. Moreover, the optimal allocation of one resource type depends in part on the allocated amounts of other resources, requiring coordination among different resource allocators.

The scheduling problem, presented in Chapter 5, can be cast into resource allocation, as the resource to be distributed among the tasks is the CPU time. Keeping this example in mind, we can divide the resource allocation problem into two classes.

1. **Resource–resource**, where the control action amounts to allocate a resource and the objective is given by some properties of said distribution (e.g., fairness in scheduling)
2. **Resource–work**, where still the control action is the allocation of a resource, but the issue is how much 'useful work' – whatever is meant for that – the application does with that resource

In resource–resource problems, the model of the uncontrolled system is normally very simple – think about the scheduling problem, in which the model of the core phenomenon is just a unit delay – and there is a negligible (if any) uncertainty. In the mentioned example of scheduling, the only source of uncertainty can be the timers' imprecision, but as long as we are concerned with the system operation *as quanti-fied based on the same timers*, clearly there is no uncertainty at all. As discussed in Chapter 5, in such problems the control-exogenous facts that can affect the con-trolled system's response, thereby requiring feedback to intervene, can be modelled as disturbances (recall the definition given in Chapter 2).

In resource–work problems, conversely, the relationships between the assigned resources and the amount of useful work done, are quite often far from being trivial. First, the resource and the useful work are normally heterogeneous quantities: for example, the former could be the amount of memory reserved for an application, and the second the number of data blocks processed by that application in a certain time span. In such situations, the process model cannot apparently be as simple as a delay, and it will invariantly include some parameters. In turn, these parameters will depend on the internals of the entity utilising the resource: for example, if the utiliser is again an application, useful work is still measured as a throughput, and the resource is the number of CPUs allotted to the application, then different degrees of parallelism will cause the same variation of the resource allocation to produce different variations of the useful work. Moreover, an application generally traverses different operation phases, being, e.g., CPU-bound when performing computations, I/O bound when exchanging data over the network, and so forth: as a result, the resource-to-work relationship is most often time-varying.

From a merely modelling point of view, in particular when models do not come only from first-principle physics as is the case herein, it has to be stated that some-times the decision of modelling some phenomenon as a disturbance or as a variation of the controlled system can be a bit subtle. At the level of this book we could just notice that when the required model can be *de facto* taken from first principles and is practically parameter-free, as is the case with scheduling, then exogenous actions tend to be preferably modelled as disturbances. Probably the fact just men-tioned is more general than the scheduling case, but investigating the amplitude of said generality is outside our scope. In other cases, it is conversely evident that the resource-to-work relationship needs to be dynamic,[1] and the effect on it of unex-pected actions – be they originated in the utiliser or outside – is better described as uncertainty and/or time variability of the used model.

Summarising to avoid discussions that would further stray from our scope, models for resource–work problems are usually affected by uncertainty, so that the techniques used so far in this work are not capable of coping with them.

If some equivalent in classical control applications is sought for resource–work problems, one finds that a very relevant idea to describe the 'usefulness' of a resource is that of *efficiency*, typically defined as something like 'what one gets over what one spends'. In classical situations, efficiency is in fact quite easily related to the plant physics – think, e.g., to the efficiency of a motor. In general it is possible to define a relationship between efficiency and the working condition of the plant, and normally such a relation is quite smooth.

---

[1] This means that the static maps often used, in some cases may prove not totally adequate to the problem.

In computing systems, conversely, the concept of efficiency cannot be defined by means of high-level physics – recall the example of Chapter 3 – and only a fine-grain level efficiency can be naturally expressed. In other words, in resource allocation problems, there is a gap between very low-level concepts (e.g., the instruction set) and high-level ones (e.g., Quality of Service metrics). This hinders the possibility of defining efficiency in a similar way with respect to the one present, e.g., in thermodynamics. In resource–work problems, indeed, the lack of a physics – in the sense sketched out in Chapter 3 – is even more evident than it was for those treated previously.

However, the resulting (and unavoidable) uncertainties and time-varying behaviours coming from the mentioned problems, can be tackled with more advanced and powerful control techniques – essentially the ones described in Chapter 7 – obtaining encouraging results (despite quite a bit of further work is needed in the future).

In the rest of this chapter, the problem of controlling an application's progress towards its goals by assigning the 'right' amount of resources is considered. In the computing systems community this problem is well known and studied in the domain of *autonomic computing*.

8.1 Literature review

Autonomic computing is a very promising research area for confronting the complexity of modern computing systems. Autonomic systems manage themselves without human intervention, and their development involves a variety of exciting challenges [64]. One of the most important of these challenges is the establishment of systematic and reproducible processes for the design of autonomic systems.

In the literature, the autonomic paradigm is characterised by the presence of three distinct phases: *sensing, deciding* and *acting*. Notable examples of this division are the Monitor, Analyse, Plan and Execute (MAPE), or Observe, Decide, Act (ODA) loops [63]. Another contribution is the Sensing, Modelling, Actuating, Regulating and Tuning design framework [65,66], which is the main reference for the topics developed in this chapter. Whatever is the case, the 'decide', or equivalently the 'analyse and plan' or 'regulating', phase is responsible for providing and enforcing the desired properties of the self-managing system. Thus, the design of the decision phase is essential for obtaining the desired self-configuring, self-healing, self-optimising and self-protecting autonomic system [67].

It has been noted that the design of closed-loop autonomic systems shows impressive convergence with control engineering, which to date has been only marginally exploited in the design of computing systems [65,66,68,69], and this book is intended to increase the convergence also with respect to this relevant topic. In fact, modern control engineering may provide useful complements or alternatives to the heuristic and machine-learning decision methods used to date.

Although autonomic systems based on the feedback control theory have been proposed [70], the corresponding engineering tools and processes are far from being fully exploited. Controlling the behaviour of applications requires application-level sensors if we want to take full advantage of control theory's capabilities. In addition, the exploitation of a control-theoretical framework requires a modelling phase involving all system components prior to the algorithmic design of the computing system. Having a model of the system, in the control-theoretical sense, means writing the equations that describe system behaviour. As it often happens in resource–work problems, in the case of autonomic computing systems, developing such a model may be tough. This is why machine learning techniques have been usually adopted in autonomic computing, since they require little to no explicit modelling. However, as it will be shown in this chapter, the results that can be obtained spending a little effort to identify the core phenomenon are significantly better than using the mentioned techniques.

8.2 Control-based design

The problem addressed in this chapter is to complement a multitasking operating system with an application-aware resource allocator, with the purpose of making an application reach its goal not only within a certain time, but also with a prescribed progress rate. The problem is quite general, as it emerges whenever the rate of processed data delivery is of concern. A notable case, e.g., is the encoding of video streams.

Before going into the details of how to design control-based components for resource allocation, some relevant and general issues that appear in that domain are in order, i.e., we need to address the problem of sensing and actuating.

8.2.1 Sensing

In problems like those addressed in this chapter, the system behaviour is quantitatively indicated by the application 'progress rate', which however is not – to date – directly measured by the operating system *as is*. Operating systems typically provide information on what resources an application is engaging, by measuring the used CPU time, the number of assembler instructions executed per second, the cache miss or memory page fault rates, and so forth. This however does not tell whether the application is using resources to do useful work, or for example just spinning on a lock. Many workarounds were attempted to infer the application progress from the taken resources but these are invariantly architecture-specific, to the detriment of portability, and above all miss the core issue: the use of resources ultimately depends on the application, hence the application is where sensing must be located.

For sensing, the recently proposed Application Heartbeats (HB) framework [71] is here used. In HB, applications are instrumented to emit a 'heartbeat' when something relevant to appreciate their progress is accomplished (e.g., a video encoder could signal each frame completion). Using HB is quite simple for the application programmer, who knows what the application is meant for. Also, and most important, doing so naturally locates sensing at the correct level – a small modification for a system, a significant simplification for its control.

8.2.2 Actuation

The allocator can exert control actions by allotting an application more or less resources. Here too, it is first required to observe what the system *as is* provides as possible actuators, limiting however the choice to what acts on the desired behaviour directly. For example, the number of CPU cores and their clock frequencies are suitable actuators, in that their effect mostly (not to say only) depends on what the application is doing. The CPU time fraction is less suited, as the actual (not the desired) distribution of the CPU also depends on the scheduler operation; incidentally, the same quantity becomes more suited if a control-based scheduler like I+PI is used. Other quantities like the nice number are finally totally inadequate, as their influence is even more indirect than that of the desired CPU time fraction, and difficult to model.

In the case at hand, the number of cores and the frequency are adopted as actuators. This is a reasonable choice as confirmed by the subsequent modelling and control design phases. Hence, for actuating, no intervention on the system is here introduced.

8.2.3 Control

Before going into the details of the solutions devised here, a heuristic approach – discussed in Reference 69 – is presented so as to provide a counterpart for the following comparative considerations. In fact, in Section 8.3, the experimental results obtained with the heuristic approach can be considered as a baseline to better understand the improvement in terms of performance that can be achieved with control-based techniques.

8.2.3.1 Heuristic

Heuristic methods are often used to speed up the search for a solution whenever an exhaustive search of the solution space is not affordable.

The values of every decision variable (knob) can be numerically ordered for increased capabilities of affecting the used performance metric. Whenever it is not possible to provide a sort function, the different values could be just listed. An heuristic method could measure the actual performance and compare it with the target levels. If the actual performance value is below the minimum threshold, the heuristic chooses a dimension, corresponding to a single knob value, and performs a move in that direction increasing the amount of resources allocated to the application. With the same *rationale*, if the actual performance value is above the maximum threshold, the heuristic selects a knob and diminishes its value.

The knob selection can be provided with a priority-based mechanism, that first changes the actuator values that are considered more effective on the application, and then moves to less effective actuators, or does a random selection, or uses other techniques. Intuitively, if the knob values cannot be ordered, the search could take much more time with respect to the amount of time it would take in the opposite case. According to the *heuristic* nature of this solution, no guarantees are given that the system will enter the best state to attain the performance goal with the minimum amount of resources possible.

Coming to our example, we first suppose there is a single knob on the machine, being this the number of cores allotted to the single application processes. In this case the heuristic setup is straightforward, and the system can be found in $1 + c_{max} - c_{min}$ possible states. Formally, the number of cores to be allotted at the kth step of the algorithm execution $c(k)$ is given by

$$c(k) = \begin{cases} \min(c_{max}, c(k-1)+1) & hr(k) < hr_{min} \\ c(k-1) & hr_{min} \leq hr(k) \leq hr_{max} \\ \max(c_{min}, c(k-1)-1) & hr(k) > hr_{max} \end{cases} \tag{8.1}$$

Informally, whenever the heart rate signal we use as a sensor of the application progresses is below the minimum threshold, the number of cores is increased, limiting this value to c_{max}. If the signal is above the maximum threshold, the value is decreased, to a minimum of c_{min} cores allocated to the running application.

Then, we add to the previous system the frequency knob. In so doing, we need to select how to explore the solution space. We define a priority on the two actuators, assuming that frequency changes are more invasive on the system in its entirety, and should be done less frequently and we use the heuristic formalised in Algorithm 8.1.

This means that whenever the number of cores reaches c_{min} and the system capabilities need to be diminished, the clock speed of the cores is diminished. If the system resources are to be augmented and the number of cores is c_{max} the frequency of those cores is augmented. Another possibility could be to randomly choose the actuator to act on, which probably makes more sense when a large number of knobs are available.

8.2.3.2   Basic control

Apart from the particular approach proposed herein, autonomic and self-optimisation capabilities have been added to computing systems via feedback control [7]. Different approaches were developed in the literature up to date to solve a variety of specific problems, although a general lack of generalisation could be noticed. An attempt to generalise these solutions was proposed [72]; however, its success was limited, probably due to some of the limitations discussed in Reference 73.

For the considered problem, a preliminary control result was published [74], that addresses the number of cores as a single knob and uses a basic control scheme. In the following, we extend these results proposing a more flexible model and we synthesise a controller that is much more general and could in principle manage any kind and combination of resources.

Probably one of the best reasons to use a control-theoretical framework for a decision mechanism is the performance guarantees control provides. In fact, when modelling and analysing the closed-loop system, proving stability means proving

---

Algorithm 8.1 Multiple actuators (cores and frequency) heuristic solution.

Input: hr_{min}, hr_{max}, c_{old}, c_{min}, c_{max}, f_{old} f_{min}, f_{max}, f_{step}
Output: c, f
  $hr \leftarrow$ measured application heart rate
  if $hr_{min} \leq hr \leq hr_{max}$ **then**
    $c = c_{old}$
    $f = f_{old}$
  else if $hr > hr_{max}$ **then**
    if $c = c_{min}$ **then**
      $f = \max\left(f_{min}, f_{old} - f_{step}\right)$
      $c = c_{max}$
    else
      $c = c_{old} - 1$
      $f = f_{old}$
    end if
  else if $hr < hr_{min}$ **then**
    if $c = c_{max}$ **then**
      $f = \min\left(f_{max}, f_{old} + f_{step}\right)$
      $c = c_{min}$
    else
      $c = c_{old} + 1$
      $f = f_{old}$
    end if
  end if

---

that the heart rate value would reach the desired point, if the control system is well-designed and the set point is feasible.

We define the model for the open-loop behaviour of our system as follows. The performance of the application at the kth heartbeat is given as

$$hr(k+1) = \frac{\sigma(k)}{w(k)} + \delta hr(k) \tag{8.2}$$

where $\sigma(k)$ is the relative 'speedup' applied to the application between time $k - 1$ and time k, and $w(k)$ is the *workload* of the application. The workload is defined as the expected time between two subsequent heartbeats when the system is in the state that provides the lowest possible speedup. In this model, a speedup is applied to the system and it clearly controls the heart rate signal. This formulation is general so the source of speedup can vary, and may include the assignment of resources, such as cores, servers and memory, or the online modification of the algorithms used in the application.

The simplicity of this model is both an advantage and a disadvantage. Obviously we are not modelling all the components that may interact with the application and change its performance value, but a model does not need to be complete to serve its control purposes (as decades of experience in other domains like process control have shown). We introduce the term $\delta hr(k)$ as an exogenous disturbance that may vary the application behaviour in unexpected ways to deal with the unknown. However, using a simple model to describe a much more complex behaviour may be effective, if we are correctly describing the main components that interact with the modelled object.

Probably the easiest control solution would be a PID controller (see Chapter 4). This kind of controllers are usually very easy to build, as the only action involved is the choice of their parameters (e.g., the degree of proportionality of the various terms). There are several techniques, named 'autotuning techniques', which allow to build and parameterise such controllers [75–78].

Another standard control solution is a Deadbeat controller. Its synthesis involves the specification of the $\mathcal{Z}$ transfer function between the input data (the desired heart rate, $hr°$) and the output (the measured heart rate hr). In our case, we specify that function as

$$\frac{HR(z)}{HR°(z)} = \mu \frac{z - z_1}{(z - p_1)(z - p_2)} \tag{8.3}$$

where z^{-1} is the delay operator and $\{z_1, p_1, p_2\}$ are a set of customisable parameters which alter the transient behaviour. We want to shape the function so that the overall gain of the closed-loop system is 1, meaning that the input signal is reproduced to the output one, therefore we choose $\mu = (1 - p_1)(1 - p_2)/(1 - z_1)$.

The Deadbeat control is straightforward to synthesise, in that the closed loop transfer function

$$\frac{HR(z)}{HR°(z)} = \frac{HR(z)C(z)}{1 + HR(z)C(z)} \tag{8.4}$$

where $C(z)$ is the controller transfer function and can be obtained solving the equation. The control equation is then found by taking the inverse $\mathcal{Z}$ transform of $C(z)$ to find the speedup $\sigma(k)$ to apply at time k:

$$\sigma(k) = F \cdot [A\sigma(k-1) + B\sigma(k-2)$$
$$+ Ce(k)w(k) + De(k-1)w(k-1)] \tag{8.5}$$

where $e(k)$ is the *error* between the current heart rate and the desired heart rate at time k and the values of the parameters $\{A, B, C, D, F\}$ come from the controller synthesis and are

$$A = -[-p_1z_1 - p_2z_1 + p_1p_2]$$
$$B = -[p_2z_1 + p_1z_1 - z_1 - p_1p_2]$$
$$C = +[p_2 - p_1p_2 + p_1 - 1] \tag{8.6}$$
$$D = +[p_1p_2 - p_2 - p_1 + 1]z_1$$
$$F = +[z_1 - 1]^{-1}$$

The choice of the parameters $\{z_1, p_1, p_2\}$ allows customisation of the transient response. A preliminary discussion on different viable ways to impose the desired speedup value can be found in the technical report [79].

However, it is evident that the speedup equations depend on $w(k)$, the workload value. It is not always possible to have an offline estimate of the workload value, so a robustness analysis is in order.

Suppose to use w_o as a nominal value for the workload. Trivial computations show that if the actual workload w is expressed as $w_o(1 + \Delta w)$, thereby introducing the unknown quantity Δw as a multiplicative error, then the eigenvalue of the closed-loop system is $\Delta w/(1 + \Delta w)$. Requiring the magnitude of said eigenvalue to be less than unity, one finds that closed-loop stability is preserved for any Δw in the range $(-0.5, +\infty)$, hence if the workload is not excessively overestimated such a simple control law can effectively regulate the system despite its variations.

The speedup signal $\sigma(k)$ can be translated into the value of a single actuator, defining a relationship between the value of the knob and the speedup. In the case of the number of cores, we could for example assume that the application speeds up linearly with $c(k)$. Therefore, in the test hardware, the maximum speedup that can be applied is c_{max}, while the minimum one is c_{min}.

Different maps from the computed $\sigma(k)$ to be applied on the system and the couple $c(k), f(k)$ can be defined. We choose to set

$$\hat{\sigma}(k) = c(k) \frac{f(k)}{f_{min}} \tag{8.7}$$

where $\hat{\sigma}$ is the estimated speedup given in the state $c(k), f(k)$. The minimum speedup applicable in the system is therefore c_{min} while the maximum one is $c_{max} \cdot f_{max}/f_{min}$. Therefore, given the speedup value computed by the controller, we map that value into the couple of values for our knobs.

8.2.3.3 Adaptive control

A standard control solution may be sufficient for many systems and applications, but much more can be done by introducing more articulated (e.g., adaptive) techniques. Suppose that the proposed control system is augmented with an identification block, which provides an online estimation of the workload. Adding this capability to a standard control system turns it into an *adaptive* one. Different techniques can be used for identification; we implement a Recursive Least Squares (RLS) filter to estimate the workload value [80] and turn the standard Deadbeat controller into an adaptive one. The adaptive controller computes the desired speedup value, which is subsequently translated into the control signal with the same rationale of the basic methodology.

Adaptiveness is not influenced in this case by the number of actuators. However, even more complex solutions may be envisaged, where more parameters describe the relationship between the control entities (number of cores assigned to the application and their clock speed) and the performance metric, to build a more sophisticated controller. One could, for example, identify regions of the solution space where adding a single core does not influence the application performance and more than one computing unit is needed to speedup the application. At the same time, one may see that adding cores and changing their frequencies does not influence the application, therefore discovering that said application can be for example memory bound.

8.2.4 Modelling for advanced control

It was stated in Chapter 3 that, if sensors and actuators are introduced at the right level, i.e., as near as possible to the core phenomenon, the model required for control synthesis 'tends to be simple'. This is now demonstrated in the addressed problem.

The required model is a MISO dynamic system, having as inputs the actuators' actions $a_i \in \mathbf{a}$, and as output the sensor output $s_j \in \mathbf{s}$. The main problem is a variable and hard to predict actuator efficacy. For example, if an application switches from a CPU-bound to a memory-bound behaviour, the efficacy of a 'number of cores' actuator will drop. Such variability occurs at a time scale dictated by the application code, and sometimes by the processed data. Only the application itself could notify about actuators' effectiveness, but from a technological viewpoint this is quite unrealistic.

However, in the example two time scales exist: one at the *code level*, where most of the unpredictability resides, the other at the *observed behaviour* level, where sensors' measurements in fact average code-level facts over convenient time spans (e.g., the number of heartbeats in the last second). The time scale of actuator actions is the code-level one, hence at the observed behaviour level the effect of actuators can be safely regarded as instantaneous, or ruled by very simple dynamics. It is thus reasonable to assume for the model the form

$$\mathbf{s}(k) = \phi \left(\mathbf{s}(k-1), \mathbf{s}(k-2), \dots; \psi \right) + \gamma \left(\mathbf{a}(k-1), \mathbf{a}(k-2), \dots; \vartheta \right) \qquad (8.8)$$

where the discrete time index k counts the measurement (and control) instants, while ψ and ϑ are parameter vectors. A key point, further stemming from the remark above, is that in many cases one can assume $\phi = 0$ (thus no dynamics at the control time scale except for a delay) or at most $\phi = p\,\mathbf{s}(k-1)$, i.e., a first-order dynamics. Moreover, ψ – or p in the simplified case – are more connected to the time span over which sensors measurements average the code-level behaviour, than to that behaviour in detail: as a result, p can generally be considered time invariant. Adopting from now on these simplifications, and specialising to the example, the required model can be written as

$$hr(k) = p \cdot hr(k-1) + (1-p) \cdot \sigma(k-1), \quad 0 \le p < 1 \qquad (8.9)$$

where hr is the application heart (beat) rate, and σ is speedup[2] yielded collectively to the application by the resources allotted through the actuators.

The problem is therefore confined to determining a suitable map $\{a_i\} \mapsto \sigma$, possibly time-varying due to the variability of ϑ. Here too, the problem can be made more tractable if instrumentation is carried out properly. In fact, actuator efficacy variability

---

[2] The concept of speedup will be discussed more clearly in Section 9.1; for the purpose of this chapter, the intuitive meaning of the word is enough.

is due mostly to the application, and generally undergoes modifications that may be abrupt and of remarkable entity, but are however sporadic with respect to the control time scale. To explain, first think again to a video encoder. During the management of each frame, it will more or less traverse the same sequence of operations: first read data, being thus bound essentially to some peripheral, then compute, which is basically CPU-bound, and finally write, which is again peripheral-bound. If such an application is instrumented by making it emit a heartbeat per frame, large variability of a 'number of cores' actuator efficacy are not to be expected. Consider, conversely, an application that reads a lot of data, and then performs some mathematically intensive processing of them in a batch fashion. If the code is written by exploiting an available parallel architecture, the same actuator will be of hardly any efficacy in the read phase, but very relevant in the processing one. If the control time scale is chosen properly, there will be several control steps in both phases, and so a single abrupt system variation will be observed. Clearly in both cases things could complicate a lot if instrumentation is done differently, but this just testifies that instrumenting an application requires knowledge of it.

For completeness, one could object that also external facts (e.g., an unavailable lock) could introduce variability. However, the only major difference with respect to the second example just given is that such facts cannot be forecast even knowing about the application. In any case, with a properly chosen instrumentation and control time scale, the sporadic character of variations still carries over – and anticipating a bit, standard adaptive controllers can handle such situations successfully.

As for the $\{a_i\} \mapsto \sigma$ (static) map, in most cases synthetic considerations are sufficient to devise a structure for it, resorting then to a *grey box* modelling paradigm, and then use identification to obtain the required parameters.

In the literature, different definitions for 'white-', 'grey-' and 'black-box' models can be found, and we do not intend here to report a discussion. In our context, anyway, we adopt the following distinction:

- A white-box model is one whose form is dictated by knowledge of the described object's physics, i.e., a first-principle model in which some parameters can possibly need to be estimated from data.
- A grey-box model is one whose form is 'figured out' based on insight on the modelled object, but not (totally) on physical principles; in general, quit intuitively, parameters are then estimated from data.
- A black-box model is one with a standard – or better, problem-independent – structure, like for example an ARX; here one invariantly has to use data for determining the model parameters and possibly the order of the involved polynomials.

Of course there is an enormously variety of modelling and identification approaches with respect to the few examples just given, and the reader can find much additional information in the cited literature.

Coming back to the main subject, quite general form for the $\{a_i\} \mapsto \sigma$ map, according to experience, is

$$\sigma = \prod_{i=1}^{N_a} \left(k_i a_i^{\alpha_i} + o_i \right) \tag{8.10}$$

where N_a is the number of actuators, where the parameter vector $\vartheta \in \mathbb{R}^{3N_a}$ is

$$\vartheta = \begin{bmatrix} \vartheta_1 \\ \vartheta_2 \\ \vdots \\ \vartheta_{N_a} \end{bmatrix}, \quad \vartheta_i = \begin{bmatrix} k_i \\ \alpha_i \\ o_i \end{bmatrix} \quad \forall i = 1, \ldots, N_a \tag{8.11}$$

Apparently, if the actuators are the number of cores c and the normalised frequency f, (8.10) reduces to

$$\sigma = (k_c c^{\alpha_c} + o_c)\left(k_f f^{\alpha_f} + o_f\right) \tag{8.12}$$

8.2.5 *Regulating with tuning*

The framework naturally leads to a control scheme like that of Figure 8.1. The modelling phase has shown that by conveniently instrumenting the system, the problem can be addressed taking as 'process' model a MISO Hammerstein one (the cascade of blocks $\mathcal{A}$ and $\mathcal{M}$). There is a vast literature on such models, but the situation (abrupt but sporadic variabilities of otherwise smooth models with very simple dynamics) and the typical requirements of computing systems control/design (high speed and computational lightness) advise here too for a domain-specific approach. In other words, the choice is made to reason for the control synthesis as if the manipulated variable was a desired speedup σ, while at the same time taking profit of the degrees of freedom introduced by the $\sigma \mapsto \mathbf{a}$ (i.e., block $\mathcal{A}^{-1}$ in Figure 8.1) as part of the system components' design.

Quite intuitively, in fact, a given speedup value will not be yielded by a single actuator combination. If that is the case, to select the combination output by the $\sigma \mapsto \mathbf{a}$ for a certain value of σ, one can bring in, e.g., considerations regarding the consumed power, the least use of some or some other resources based on what are most 'precious' for the system, or technologically simpler to act upon, and so forth. Any such mechanism will work under the assumption that $\sigma \mapsto \mathbf{a}$ is either known or estimated reliably enough, which means that the $\mathcal{R}$ and $\mathcal{A}_{\hat{\vartheta}}^{-1}$ blocks are carried out properly.

Here too, the addressed example is useful to clarify. The number of cores and the frequency are used as the actuators. The number of cores can assume only integer values, but can be treated as real thanks, e.g., to a pulse width modulation (PWM)

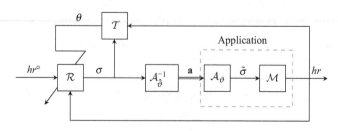

Figure 8.1   The control scheme

policy. For example, if 2.4 cores must be assigned to an application, the actuation policy allots 3 cores for the 40% of the control interval and 2 cores for the 60% of the control interval. The two actuators, however, impact the system differently, since in general the frequency is the same for all cores. Thus a frequency change is more invasive than a core re-allocation, and based on that (design) consideration, the adopted solution can be summarised as follows:

1. starting from the speedup σ computed by the controller, c is computed maintaining the clock frequency of the previous step,
2. if c is not within its saturation values, the frequency is increased or decreased (accordingly to which saturation is violated) and step 1 is repeated,
3. otherwise the computed number of cores and clock frequency are assigned to the application.

Given all the above, the chosen $\sigma \mapsto \mathbf{a}$ map and the cascaded Hammerstein MISO model composed of (8.9) and (8.10), can be viewed as a time-varying linear SISO model. The *nominal* $\sigma \mapsto \mathbf{a}$ map above is physically realised in the system as block $\mathcal{A}_{\hat{\vartheta}}^{-1}$ in Figure 8.1 and the task of counteracting variabilities is delegated to an adaptive controller designed in a linear context. In so doing, the considered problem (like many others) can be cast in the strong framework of linear adaptive MPC, to which – it is worth and important recalling – it did *not* belong prior to its structuring along the proposed approach.

The presented resource allocation example can be treated with an adaptive model predictive controller, based on an ARX-type process model of fixed structure, parameterised on line by recursive identification (see Chapter 7). The choice of the ARX orders, the prediction horizon H_p, and the two weights on the error and the control energy q and r, are the subject of the subsequent Tuning phase (block $\mathcal{T}$ in Figure 8.1), that thanks to the previous problem structuring, is completely standard.

8.3   Experimental results

The case studies presented in this paper are taken from the PARSEC benchmark suite [81] and instrumented with the Application Heartbeats framework [71]; the proposed controller is realised in user space. All experiments are run on a Dell PowerEdge R410 server with two quad-core Intel Xeon E5530 processors running Linux 2.6.26. The processors support seven power states with clock frequencies from 2.4 to 1.6 GHz.

8.3.1   Swaptions

The swaptions application is a financial software that prices a portfolio of swaptions. It employs the Monte Carlo simulation method to compute the prices. The program uses an array to store the prices. As for parallelism, the application partitions the array into a number of blocks equal to the number of threads and assigns one block to every thread. Each thread then iterate over its block.

For our test, we decided to price 500 swaptions with 1,000,000 simulations each. This corresponds to the application emitting 500 heart beats over time. We set a desired heartrate of 9 beats per second, specifying hr_{min} equal to 7 and hr_{max} equal to 11. Figures 8.2 and 8.3 report the test results. In each of the plots (and also in the following ones for other applications), the x-axis represents the application progress, expressed in heartbeats (which could correspond to a measure of time). Each application is emitting a series of heartbeats at non-regular intervals, and the controller strategies are acting when the application completes a prescribed number of heartbeats, trying to adjust the progress rate of the software, depicted in the y-axis through the heart rate signal.

Figure 8.2 shows the results of the heuristic and basic control approach. The heuristic single actuator technique is initialised outside the desired area and is not able to drive the performance signal while the heuristic multiple actuators approach performs better, it starts when the heart rate is in the desired performance range and is able to attain an average heart rate; however, bouncing between the upper region and the lower one. The control basic single actuator technique and the control basic multiple actuators are able to attain the set point with few oscillations.

The sole workload adaptation fails in obtaining stable performances as can be noticed in Figure 8.3 for the control adaptive single actuator and the control adaptive multiple actuators. The same figure reports also the execution of the model predictive controller both for the single and for the multiple actuation mechanism. As can

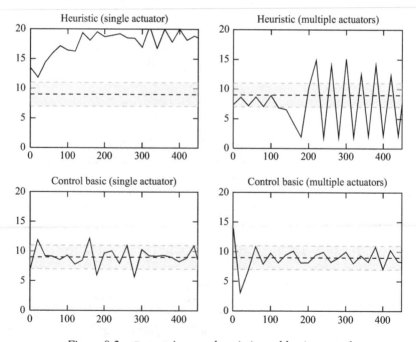

Figure 8.2   Swaptions – *heuristic and basic control*

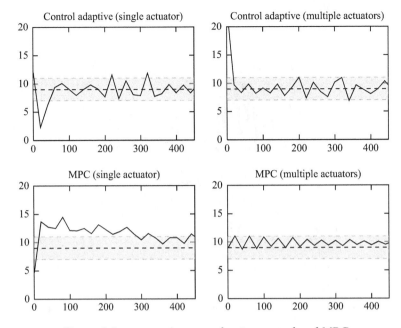

Figure 8.3   Swaptions – *adaptive control and MPC*

be seen, the use of a more complex control technique allows to attain the set point with much more precision than with simpler control structures.

8.3.2 Vips

The vips benchmark is a software application based on the VASARI image processing system. It includes fundamental image operations such as an affine transformation and a convolution and constructs multithreaded image processing pipelines transparently on the fly. The pipeline used for this test has 18 different stages. In our tests the vips application is supposed to emit 70,000 heartbeats and we desire to attain a set point of 2000 heartbeats per second, being the acceptable range between 1500 and 2500 beats. Moreover, in the test, we use the native input configurations, acting on a 18,000 × 18,000 pixels image.

Notice that vips is way harder to control an application with respect to swaptions, because the parallelism model is much more complex. In fact, the introduction of a pipeline and of worker threads makes the control much more difficult. Not all the threads, in fact, are experiencing the same amount of work and the asymmetry of the workload affects the application performance.

Figures 8.4 and 8.5 show the results of this test and are organised as the swaptions test case ones. It is noticeable that the heuristic solutions, as well as simple control ones, fails in stabilising the application performances. On the contrary, the adaptive and predictive controllers are able to attain the desired set point, with some oscillations.

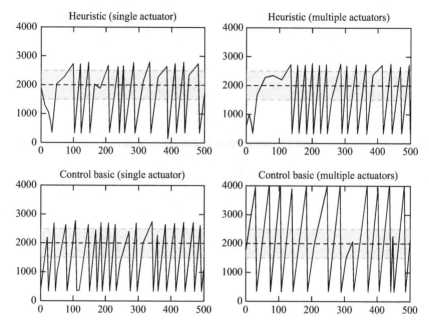

Figure 8.4   Vips – heuristic and basic control

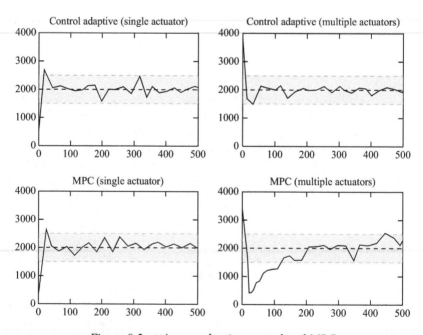

Figure 8.5   Vips – adaptive control and MPC

8.4 Concluding remarks

Even if this chapter focused only on a specific problem, the presented concepts are more general, and can be easily applied also in other ones. In particular, it should be apparent that resource–work problems – e.g., the heartbeats control – are much difficult to handle from both the modelling and the control viewpoints, since they exhibit uncertainties and time-varying behaviours that cannot be neglected. Thus, more advanced control techniques were brought into play, showing their effectiveness.

It is worth mentioning that in the literature, this kind of problems are typically addressed with machine learning techniques. In References 66 and 69, the control-theoretical approach presented herein was also compared with neural networks and reinforcement learning techniques, showing that in many cases a suited control design results in higher performance.

Some conclusions can be drawn from the presented experiments. First, instrumentation is crucial, and whenever an application cannot be instrumented in a sensible manner, there is simply no way out.

Second, the relative performance of the various techniques is influenced by application variability in quite predictable a way. In other words, forecasts on the application variability can easily be turned into choices of the most appropriate technique(s).

Third, the same remark above applies up to different extents, depending on how many and which actuators have the most significant influence on the application. When there is more than one actuator, techniques that in some sense resort to a space search, suffer significantly if not properly initialised.

Fourth, and last, control-based methods deserve being considered as viable alternatives to more often used ones. In fact, they invariably perform comparably with all the other techniques: sometimes *slightly* worse, which is a problem to be addressed although differences are small indeed, but usually better, and often *significantly* better.

To summarise, the presented results indicate that the best decision method can vary depending on the specific application to be optimised; however, adaptive and model predictive control tend to produce good performance, and may work best when the applications to be controlled are *a priori* unknown.

Chapter 9
Power-awareness

After scheduling, memory management and resource allocation, we consider in this chapter another application of the proposed design approach, namely that aimed at realising 'power awareness'. Such a capability is of particular relevance nowadays, since operating systems run on a variety of devices that are not designed for a single purpose, but rather host different applications, each with its own requirements. In this context, an incorrect use of the functionalities made available by the host architecture could easily result in an undue power consumption, or even in the inability of satisfying the applications' needs. In a battery-operated device the relevance of the mentioned problem is apparent, and also larger systems can be affected. In the former case the energies coming into play are small, and the main issue is battery life, in the latter the same energies are instead relevant, and the main concern is their cost. Given also the need for an operating system to scale on differently sized architectures, which is nowadays another important characteristic in a view to application portability and user experience uniformity, a unitary framework to cast the power awareness problem into, is thus highly desirable.

The *scenario* just sketched poses nontrivial design problems, tackled in the literature at different levels, from energy-efficient code generation [82,83] to consumption estimates [84], battery optimisation [85] and much more.

The main issue is that, ideally, a device should activate a different subset of its architectural capabilities – i.e., the required ones and nothing else – depending not only on the applications that are being executed, but also on the particular data that they are processing [86]. This makes it impossible to design the architecture based on some 'general' consideration, whatever is meant for that: strictly, on the contrary architecture tailoring is needed *on-line*, and this should conceptually be done not only for each application, but for each particular *run* of that application.

The purpose of this chapter, that deals with power-aware resource allocation, is to show that the proposed design approach can be also used to induce 'power awareness' in the management activity of an operating system.

To put the proposed concepts to work in such a context, the basic idea is to size the architecture for the heaviest load case, and then allow a feedback control mechanism to turn on just the required features at any given time. Doing so complements classical design methodologies, and the presented *modus operandi* can be seamlessly applied to both new and existing devices. Also, since one can size for the worst case and then be sure that nothing useless will be on and consuming power at runtime, it can be conjectured that a smaller number of architectures will be able to fit all the possible different needs, and somehow symmetrically, already designed architectures can be extended to new applications without undue power losses. In other words, and to summarise, we are here separating 'sizing' from 'online allocation', which is quite common an idea, e.g., in the process industry, thus another example of porting the process/control co-design idea into computing systems.

9.1   A case study

Given the somehow peculiar nature of this particular use of the proposed approach, especially for the actuation part, we proceed by first presenting a case study, and then generalising the idea based on some considerations made while devising the case-specific solution. Correspondingly, in this chapter we privilege a treatise aimed at clarifying the role of the proposed approach. The reader interested in more technical details can find them in Reference 87.

The considered application is a video encoder, that processes frames from a raw stream to achieve an efficient transmission. When encoding a frame, depending on its type along a classification irrelevant to discuss here, three cases are possible:

- information is produced for all pixels (and these are termed I frames),
- or by difference with respect to the previous frames (P frames),
- or by difference with respect to both the previous and the subsequent ones (B frames).

Such differences obviously lead to a high workload variability. For example, a sequence of quasi-static frames like the video of a conference has very different requirements with respect to high-variation sequences like those in the video of a sport event. Also, to limit the need for buffering on the receiving side, a constant encoding rate is desired; the National Television System Committee (NTSC), for example, recommends 30 frames per second.

The proposed approach is here applied in a three-steps procedure. First, based on a problem and architecture analysis, sensors and actuators are defined. Then a control structure is devised based on a simple model of the controlled device, as usual, and finally that structure is parameterised. The data required by the procedure are obtained by profiling the targeted architecture offline.

9.1.1   Step 1: Analysis, sensors and actuators

In the study, the architecture to run the video encoder was a multi-core one with variable frequency. The software to use was a library for encoding video streams into the H.264/MPEG-4 AVC format, named x264 and released within the GNU GPL license. A first definition of the goal came out very naturally as the achievement of a desired encoding rate (30 frames per second) with the least power consumption.

Then, as usual when process/control co-design is included in the paradigm, attention was focused on the plant *as it was*, to figure out what to measure and how to act in order to attain the goal, and – which is particularly important – which aspects of the plant could make it unduly rigid from the control standpoint for the problem being defined.

Quite often, some actuators are offered by the plant in a natural way, and here this is the case, since the encoding speed can apparently be affected by allotting more or less cores, and altering their frequency. In a view to minimise intrusiveness, it was therefore decided to continue the study with those two actuators. With the hardware used for the presented tests, from one to eight cores can be allotted, while seven frequencies are available in the range [1596–2394]MHz. The first actuator is implemented via the `taskset` Unix command, while the second is realised through the `cpufrequtils` Linux package. The controller was realised in user space for implementation simplicity reasons.

Coming to plant rigidity issues, the major one evidenced in this analysis was the strict real-time character of the *original* goal, i.e., encode 30 frames per second processing *every* frame. Since skipping a few ones can still result in an acceptable user experience, the decision was taken to turn x264 into a soft real-time application, by giving it the capability of dropping frames in the case of a too low encoding rate with respect to the goal – in the reported tests, the limit was decided to be 25 frames per second.

Performance was hence defined more precisely as the achievement of a frame rate as close as possible to the desired value with as low a consumption and a percent of dropped frames as possible. And again as usual, the definition of a performance metrics led to that of the candidate sensors: one for the frame rate, one for the drop rate, and one for the consumed power.

The first two proved easy to realise at virtually no cost. To measure the frame rate, x264 was instrumented with the Application Heartbeats framework [88] (already used in Chapter 8), while the frame drop ratio measurement simply required to introduce a counter in the code. As such, the assumption was made that the frame and drop rate sensors could be present.

On the other hand, things proved quite different for the third sensor. Measuring the consumed power in a laboratory setup is easy, and was done here with a WattsUp device [89], but for apparent size and cost reasons, such a sensor could not be considered for inclusion in the production architecture.

Similar situations, namely the availability of some measurement only in the 'pilot plant' – here, the laboratory architecture – are not uncommon also in classical control problems. Note that this is not the case for actuators: the pilot plant can have additional sensors for control design and setup provided the production one can cope without them, but if the production plant is missing an actuator, no control policy devised on the pilot one can be realised.

When a sensor is relevant for control setup – as here the power one is – but cannot be deployed into production, broadly speaking to serve just the purpose of this book, two are the possible situations. In the first one, no control strategy can be devised without feedback of the quantity under question. If this is the case, some estimator will clearly need to be created, and it will also become part of the control loop. This can make the estimator's correct operation critical, and its dynamics relevant for the overall result: it is not frequent that stability and/or performance properties achieved on the pilot plant, where the quantity is really measured, cannot carry over to the production plant, because no measurement available there can provide good enough an estimate.

The other situation, that is preferable if a thorough co-design can make it arise, is when the behaviour of the unmeasurable quantity can be reliably forecast based on offline profiling of the laboratory setup as a function of the control inputs only (not of other measurements). If this is he case, degrees of freedom on the actuation side can be exploited to set up a control strategy that requires only feedback of real measurements, while indirectly governing the quantity as forecast based on said profiling. Note that also this case implies some estimation, but not in the loop, since the forecast quantity is not fed back to the controller.

Coming to the case at hand, natural actuators are cores and frequency. Considering a certain application – not necessarily the video encoder – ran with certain data, it can be expected that allotting more cores or increasing frequency normally results in an increase of the application progress speed, measurable, e.g., with Heartbeats. If some baseline architecture is defined, and the speed increase is measured with respect to that architecture – hereinafter, this will be called the *speedup* – then it is possible to determine which cores/frequency couple achieves a certain speedup with the least consumption. If many applications are profiled in this way with many different data sets, the result will tend to characterise the architecture, thus allowing to have the controller produce a speedup, that the actuation mechanism turns into the best core/frequency couple. Such a couple is called in the following a Power Optimal (PO) state for that speedup, and a controller acting this way will achieve the required speedup (i.e., performance) by consuming the least possible power.

9.1.2   Step 2a: Data collection

First, in a view to the following tests, an upper bound to the amount of resources needed to meet the requirement was found. The so determined 'upper bound architecture', that can encode all the videos without dropping any frame, turned out to have eight cores and a clock frequency of 2394 MHz. To define a baseline for the following comparisons, also a 'lower bound' architecture was determined, as the one with which at least one of the videos was encoded maintaining the minimum frame rate; this architecture resulted to have three cores, and the same clock frequency as the upper bound one.

For the profiling phase, the architecture was subjected to the PARSEC benchmark suite [81]. The used benchmark is a collection of applications presenting a wide variety of workloads (recall that this is an offline activity, thus a huge set is not detrimental, and in principle one could even think of trying 'any application that the device can be expected to run'). Those applications were executed with various data and in all the 56 power states, collecting power and performance measurements. States were finally sorted based on power consumption, and the set of PO ones was determined as follows. A state was included in the PO set if, for at least one of the runs, any other state consuming more power also produced a higher performance. In other words,

Table 9.1 Summary of power-optimal (✓) and non-power-optimal (–) states

	1	2	3	4	5	6	7	8
1596 MHz	✓	✓	✓	✓	✓	–	–	✓
1729 MHz	✓	✓	✓	✓	–	✓	–	✓
1862 MHz	✓	✓	✓	–	–	–	–	✓
1995 MHz	✓	✓	–	–	–	–	–	✓
2128 MHz	✓	✓	–	–	–	–	–	✓
2261 MHz	✓	–	–	–	–	–	–	✓
2394 MHz	–	–	–	–	–	–	–	✓

PO states are the combinations of control input values for which, in all the runs of all the applications with all the data sets, allotting less resources diminishes the achieved performance.

As shown in Table 9.1, only 25 of the 56 possible states are PO. Surprisingly enough, and thus as a proof for the usefulness of a systematic approach, no state with seven cores is PO, while assigning eight cores is PO with any frequency. Anticipating a bit with respect to the general considerations reported later on, the used control *rationale* based on PO states can be outlined as follows:

- At design time, each PO state is provided with an estimated value of the speedup – i.e., recall, of performance increase with respect to the baseline. To provide such estimates, assumptions are of course needed. In this work, it was supposed that application performance scales linearly with frequency, and a speedup of

$$\sigma_c = c^{\frac{N-1}{N}} \tag{9.1}$$

is obtained when c cores are allotted, N being the total number of available ones. This is clearly an empirical relationship, suitable for the presented case, but it is equally clear that the idea can be applied to other situations by just reconsidering the assumptions, and designing the (offline) experiments accordingly.
- At runtime, at each control step the controller produces a speedup request. The two values nearest to that request (one lower and one higher) are found among those obtained from the profiling, thus selecting a couple of PO states. Those two states are applied, each one for part of the subsequent control sampling period, so that the time-weighed average of their speedups equals the requested one.

Hence, the feedback controller – described in the following – decides the quantity of resources to collectively allot to the application in terms of speedup. Then, the map from speedup to PO states, obtained from profiling, is used to achieve the desired speedup by keeping the system always in a PO state. In some sense, this decouples power from performance: the controller reasons like if it had just to allot a 'comprehensive resource', and the offline profiling is exploited at runtime to select the most power-efficient input combination with the desired effect.

9.1.3   Step 2b: Control design

Performance is measured by the frame encoding rate (fer) output, while actuation is designed to select only control actions yielding PO states for any admissible speedup value. Hence, as already envisaged in the analysis phase and confirmed by the profiling one, control structuring just requires to introduce a feedback block acting on the speedup request, having as controlled variable the frame rate, and with a set point fixed at 30 frames per second.

Assuming here fixed-rate control, denoting with k the discrete time (*stricto sensu*) index, and assuming that the control period is long enough for the applied speedup to fully exert its action, the speedup-to-fer relationship is expressed as

$$fer(k) = \frac{\sigma(k-1)}{w(k-1)} + \delta(k-1) \tag{9.2}$$

where $w(\cdot)$ is the (time varying) application *workload*, i.e., the (nominal) time between two subsequent frame encodings, and δ a disturbance accounting for any non-nominality in said time behaviour. Clearly w is in general unknown, but the profiling activity can provide reliable bounds for it. In the specific case treated here, it was decided for practical reasons to treat w as an unknown parameter – denoted in the following by w_o – instead of a time-varying quantity, but this particular choice does not impair the general idea.

From (9.2), the transfer function from s to *fer* is

$$\frac{FER(z)}{\Sigma(z)} = \frac{1}{w_o z} \tag{9.3}$$

and for the controller, the very simple deadbeat solution $R(z)$ is found by solving

$$\frac{FER(z)}{FER°(z)} := \frac{R(z)\frac{1}{w_o z}}{1 + R(z)\frac{1}{w_o z}} = \frac{1}{z} \tag{9.4}$$

with respect to $R(z)$, $FER°(z)$ being the $\mathcal{Z}$-transform of the desired frame rate. This produces

$$R(z) = w_o \frac{z}{z-1} \tag{9.5}$$

In the time domain, this corresponds to the law

$$\sigma(k) = \sigma(k-1) + w_o \left[fer°(k) - fer(k) \right] \tag{9.6}$$

and the control saturations resulting from the minimum and maximum possible speedup values are managed with standard antiwindup techniques.

As w_o is just a nominal workload value, at least a minimal robustness analysis is advisable. This can be done in the same way illustrated in Section 8.2.3.2. As a result, if the workload is not excessively overestimated, and varies slowly (or abruptly but sporadically) enough with respect to the control time scale, the simple control proposed can effectively handle the system despite 'acceptable' variations (note that this also gives a practical justification for treating w as a time-varying parameter). Strictly speaking, the system is a linear discrete-time switching one with state-independent switching signal, so that a deeper analysis should be done if full detail is desired. Nonetheless, if all the closed-loop eigenvalues lie in the unit circle for any value of the switching signal, there surely exist a finite dwell time (i.e., a time for which the system has to 'dwell' in one of the possible conditions among which it switches) that ensures stability [90]. Estimating that time would, however, stray from the scope of this section.

A final point to address is that the speedup values obtained by profiling are isolated points, while the output $\sigma(k)$ of (9.6) lies in the continuous range from minimum to maximum speedup. However, denoting by $\bar{\sigma}$ the output of (9.6), it is by construction possible to find two actuator values $\mathbf{a}_{i+1}$ and $\mathbf{a}_i$ such that

$$\sigma(\mathbf{a}_{i+1}) = \sigma_{i+1} \qquad \sigma(\mathbf{a}_i) = \sigma_i; \qquad \sigma_{i+1} \geq \bar{\sigma} \qquad \sigma_i \leq \bar{\sigma} \qquad (9.7)$$

This, indicating by τ the time between two control actions, a PWM actuation mechanism can be used, as already shown in Section 8.2.5 computing the time spans τ_{i+1} and τ_i in which to apply respectively $\mathbf{a}_{i+1}$ and $\mathbf{a}_i$ as

$$\tau_{i+1} = \tau \frac{\sigma_{i+1} - \bar{\sigma}}{\sigma_{i+1} - \sigma_i}; \qquad \tau_i = \tau - \tau_{i+1} \qquad (9.8)$$

9.1.4 Step 3: Control structure parameterisation

In the considered situation, the parameterisation activity simply consists of inserting the profiling phase output in the control law (9.6) and in the actuation policy. This can be realised in many ways, depending on the particular application. For example, in very simple devices where no 'configuration' of the introduced controls is envisaged online, the parameterisation can be realised by suitable inclusion in the compiled code of a header file (to use the C jargon) containing the required parameter values. No matter how the parameterisation is actually realised, however, the controller is inherently modular, and there is no need to change its code if the architecture changes.

9.2 Experimental results

As an example of the achievable results, we briefly present here an evaluation campaign. The encoder endowed with resource control was tested with 16 different videos.[1] Each of them was encoded 25 times, and the results were averaged to improve the meaningfulness of the analysis. In particular, the used videos for the benchmarking, their brief description, and the correspondent numeric identifiers used in the following, are reported in Table 9.2.

---

[1] The benchmark of videos used here is available at http://xiph.org.

Table 9.2   Video used for the benchmarking. They can be found at
http://media.xiph.org/video/derf/

ID	Name	Frames	Description
1	blue_sky.yuv	250	Top of two trees against blue sky. High contrast, small colour differences in the sky, many details. Camera rotation.
2	crowd_run_1080p.yuv	500	
3	dinner.yuv	950	
4	ducks_take_off_1080p.yuv	500	
5	factory.yuv	1339	
6	in_to_tree_1080p.yuv	500	
7	life.yuv		
8	native.yuv		
9	old_town_cross_1080p.yuv	500	
10	park_joy_1080p.yuv	500	
11	pedestrian_area.yuv	375	Shot of a pedestrian area. Low camera position, people pass by very close to the camera. High depth of field. Static camera.
12	riverbed.yuv	250	Riverbed seen through the water. Very hard to code.
13	rush_hour.yuv	500	Rush-hour in Munich city. Many cars moving slowly, high depth of focus. Fixed camera.
14	station2.yuv	313	View from a bridge to Munich station. Evening shot. Long zoom out. Many details, regular structures (tracks).
15	sunflower.yuv	500	Sunflower, very detailed shot. One bee at the sunflower, small colour differences and very bright yellow. Fixed camera, small global motion.
16	tractor.yuv	761	A tractor in a field. Whole sequence contains parts that are very zoomed in and a total view. Camera is following the tractor, chaotic object movement, structure of a harvested field. Very red wheels of the tractor.

For each video, the encoding procedure was carried out first with 1 enabled core and the minimum frequency, to obtain the lowest performance and power consumption, and then with different *fixed* (i.e., uncontrolled) architectures, with a number of cores ranging from 3 to 8, and the maximum clock frequency. The procedure was finally repeated with the resource control activated.

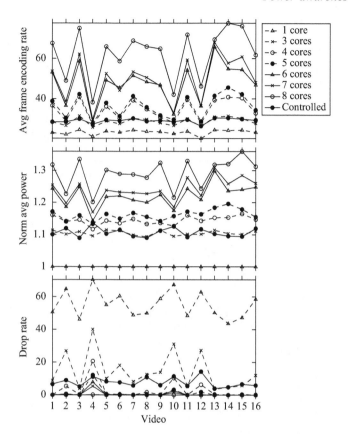

*Figure 9.1   Average fer (top row) and normalised power consumption (bottom row)
of the x264 video encoder with 16 different videos, over 25 runs per
video © 2013 IEEE. Reprinted, with permission, from paper [Power
Optimization in Embedded systems via Feedback control of resource
allocation] appears in Control Systems Technology, IEEE
transactions on*

The outcome is shown in Figure 9.1. The top row reports the average fer, while
the middle row provides the power consumption, normalised to the minimum value
defined above. The last row represents the drop rate. All plots are shown with respect
to the different videos. The controlled architecture almost invariantly maintains the
encoding rate, while not consuming more power than the uncontrolled architecture
best attaining that rate (which, it is worth stressing, is not the same as the video varies).

To further appreciate the obtained improvement, Figure 9.2 reports the same
results with boxplots, but organised by architecture instead of by video: '1c' stands
for one core, '3c' for three, and so on, while 'C' denotes the controlled architecture.
The top, middle and lower plot refer, respectively, to the fer, with the dotted line
marking the desired rate of 30 frames per second, the normalised consumption and

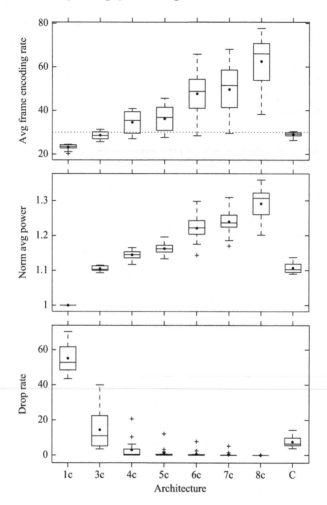

*Figure 9.2   Boxplots of the average fer (top), normalised average power (middle)
and drop rate (bottom) with respect different architectures*

the dropped frames percent. In each plot item the top and bottom segments indicate
the maximum and minimum value for each architecture across the 16 videos, the
rectangle marks the 25th and the 75th distribution percentiles, the segment across the
rectangle denotes the median, and the dot the average. The controlled architecture
best keeps the set point – which is in fact not surprising – followed by the three-cores
one, that has a comparable power consumption, but a definitely worse drop rate. The
one-core architecture simply cannot keep the set point, while more powerful ones
than three cores consume too much power to yield uselessly high frame rates.

Figure 9.3 finally summarises the results by giving a 3D representation of
them, where the axes report the (average) normalised power, fer, and drop rate.

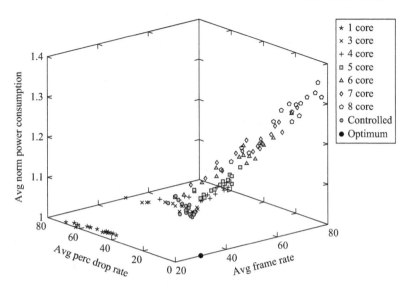

Figure 9.3   Summary of the x264 video encoder results. Average fer, percentage of dropped frames, and average power consumption for the 16 considered videos. The black dot represents the optimum point © 2013 IEEE. Reprinted, with permission, from paper [Power Optimization in Embedded systems via Feedback control of resource allocation] appears in Control Systems Technology, IEEE transactions on

Each architecture produces 16 points, each one corresponding to the average over 25 runs of one of the 16 benchmark videos. The black point in the same figure identifies the 'optimum' point, which means zero drop rate, 30 encoded frames per second, and the lowest possible power consumption.

The figure confirms once again that a fixed low number of cores is better for consumption but tends to miss the frame and drop rates, while a fixed high number of cores drops few or no frames, but consumes more power and yields a too high fer. The controlled architecture conversely remains in the vicinity of the optimum, and which is at least equally relevant, its results are much nearer to one another, i.e., much more uniform for the different videos.

To further witness and quantify this idea, one can also compute the distance between the points in Figure 9.3 and the optimum one. Table 9.3, where each row refers to an architecture, reports the result. The first two columns contain the minimum and the maximum value of the distance above, giving an idea of the performance range that each architecture produces. The third and fourth column contain the average distance and its variance, to also give an idea of the performance distribution. The controlled architecture invariantly produces comparable ranges with respect to the *best* uncontrolled one for the considered case, and in addition it results in a significantly lower variance.

Table 9.3   Summary of distances between the video encoder points and the optimum one as identified in Figure 9.3

		Minimum	Maximum	Average	Variance
1)	$c:1, f:1596$	43.9414	70.8640	55.5421	69.0430
3)	$c:3, f:2394$	3.6907	40.1393	14.6116	124.2050
4)	$c:4, f:2394$	0.4949	20.8357	7.8127	23.9182
5)	$c:5, f:2394$	0.6499	15.5612	7.5859	23.6922
6)	$c:6, f:2394$	3.3815	35.7312	18.3023	78.8064
7)	$c:7, f:2394$	3.2127	38.0173	19.9814	108.2678
8)	$c:8, f:2394$	8.1801	47.6131	32.4297	152.1449
C)	Controlled	3.9713	14.8207	7.7699	9.2831

9.3   Generalisation

Based on the case study above, a general methodology aimed at power-aware designing can be abstracted. As anticipated, it has to be assumed that the hardware architecture has already been designed in such a way to be able of covering the heaviest utilisation case. Note, incidentally, the tight relationships with the general resource allocation design guidelines of Chapter 8.

9.3.1   Step 1

The first step is to define which measurements are needed to online assess the desired behaviour, and quality of resource use. Also, it is necessary to define the actions to be taken in order to influence those quantities, such as enabling or disabling cores, or scaling frequency. In this phase, possible interventions on the 'plant' are to be considered, as they can significantly ease the subsequent steps (think of the frame dropping capability in the reported study).

This is again defining 'sensors' and 'actuators'. In the following we shall denote by N_s the number of sensors, each yielding a measurement of value s_i in a set S_i, and by N_a the number of actuators, each exerting an action of value a_j in a set A_j. Notice that S_i and A_j can be physically heterogeneous.

9.3.2   Step 2a

Then, conveniently designed (*offline*) tests are to be performed, to assess how a generic application, in the set envisaged to be of interest, exploits the architecture capabilities in the absence of control (i.e., of online tailoring).

This activity provides what we may call an *uncontrolled hardware profile (UHP)*, defined as follows. Denoting by $\mathbf{a} := [a_1, a_2 \ldots a_{N_a}]$ the vector of actuator values, with $\mathbf{p}(\mathbf{a}) := [p_1(\mathbf{a}), p_2(\mathbf{a}) \ldots p_{N_p}(\mathbf{a})]$ that of performance metrics, each p_i being in a set $P_I \subseteq \mathbb{R}^+$ and obtained from the sensor outputs or elaborations of them, and finally denoting with $\underline{\mathbf{a}}_j$ a value of $\mathbf{a}$ providing the worst value $\underline{p}_j$ of p_j, the UHP is a map

$$\mathbf{a} \in \mathcal{A}_1 \times \mathcal{A}_2 \cdots \times \mathcal{A}_{N_a} \mapsto \mathbf{r} \in (\mathbb{R}^+)^{N_p}$$

where $r_k = p_k(\mathbf{a})/\underline{p}_k$.

Somehow contrary to intuition, but as confirmed by experience, the tests here considered are not very strictly tied to any specific application, and are best performed on a wide application set. Tests can be in fact designed on the sole basis of sensors, actuators, goals and performance indices, and only some broad assumptions on the applications to be run are generally enough to produce the UHP. The presented study definitely backs up this statement, although the matter surely deserves further research in the future.

9.3.3   Step 2b

In parallel with Step 2a above, whence the shared number, devise a *control structure (CS)* capable of controlling the hardware to achieve the desired performance. This amounts essentially to turn preliminary ideas on the control scheme, as coming from the analysis of the first step, into a full-fledged block diagram. Also, possible 'virtual' quantities (like the speedup above) can be defined and used.

It is worth noticing that if the previous activities were carried out thoroughly, then the CS is very often surprisingly simple. This is a merit in practice, as time and resources are an issue in virtually any system, and also from a methodological point of view, as simplicity allows for systematic domain-specific designs, that are generally safer and more effective than those based on mere heuristics.

9.3.4   Step 3

Based on the UHP, the final step is to parameterise the CS for the architecture under question. Notice that if the hardware changes, *only Step 2a* needs repeating.

Also, Step 3 intrinsically yields dynamic models of the (controlled) hardware, the controller, and the closed loop. This allows to analyse the system to assess its behaviour, also (e.g., via simulation) in a general manner with respect to subsequent, possibly different, uses.

As a result, the overall system looks like Figure 9.4, where one can distinguish sensor(s), actuator(s), and the role of the speedup signal.

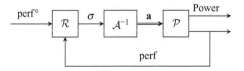

Figure 9.4   General scheme representing the proposed solution

9.4   Concluding remarks

In the first place, this chapter should have further evidenced the importance of a control-centric *analysis*. It should also be clear that control-based *design* is frequently an iterative process, since assumptions made in the analysis phase could be confuted by the subsequent profiling. However, once the process has converged, the creation of the control algorithm is once again quite straightforward an operation, and normally the obtained law is quite simple.

Although the presented study requires some extensions, for example in the case of multiple running applications, the proposed design methodology can be considered an effective way to attain power-awareness. Its generality is already remarkable, as in fact the multiple application case will most likely affect essentially the profiling phase, as not only single applications but also their combinations will affect the UHP. No doubt this makes the exploration space much wider, but the main problem is to find some ways to explore it 'cleverly': the validity of the approach is not affected. All in all, thus, we have seen another application of process/control co-design, thereby further confirming that computing system are a potential domain of election for a so powerful idea.

Chapter 10

An experimental OS: Miosix

As already stated, and as the reader should now hopefully convene, several important parts of operating systems can take profit from a control-based (re-)design. Quite intuitively, an operating system should then be used to test the mentioned statements in the real world. This chapter describes the Miosix kernel, that the authors are currently using for that purpose.

The Miosix kernel is released as free software within the terms of the GNU General Public License version 2 (GPLv2), and can be downloaded from http:// miosix.org. The same web page contains a link to its documentation.

The chapter is organised as follows. First, the motivations for the introduction of a new kernel are presented. Then, the requirements that led to its design choices are discussed. Some words are subsequently spent illustrating the kernel architecture, and in particular its scheduling API (Application Program Interface). The chapter ends with expected future directions, and work in progress.

10.1 Motivations

In the previous chapters, it has been shown how describing the phenomena that dictate the behaviour of a computing system by using dynamic models, can be a powerful tool not only to design a suitable controller for them but also for simulation purposes. Such simulations allow to quickly obtain preliminary results to assess the performance of a control scheme, as well as to compare different possible schemes for a given problem, and also to fine-tune the parameters of the selected one.

However, it is often difficult to use simulations to compare a control-based operating system component with existing state-of-the-art solutions, which are often *not* designed as controllers, as already noticed several times, and are therefore difficult to analyse with the formalisms of dynamic systems. Moreover, without questioning the value of simulation as meant herein (see Section 3.2), there are some metrics – such as the context switch overhead in the case of the scheduler – that are only measurable after the controller has been implemented and profiled on the target architecture(s).

For those reasons, a software implementation of the proposed controllers is desirable, and in some sense necessary, to provide a proof of concept for their feasibility, as well as to profile them in real-life conditions, and obtain operation data that cannot be produced via simulations, that for example are not – and must not be – tied to the detailed behaviour of a specific application. More or less, keeping the parallel with more classical control problems, this is the same reason why, after assessing a process and control solution, one wants to build and commission a pilot plant before addressing industrial size realisations.

However, modifying an existing kernel (think for example of the Linux one) to replace a core functionality with a significantly different implementation is never an easy task. Kernels are extremely complicated objects, where some design decisions are almost set in stone, for example because some data structures are so widely used to make it very difficult to apply any changes. This issue is somehow worsened by the fact that most kernels are written in the C language, that does not strictly enforce information hiding.

Moreover, kernels often have to support so different hardware platforms that core functionalities are frequently implemented using the lowest common denominator of what all these architectures provide. Incidentally, this conveys the disadvantage that although a platform may have an hardware feature necessary for the implementation of a controller, it may not be available in software (another reasons to port around *models*, not algorithms).

An example of this situation, as anticipated, is the way the Linux kernel initially used to implement context switching. That ancient solution relied on a periodic interrupt timer, which decremented a software counter used to know when the time quantum of a process had expired. As can be easily understood, such a solution limits the granularity of actuation in terms of CPU burst – a problem that cannot be neglected when implementing the I+PI scheduler. The context switch implementation in the Linux kernel has now changed, but at the time when the I+PI scheduler was first implemented in Miosix, it was still the one here described.

For a number of reasons like those just exemplified, the decision was taken not to select Linux as the primary target for testing the proposed control strategies, at least for the moment. Instead, a different – and much smaller – kernel was chosen, named Miosix. This choice may change in the future, but surely development will continue also on Miosix, that is progressively taking the role of an example of control-based kernel.

The choice of a small and simple kernel, or even the development of a completely new one, is in fact not uncommon when the main purpose is research, and other examples could be given, like for example the barrelfish OS [91], which was developed as a testbed for a kernel aimed at a straightforward scale-up towards many-core systems.

10.2   Requirements and design decisions

The fundamental requirements that were sought in an operating system kernel for use as a testbed for our purposes are summarised in the following:

The first requirement is to ease as much as possible the implementation of components designed as controllers, and allow comparisons with more traditional solutions to quantify the achieved improvements. This calls for a small and well-structured kernel. In fact, the combination of these two features can greatly reduce the effort required to replace an existing component with its control-based counterpart, as well as implementing more versions to compare their performance, as has been done with the scheduler.

The second necessity for the kernel is to be, whenever possible and/or convenient, compatible with existing software standards, for example providing support for the C and C++ standard libraries, and for POSIX threads. This is mainly to ease the porting of existing software, and in particular benchmark suites, to the selected kernel, so as to assess the performance of the new components. As an example, benchmarks such as the MiBench one presented in Section 5.4.1, are often composed of simplified versions of real-world software programs, and therefore heavily rely on the libraries just mentioned.

A third need is to also support small embedded systems. This was considered relevant because we believe that some of the control schemes presented in this book could scale very well from performance-oriented systems, such as servers, down to resource- and cost-constrained embedded ones. To be able to support this claim, however, an OS was needed that could also support such systems. In addition, embedded systems have different requirements when compared to general purpose ones, including more emphasis on real-time operation, as they often need to interact with the physical world, and stricter energy-related requirements. It is therefore interesting to test some of the control schemes, for example the scheduler and the power-aware resource manager, also in this context.

To fulfil the above requirements, the Miosix kernel was therefore developed. The kernel is simple and small in size. By consisting of less than 100 thousands lines of C++ code, it is well suited to rapid prototyping with low development time. Also, being developed in C++, Miosix is entirely built with information hiding in mind. This reduces the coupling among software components, and eases the introduction of different implementations.

Miosix is also an operating system kernel targeting microcontrollers. A microcontroller is an integrated circuit that contains a CPU, a small amount of both volatile (i.e., RAM) and nonvolatile memory and some I/O interfaces. Due to that, Miosix meets the requirement of testing the proposed schemes on embedded systems.

Finally, the kernel has an explicit focus on providing full support for the C and C++ standard libraries, including an effort to ensure thread-safety of those libraries – two other distinctive features with respect to the typical microcontroller operating systems.

10.3   Architecture of Miosix

An overview of the Miosix kernel architecture is depicted in Figure 10.1, assuming that the host architecture is a microcontroller-based board.

At the lowest level there is the board support package, which abstracts the details of the specific microcontroller and board. This package mainly contains interrupt handlers low level assembly code to perform context switches, and the board-dependent part of the boot code. Moreover, it also contains the drivers for the key peripherals, including the timer used for context switches and those to allow console and disk access by the higher layers. This particular structure eases portability; for

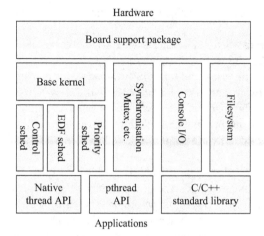

Figure 10.1   The architecture of the Miosix kernel

example, the kernel has been straightforwardly ported to a variety of boards with ARM microcontrollers.

The base kernel is built on top of the board support package, and provides the architecture-independent boot code and utilities. At this level multithreading is implemented, which is a key feature of the kernel. This part contains – as will be explained later more in detail – multiple task schedulers with different characteristics. Also, two threading API – the POSIX API and a Miosix-specific one – expose the threading and synchronisation services to applications. Besides threading support, the kernel offers an implementation of processes, although at present this is not fully completed owing to the limitations typical of microcontroller systems (most notably the lack of a full MMU to enforce memory isolation, and the small amount of available RAM).

Filesystem support is also available, for code size constraints currently only supporting the FAT32 filesystem. Console input/output is the main way to interact with the system; this is usually redirected on a serial port on the hardware side, while on the software side it is made available through the standard C and C++ libraries (e.g., `printf()`/`scanf()`). A prototype GUI library is also available, supporting boards with a display.

Finally, for what concerns connectivity, a USB library is available, currently supporting the USB *device* mode, which is expected to be further improved to include the *host* mode, so as to test bandwidth allocation control.

10.4   The Miosix scheduler

In most operating systems, be they targeted to microcontrollers or larger machines, the scheduler is tightly coupled with the rest of the kernel. From an engineering point of view, there are solid motivations for this choice. The first one is to maximise the scheduler performance; the second is that normally only one scheduler (not necessarily policy) is present in the system; the third is the complexity of designing an API to separate the kernel from the scheduler.

However, especially in embedded systems, the ability to choose a suitable scheduler for the application (in broad sense) being developed can be a significant benefit. Moreover, while doing research on schedulers, it is essential to be able of comparing two or more schedulers under the same hardware and software conditions, to obtain meaningful results regarding their performance.

Therefore, one of the features introduced in Miosix is the so-called 'pluggable scheduler' API.

The idea of having more than one scheduler in the same codebase can be implemented in (basically) three ways. The first possibility is to allow scheduler selection at compile time only, the second is to allow to switch scheduler at runtime, moving tasks from one scheduler to another during the switch, while the third one is to have more schedulers running at the same time, each one with its own pool of tasks.

Each implementation has its advantages and drawbacks, that are briefly summarised in the following. The third possibility above might seem the more flexible, and at least for 'clients' of a so conceived API, this is true. However, having more schedulers that coexist at the same time requires coordination between them. This would add a lot of complexity to the schedulers' implementation, and that complexity may quite likely result in an undesired coupling between different schedulers, as well as in a performance penalty. Additionally, the need for cooperation would somewhat limit freedom in the implementation of said schedulers, imposing uniformity for example on the way context switches are implemented, or even prescribing the same data structure for all schedulers. Therefore, this solution is significantly unfit for research on new schedulers.

The runtime switchable scheduler option simplifies the implementation with respect to the coexistence one, but creates problems during the switch between one scheduler and another. For example, in a real-time system, it would be quite complex to guarantee that no deadline misses may occur during such a switch. In addition, even this solution requires some runtime indirection, that results in a performance penalty as well.

The compile-time option, which is the one selected for implementing the Miosix pluggable scheduler API, has many advantages. First, it is well suited for embedded systems, which is the first and major domain Miosix is targeted too. It is the option with the lowest possible performance and code size penalty, because after the compile phase, the kernel has only one scheduler. Also, embedded systems are used to perform specialised tasks (unlike general purpose personal computers) so the need to change scheduler dynamically is usually not present. Finally, for the research and testing of new schedulers, this option offers the highest possible design freedom, allowing to change almost everything including the context switch code, data structures, and so forth.

After explaining the design choices that led to the selection of a compile-time pluggable scheduler API, said interface will now be outlined, along with the list of implemented schedulers.

10.4.1   Pluggable schedulers in Miosix

Realising a scheduler in Miosix requires to declare and implement three classes. The first is the `Priority` class, the second one is `SchedulerData`, while the third is `Scheduler`.

The `Priority` class has this name only for backward-compatibility reasons. This class is meant to represent 'hints' that tasks pass to the scheduler. In traditional schedulers this information is, in fact, a priority value, but it doesn't necessarily need to represent such an entity. For example, in the EDF scheduler the information passed from tasks to the scheduler is a deadline, while for the I+PI scheduler this can be for example the (*CPU%, relative_importance*) tuple, although the exact details depend on the chosen set point generator. By redeclaring this class, a designer has the maximum flexibility in choosing the information passed from applications to the scheduler.

The Miosix kernel keeps an instance of the `Thread` class for each thread in the system. Each `Thread` class contains an instance of the `SchedulerData` class. The `SchedulerData` class therefore contains the private per-thread information that the scheduler needs. For example, in the I+PI controller, it contains the state variables for the inner integral controller, the α value for the thread, its CPU time set point, and its actual CPU time in the previous round.

The `Scheduler` class is the place where the scheduling logic is realised. This class has to implement a specific interface, shown in Figure 10.2. To allow each scheduler to use its own customised data structure, the list of currently running threads is part of the scheduler and not of the kernel. Therefore, the scheduler API includes functions to manage the addition and removal of threads, as well as to query existing threads. Those are the `PKaddThread()`, `PKexists()` and `PKremoveThread()` member functions.

To support the ability of a thread to change its scheduler hints during its lifetime there are the `PKsetPriority()`, `getPriority()` and `IRQgetPriority()`

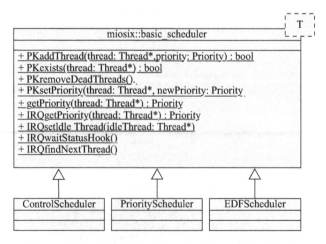

Figure 10.2   The pluggable scheduler API in Miosix

member functions, with obvious meaning once 'priority' is intended in the abstract sense explained above.

There is then a member function, `IRQfindNextThread()`, that needs to be called by the low-level interrupt handling code in order to ask the scheduler to perform a context switch. This function is called from the timer interrupt service routine, or when a thread yields the CPU, or gets blocked on some resource. The function selects the next thread that will run, the main task a scheduler is designed to solve. In the I+PI scheduler this function selects the next task in the round, and if the current task is the last one, it runs the I+PI scheduler so that a new round can begin.

Lastly, there are a number of 'notification points' or 'hooks', functions that the kernel calls to inform the scheduler of certain events it may be interested in, like a thread blocking or unblocking.

The Miosix codebase currently has three schedulers that implement the pluggable scheduler API. The first is the I+PI one, completed with feedforward and regulator reinitialisation. Then there is the EDF scheduler. Finally, there is a priority-based scheduler that always schedules the thread with the highest priority, and if there are more threads with the same priority, turns itself into a Round Robin one to manage them.

10.4.2 I+PI implementation in Miosix

The I+PI scheduler has been implemented in the Miosix kernel. The full code concerning this part can be found in Appendix A.2. The scheduler description found in Chapter 5 is here complemented with some relevant implementation details.

10.4.2.1 Sensors and actuators

The I+PI scheduler requires measurements of the tasks' CPU time usage, and acts by assigning their burst at each round.

The quality of so defined sensing and actuating mechanisms affects the scheduler's achievable performance, so it is important to understand their requirements, how they differ from the requirements of a traditional scheduler, and how they can be met in a real implementation such as the Miosix one. To this end, we shall adopt for this chapter a totally implementation-centric view. However, we shall never violate the system theoretical foundations of the design being implemented.

First, consider a simple Round Robin (RR) scheduler. Such a scheduler assigns the CPU to tasks always for a fixed amount of time (unless the scheduled task blocks). Therefore its actuator is a generic API call that gives the CPU to the task selected by the RR algorithm for a fixed and constant amount of time. RR, not being a feedback scheduler, does not make use of sensors.

The EDF scheduler, instead, requires an actuator that assigns the CPU to a task with no timeout. As EDF always schedules the task with the earliest deadline, only the arrival of a task with a closer deadline, not the expiration of a timeout as it was for RR, would cause a context switch. Typically, this scheduler does not make use of sensors, as deadlines are usually passed to it by the tasks themselves.

The I+PI scheduler, on the other hand, computes a desired burst value for each thread, and this value changes over time. Therefore the required actuator is similar to the one required for a RR scheduler, in that it needs to give the CPU to a task selected by the scheduler and to preempt it after a timeout expires. However, a notable difference between the two actuators is that the timeout is no longer a fixed, constant value, but is dictated by the scheduler to be equal to the desired burst. Also, the I+PI ability to give an exact CPU share to tasks even in the presence of unpredicted runtime disturbances is grounded on the availability of a measure of the *actual* CPU time values, which are the actual times a task has run.

10.4.2.2 Context switch implementation

The idea of varying the burst values is not new in the scheduling world. Such a modification is often done to basic schedulers like RR [92], as well as more complex ones such as the multilevel feedback queue one, to achieve various goals including increasing responsiveness, reducing cache misses, and so forth. Also the idea of using sensors to measure the effective execution time of a task is widely used. For example, in the Linux kernel, the 'completely fair' scheduler always schedules the task with lowest accumulated execution time, with the aim of improving fairness.

However, in most cases, the assignable burst value is a multiple of a fixed time quantum. This is because the actuator is still implemented as a periodic interval timer that generates interrupts to preempt tasks, and the variable burst is implemented by counting a given number of interrupts before doing a context switch.

Despite the advantage of simplicity, this approach has the disadvantage that both task execution time sensing and burst assignments are relatively coarse-grained, with a resolution that can hardly go below the order of milliseconds. Also, performance is hampered by the need of generating more interrupts than is strictly required to perform context switching.

In a control-based scheduler, the coarse-grained sensing and actuation of task bursts is seen as a quantisation, which adversely affects the scheduler's ability to maintain its set points. Worse, this quantisation is of the same order of magnitude of the computed burst values.

For quantisation to be of negligible impact, the resolution of sensors and actuators must be suitably lower than the typical assigned burst values. Therefore, if burst values are in the order of milliseconds, sensors and actuators need to have a resolution at least in the order of microseconds. This resolution cannot obviously be reached by 'polling' the running task with a periodic timer, as the overhead caused by the time spent in a so frequently called interrupt service routine would be unacceptable.

Hence, a completely different approach to context switches is used in the Miosix implementation of the I+PI scheduler. An hardware timer is always used, but it is configured at the start of each burst to generate exactly one interrupt at the end of the burst.

To understand the details of the implementation it is better to explain how a hardware timer works. Timers are usually composed of three parts, a prescaler whose aim is to divide the system frequency before feeding it into the actual counter, a counter which is a readable and writeable peripheral register that is incremented (or decremented) in hardware, and a configurable interrupt generation logic.

In the Miosix implementation of I+PI, at least with the currently targeted boards, the prescaler is configured to output a 100 kHz frequency; in this way the counter has a resolution of 10 μs. At the start of each burst the counter is reset to zero and the interrupt logic is configured to generate an interrupt when the counter reaches the desired burst value. When the scheduler is called again, either because the burst expired or because the task has blocked, it first reads the timer's counter, obtaining a measurement of the task's execution time. Of course, in the absence of blocking, the read value would equal the desired burst value, while in case of blockings (calls to `yield()`, `sleep()`, and so forth) the value would be lower. The read value could also be greater than the desired burst value, for example if the thread was caught by the preemption interrupt while being in some critical section with interrupts disabled.

It is noteworthy to outline the benefits of such an approach. First, a single hardware timer is used both as sensor (by reading the counter at the end of a task's *actual* burst) and as actuator (by generating an interrupt at the end of a task's *nominal* burst). Second, the approach allows to achieve the fine grained resolution the I+PI scheduler requires. Even a 16-bit timer as the one used in the Miosix implementation allows to impose/measure bursts of up to 655.35 ms with a 10-μs resolution. Third, it allows to implement context switching efficiently, interrupting the task only when it has to be preempted.

10.5   Future directions

The Miosix kernel will continue to be used as a testbed for the implementation of control-based components, and future development are expected to add the parts that are currently missing. One such example is the porting to MMU-capable hardware and the implementation of a virtual memory system, to test the memory manager of Chapter 6.

As the process of formalisation of operating system management problems as control ones goes on, additional components will be added and tested. A foreseeable example is the bandwidth allocation problem, in both network and peripheral management, which will call for an implementation of a TCP/IP and a USB host stack.

Lastly, the kernel is being used also for other research purposes, including the field of Wireless Sensor Networks (WSNs), with specific reference to time synchronisation, and more in general to the control-based design also of communication stacks.

Chapter 11

Future perspectives and cyber-physical systems

This work started out by stating that in the design of operating systems a perspective shift would be beneficial, and that a deeper and more pervasive use of system- and control-theoretical concepts can provide the necessary background and *modus operandi*. Also, it was stated that the entire book is in fact the first step of a long-term research. The aim of this research is to bridge the gap between the 'parallel lives' of the computer science and the control communities. This is however attempted here in a novel way, i.e., by adopting a fully control-theoretical attitude right from the design stage of computing system components. Given that, we think that a few words on future perspectives, thus possible research directions, are now in order.

11.1   Control-related concepts coverage

In operating systems, not to say in computing ones at large, it is possible to associate to each problem a degree of abstraction with respect to 'strict' physics. Deferring a more quantitative study of the matter to future works, we can, however, qualitatively sketch out the situation by imagining an $x - y$ graph where the horizontal axis reports the mentioned level of abstraction, while the vertical one indicates to what extent system- and control-theoretical methodologies are used by the research that refers to the objects encountered therein (see Figure 11.1). Said measure of the presence of control was for the moment drawn from qualitative considerations on the reviewed literature. One may want to carry out a more quantitative analysis, but the conclusions reached so far are sufficient for the particular purpose of this chapter.

At the lowest level clearly stand problems tightly related to the used electronic devices. For example, one can find here the design and assessment of processor components, bus transceivers, and so forth. Since handling such problems involves a significant interplay with electronics in the strict sense of the term, many papers can be found where the control theory provides a major tool for the presented research. The used dynamic models are quite different from those presented herein, however, as they directly refer to strict physics, and for example live very frequently in the continuous time domain. Nonetheless, the idea of designing and assessing systems via dynamic models, and frequently control loops, is very well represented. Notice that research works of this type naturally adhere to the principle mentioned here of 'just model strict physics—the rest is control', simply because they are in fact homogeneous with problems termed in the first chapter of this book the 'classical' ones.

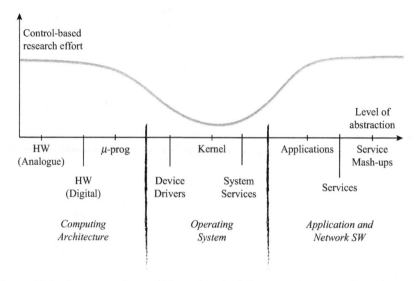

*Figure 11.1   Presence of control-based methodologies in the research on the
design of computing systems components at different abstraction
levels*

At the highest level, one conversely finds problems involving the design of
services – e.g., web-based ones – and the quality of their operation, addressed in
totally abstracted a manner with respect to the underlying hardware, and system software. Also at this level it is possible to find many works that make a significant use
of control, but typically *not* along the approach proposed here. Sometimes this may
not be possible due to the peculiar nature of the encountered problems, of course,
and entering such a discussion is not the purpose of this section. However, the general
fact just mentioned remains, and most interesting for us is another remark.

In the middle with respect to the two extremal levels just evidenced, there are
in fact a number of problems, among which those addressed in the previous chapters
play a major role. At this level, although the use of control tools in the way here
suggested seems a promising idea, a minority of works do follow compatible reasoning
paths. Indeed, in control coverage of the addressed context, a gap is observed. And
broadly speaking – but in the end, not so broadly – the boundaries of said gap more or
less coincide with those of the operating system below and above (as for abstraction)
control – especially for *design* – is used much more than inside. In this book we have
shown that bridging the gap is possible, and provided some initial solutions.

As such, a first open issue – probably perceived as a bit philosophical, but in the
authors' opinion relevant – is not only to fill the gap up to the necessary and possible
extent, but more ambitiously to provide a systematic taxonomy of the encountered
problems, far beyond the initial attempt of this book, and possibly to develop some
ad hoc systems and control theory to cover them.

11.2　Problems not treated herein

Taking more practical an attitude with respect to Section 11.1, there are a number of problems not treated herein that would benefit from an analogous approach. A minimal overview of them – or at least, the major ones from the authors' viewpoint – is reported below.

11.2.1　Time synchronisation

A relevant problem, e.g., in wireless sensor networks, is that of time synchronisation, meaning for that a mechanism thanks to which all the network nodes – despite having each one its own clock with unavoidable imperfections such as skew and thermal drift – share a reliable common time. In the literature, mainstream approaches are based on the transmission of timestamps, followed by local clock corrections that are seldom performed based on a dynamic model. This is because the problem is typically faced from outside the communication protocol, which is more or less like attempting to control the CPU distribution by leaving a previously existing scheduler in place.

Research is at present underway on this subject, and preliminary results appear to indicate that synchronisation functions can be designed as feedback controls with low-order 'plant' models and regulators, leading to extremely lightweight solutions from both the transmission overhead and the nodes' power consumption points of view.

11.2.2　Bandwidth scheduling

This problem has more facets than sketched out in the brief example of Section 3.3.4, and if viewed from the resource use optimisation standpoint, reveals (once more) significant relationships with the task scheduling one. There are of course a number of technological differences, impossible to list herein, but addressing the matter could yield improvements for at least two relevant cases, namely USB-based peripherals and network devices.

Starting from the latter case, an appropriate controller design can be used as a basis for a network stack to help enforcing Quality of Service (QoS) specifications. When implemented in servers, such a controller can be used to offer guaranteed bandwidth shares to heterogeneous applications with different requirements. Examples could be web servers, that generally have a bursty network usage, sharing some communication means with video and audio streaming applications, which demand a guaranteed share of the available bandwidth per connected client. Note that this approach to bandwidth allocation could also be useful in desktop computers, to schedule bandwidth among applications with different requirements, such a web browsers, peer-to-peer file transfers, VoIP (Voice over IP), video games, and so forth.

At the opposite end, bandwidth scheduling is also necessary when handling peripherals such as USB devices. The USB is a bus architecture with a tree topology that allows hubs to connect multiple devices to the same bus. Devices can have more functionalities – termed 'interfaces' – active at the same time (think about a printer/scanner multifunction device). Interfaces are in turn composed of endpoints, which can be somehow thought of as individual sockets in TCP/IP networks. Each endpoint has, however, a type, which can either be

- *control*, used mainly for device identification;
- *interrupt*, used to transmit short and bursty information, such as mouse and keyboard data;
- *isochronous*, used for devices that require a guaranteed bandwidth allocation, such as webcams;
- *bulk*, which uses all the remaining bus bandwidth to maximise throughput, thus being suited, e.g., for storage devices.

It is quite evident that a proper bandwidth scheduling could improve bus utilisation while fulfilling the devices' constraints.

11.2.3   *Peripheral and queue management*

For space limitations, and also due to the in-progress state of the research, we have omitted from this book problems related to peripherals such as disk drives. However, it is well known that a sub-optimal use of such devices can significantly impair – and possibly *de facto* nullify – the parallelism achieved with a well-managed multitasking. Problems of this type can be apparently viewed as queue management ones, and if the focus is set on a short-time horizon, are in fact not so different (apart again from technological facts) from those previously considered. Here too, the proposed approach needs putting to work.

11.3   Envisaged extensions

Returning the focus to the subject of this book, some extensions of the presented results can be readily envisaged, and doing so opens the way to some additional considerations, as briefly discussed in Section 11.4.

11.3.1   *Multi-core and multi-CPU scheduling*

The scheduling treatise of Chapter 5 concentrated on a single processing unit. As everybody knows, nowadays there exist both multi-core and multi-CPU ones, and therefore extending the presented results to such architectures will surely be a subject for future research.

From this point of view, it is, however, to note that the way design has been tackled so far, at least to the best of the authors' knowledge, was once again not driven by the need of producing controlled objects that are easy to model in the sense meant herein. There are a number of different architectures with multiple processing units, and the way they interact and are governed obeys to different choices as for shared cache memory, program counter management, and other similar facts.

We cannot here even scratch the surface of the matter, however, the proposed design approach opens at least one possible way of extending the presented scheduling design. The most promising path in this respect seems to have each processing unit (or each set of units sharing the program counter) host a scheduler, while a further external loop, having a longer time horizon than that of said individual schedulers, should take care of synchronisation and task migration. No doubt setting up such a solution will be a difficult problem, but at least it will obey to the well-grounded idea of cascade control, already exploited at the single CPU level by I+PI, allowing for the corresponding analysis tools.

11.3.2   Bridging non-real-time and real-time

Focusing again on scheduling, the computer literature evidences a *qualitative* distinction between non-real-time and real-time solutions. Respectfully, we conjecture that a control-theoretical approach like that presented here, can prospectively bridge the two, making the distinction just *quantitative*. In other words, what is called *error analysis* in a control-theoretical framework, is potentially reflected in quite direct a manner into *response time predictability* when viewed from the computing systems' point of view. The considerations on the generation of CPU utilisation set points reported in Chapter 5 could be a good starting point to develop a deeper research on this important matter.

11.3.3   Thermal issues

Due to a steadily increasing silicon process scaling, modern CPUs exhibit an impressive power density. As such, several thermal problems that once could be practically neglected, are conversely of paramount importance nowadays. This category of problems is in some sense contiguous to the power-awareness one addressed in Chapter 9, although if issues like, e.g., temperature gradients are of concern, the use of continuous-time models as the starting point for the process dynamic description, cannot be avoided.

It is, however, to note that also in this context, based on the remark above, formulating computing-related problems as control ones makes their representation naturally keen to be joined with that of strictly physical ones.

11.4   A cyber-physical perspective

As can be seen, some of the open problems and extensions just mentioned bring into play 'strict physics' directly, or more precisely, come to state – and prospectively solve – problems where the equations governing the controlled systems come from both first principles and computing-related phenomena.

The reader should thus perceive a relationship between the design approach here proposed, and the flourishing research field nowadays collectively called 'cyber-physical systems'. In this section we would like to delve just a bit into this subject, organising the discussion somehow in parallel with the ideas on cyber-physical systems expressed in the position paper [93].

In the mentioned work, the author discusses the adequacy of *computing* foundations to this emerging domain, and the reader encounters the following statements:

'Cyber-Physical Systems (CPS) are integrations of computation with physical processes. Embedded computers and networks monitor and control the physical processes, usually with feedback loops where physical processes affect computations and vice versa. In the physical world, the passage of time is inexorable and concurrency is intrinsic. Neither of these properties is present in today's computing and networking abstractions. [...]

There are technical approaches that partially bridge the abstraction gap today (such as real-time operating systems, middleware technologies, specialised embedded processor architectures, and specialised networks), and there is certainly considerable room for improvement of these technologies. However, it may be that we need a less incremental approach, where new abstractions are built from the ground up.'

Viewing the matter from the control scientist's standpoint, one would most likely write something very similar, albeit with some slightly different – but relevant – *nuances*. One would in fact notice that the correctness of a computing system's behaviour – thinking for example of the vast *corpus* of software engineering, and accepting some simplification for space reasons – is typically decided based on a mixture of logic and temporal logic predicates, that need to be guaranteed to hold true in any possible evolution of the system. Since in cyber-physical systems the occurrence of some events in time is actually decided by a mechanism that is exogenous to the computing system itself, as the evolution of any physical process in the sense above is, any *guarantee* that relies on some assumed behaviour of said events comes to be subject to facts that cannot be modelled with the same formalisms used for the computing system alone.

As a consequence, a control scientist would focus attention on the idea of *guarantees*, and look for 'new abstractions' precisely in the domain of the systems theory, where the specific purpose of analysis is exactly to provide that type of guarantees (think of stability or performance ones, for example).

Based on these considerations, the authors conjecture that it would be beneficial to tackle the problem starting not from the technological side, which is somehow unavoidably related to the prescriptive paradigm inherent to algorithmic or algorithm-based design. On the contrary, some paradigm ought to be sought that does not need to bring technological details into play unless at the time of realisation, provided that said realisation of the devised objects can be carried out without ambiguity.

Of course, the two views just mentioned are not in contrast but complementary, and in the authors' opinion a major research task in the future will be to find a common terrain for both of them to unleash their joint potential. To this end, we think that several of the ideas expressed herein can be suitably generalised, and provide useful material for future research, that according again to the quoted position paper (see in particular its Section 4) should have among its main topics 'rethink the hardware/software split' and 'predictability' at various levels, such as memory access and concurrency.

Concerning the first mentioned aspect, the idea of 'modelling just the core phenomenon' and of disregarding the hardware or software nature of an action on the controlled system, until it comes to deciding actuation details, could in fact be a viable way to make the hardware/software distinction loose enough for an integrated design. The power-aware resource allocation problem discussed previously is, again, quite neat an example.

As for the second aspect above, i.e., predictability, taking a control attitude naturally yields the corresponding way of specifying and attaining desires. More specifically, and briefly as usual, the transition is from on/off predicates, such as 'a certain reaction time must never exceed a specified value', to control-theoretical behaviour prescriptions, like 'the system must guarantee that a certain deviation of some varying quantity does not produce a variation of a certain response time larger than a specified value'. Clearly the latter type of constraint is inherently weaker than the former, but the good news is that one can make it arbitrarily strict if possible, and in the opposite case one can quantify – by analysis – which is the limit, and on what system parameters and/or characteristics at large said limit depends. This is in some sense another way of thinking about predictability, and another means to have the two mentioned communities converge.

In the end, as already stated, most of the exposed concepts and research directions can be viewed as domain-specific applications of the idea of 'process/control co-design'. Such an idea was in fact already envisaged many years ago, with the only but relevant difference that for 'process' one meant at that time something like a chemical plant, and for 'control' the set of hardware and software devoted to govern it – equivalently, the idea of process/control co-design can be thought of as an ancestor of that of cyber-physical systems, where 'physical' is the plant and 'cyber' is the computing system devoted to its control. However, there is in principle no reason not to replicate the same viewpoint *inside* the computing system. In other words, one could well view the computing system itself as a cyber-physical one, as the previous chapters should have suggested. At this level things are frequently simple enough to provide theoretically sound solutions and *guarantees*, in turn allowing for a straightforward realisation. At more complex levels things may not be so easy but probably the experience gained in simpler cases could be generalised and somehow extended. Also the presented memory management system can serve as an example for the same purpose.

However, if we want to find out the core reason why the simple proposal of this book may be helpful in more general contexts, we should relate the presented work to another quote from the same position paper above.

'Systems theories today are either purely physical (e.g., control systems, signal processing) or purely computational (e.g., computability, complexity). A few blended theories have emerged, including hybrid systems and timed process algebras.'

In this respect, no doubt we have been using here a 'physical' theory, namely that of discrete-time dynamic systems. Nonetheless, and somehow in retrospect, we have followed two important guidelines.

First, we have mainly used discrete-time but not sampled-signals systems. Whenever this is possible, the resulting problem simplification is relevant. In simple cases like the scheduling one it is possible to treat time substantially as a state variable, so that as long as the involved part of the control system is functioning properly, guarantees are quite straightforward to obtain. Of course we are not claiming this is possible is in general, however, for more than one problem it could be a viable way to attempt.

Second, we have tried – when convenient – to divide problems in a 'how much' and a 'what' part. To explain, think of the proposed memory manager, where the proposed controller decides 'how much' to swap in or out and *on this basis* achieves its goal (see Section 6.2.1). Deciding 'what' to swap in or out is here irrelevant, and can be devoted to any underlying mechanism without hampering the mentioned achievements. The same could be stated about resource allocation.

In this respect, while researching on the subject, we came to suspect that a major reason why simple and powerful control theories, like those for discrete-time systems, seem unnatural to apply, is that problems are formulated in such a way that the 'how much' and the 'what' part stay intertwined. We additionally found that when the former of the two is isolated, most often it can be treated with the mentioned simple theories, and normally the so obtained results can be realised in a transparent manner with respect to how the latter is handled. If also the control requirements can be expressed – at least partially – as 'how much' ones, guarantees are apparently easier to achieve.

Continuing along this reasoning line, we could therefore conclude the book with a remark that in some sense originates from connecting our work to the ideas related to cyber-physical systems just exposed, but in the end is far more general, and maybe provides – again, in retrospect – quite comprehensive a claim and goal for the particular research we started.

When it is to have software run in a loop with the physical world, an idea proposed in the literature is to endow programming languages with time predicates. In fact, we are here proposing an alternative use of substantially the same concepts, by

- treating as the physical part of a cyber-physical system not (only) the world *outside* the computer, but also that *inside*, i.e., the hardware where the 'core phenomena' we sought take place,
- and dealing with time not with a prescriptive (algorithmic) attitude, but rather by having time-related quantities as state variables, so that the control of said variables become a means to fulfil desires on them.

Such a view also naturally induces a peculiar idea of 'abstraction'. By following this path, one in fact naturally aims at a hierarchical operating system structure, similar to that encountered in hierarchical plant-wide control, having very configurable control-based low levels, that by changing the control specifications are made capable of playing their role in all the different situations the overall system is expected to encounter.

Building upon said low levels, at higher ones it is possible to state and solve the problems there encountered (again) in a control-theoretical manner, and those problems are made simple enough thanks to 'encapsulation' realised below. As a result, higher levels will act on the loops of the lower ones, e.g., by providing set points and possibly block diagram configuration parameters, but the overall structure remains simple and open to modifications as long as these are specified in system-theoretical terms.

Summarising, the result is, as anticipated, an alternative view of abstraction levels, organised substantially by nested control loops, rather than by distance from the hardware.

In the end, by considering an operating system as a set of controllers governing the machine based on the physical phenomena that occur in it, we are *de facto* proposing 'cyber-physical operating systems', and strongly believe that such systems will play an important role in the future of computing.

Appendix A

Code fragments

A.1 Simulation code

This appendix contains the programs used to perform some of the simulations presented in this book. They are implemented using Scilab, a high-level programming language oriented towards numerical computation.

Interpreters are available as free software, for Linux, Windows and Mac OS X, while an introduction to the language can be found in Reference 94. The readers are encouraged to try these programs, the source code of which can also be found by navigating the authors' homepages, and use them as a starting point to learn about simulation of dynamic systems.

A.1.1 Bandwidth allocation simulation

The following piece of code implements the example presented in Section 3.3.4:

```
clear; clc;

Na      = 3;      // # Applications
Lsim    = 50;     // Simulation length

mmu     = zeros(Na,Lsim);  // Transmit time
mnt     = zeros(Na,Lsim);  // Non-transmit time
mnu     = zeros(Na,Lsim);  // Unused transmit time
mpsi    = zeros(Na,Lsim);

vk      = 1:Lsim; // Time vector

// Simulation
for k=2:Lsim
    psi       = [1;2;3];
    deltapsi  = (psi.*(rand(Na,1)-0.5)*2).*[0.5;0.2;0.1];
    mmu(:,k)  = mmu(:,k-1)+psi+min(deltapsi,zeros(Na,1));
    mnt(:,k)  = max(deltapsi,zeros(Na,1));
    mnu(:,k)  = -min(deltapsi,zeros(Na,1));
    mpsi(:,k) = psi;
end

// Plotting results
scf(0); clf;
```

```
25  subplot(311);
26     aa = sum(mmu,'r');
27     aa(1) = 1;
28     plot(vk,mmu./(ones(Na,1)*aa));
29  subplot(312);
30     plot(vk,mnt);
31  subplot(313);
32     plot(vk,mnu);
33
34  // Saving data to a file
35  M = [vk',(mmu./(ones(Na,1)*aa))',mnt',mnu'];
36  fprintfMat('bandwidthAllocation.dat',M);
```

A.1.2   Per-process swap-out partitioning

This is the full code of the *f* function that performs the partitioning of the global swap-out signal considering per-process memory limits.

```
 1  function result = integerShare(value,share)
 2      result = [];
 3      // compute the process swapout share except for the last
 4      // one, rounding to the nearest integer
 5      for i = 1:length(share) - 1
 6          result = [result, round(value*share(i))];
 7      end
 8      // compute the last so as to preserve the total
 9      result = [result, value - sum(result)];
10  endfunction
11
12  function result = f(sp,m,etilde,deltam)
13      result = zeros(sp);
14      totalover = sum(max([0,0,0], m - sp));
15      // first try to partition swap-out against processes
16      // above their limit
17      if(totalover > 0)
18          result = integerShare(min(etilde,totalover),...
19                  max([0,0,0], m - sp)/totalover);
20      end
21      // if not enough swap-out form processes that are
22      // allocating memory right now
23      if(etilde > totalover) then
24          result = result + integerShare(etilde - totalover,...
25                  max([0,0,0], deltam)/sum(max[0,0,0],deltam));
26      end
27  endfunction
```

A.1.3   Full memory management simulator

The following is the memory management simulator, used to produce the data of Figure 6.4:

```
 1  clear; clc; clf;
 2
```

```
1   // This function does the same as 'result=value*share'
2   // where value is a scalar, and share an array whose elements
3   // sum to one. It guarantees that sum(result)==value AND that
4   // result only contains integers
5   function result = integerShare(value, share)
6       result = [];
7       for i = 1:length(share)-1
8           result = [result, round(value*share(i))];
9       end
10      result = [result, value - sum(result)];
11  endfunction
12
13  k = 0;                      // Regulator intervention index
14  T = 1000;                   // Number of simulation rounds
15  n = 3;                      // Number of processes
16  M = 1500;                   // Amount of RAM in the system
17  b = 0.95;                   // Swapping threshold (beta)
18  msp=round(M*b);             // Memory set point
19
20  alfa = [0.5, 0.3, 0.2];       // Memory partitioning
21  sp = integerShare(msp,alfa); // Memory set point
22
23  m = [100, 100, 100];        // Memory occupied by process
24  s = [0, 0, 0];              // Swap occupied by process
25
26  u  = [0, 0, 0];             // Actuator value
27  a  = [0, 0, 0];             // Allocated memory
28  dm = [0, 0, 0];             // Memory deallocated form RAM
29  ds = [0, 0, 0];             // Memory deallocated from SWAP
30  pf = [0, 0, 0];             // Page faults
31
32  mh  = [];                   // Memory history
33  sh  = [];                   // Swap history
34  sph = [];                   // Set point history
35  mth = [];                   // Total memory history
36  sth = [];                   // Total swap history
37  th  = [];                   // Swapping trigger history
38  uh  = [];                   // Swapping/unswapping history
39
40  for k = 1:T
41      // Compute disturbances
42      for i = 1:n
43          if k > 700
44              a(i) = 0;
45          elseif k > 200
46              a(i) = 3;
47          else
48              a(i) = 5;
49          end
50          if m(i) > 0 & k < 700
51              dm(i) = round((m(i)+s(i))/200);
52          else
53              dm(i) = 0;
54          end
```

```
56              end
57              if(k==700)
58                  m(1) = 0;
59                  s(1) = 0;
60              end
61              ds(i) = 0;
62              pf(i) = 0;
63          end
64
65          //Compute set point
66          if k==500
67              alfa = [0.33, 0.33, 0.33];
68              sp = integerShare(msp,alfa);
69          end
70
71          //Regulator code
72          d = a-dm+pf+[1,1,1];
73          e = sum(m+d)-msp;
74          over = max(0,e);
75          swap1 = [0,0,0];
76          swap2 = [0,0,0];
77          if(over>0)
78              totalover = sum(max([0,0,0], m - sp));
79              //We need to swap some memory, first try to reclaim
80              //it from the processes that are over their set point,
81              //but recalim only what is strictly needed, not more
82              if(totalover > 0)
83                  swap1=integerShare(min(over,totalover),...
84                      max([0,0,0], m - sp)/totalover);
85              end
86              //If this is not enough, reclaim memory from those
87              //that are allocating
88              if(over>totalover)
89                  swap2=integerShare(over-totalover,...
90                      max([0,0,0],d)/sum(max[0,0,0],d));
91              end
92          end
93          u=[-1,-1,-1]+swap1+swap2;
94          for i=1:n
95              u(i)=max(min(u(i),m(i)+a(i)-dm(i)+pf(i)),...
96                  -s(i)+ds(i)+pf(i));
97          end
98
99          //Simulate the processes
100         m=m+a-dm+pf-u;
101         s=s -ds-pf+u;
102
103         //Save data for plotting
104         mh=[mh;m];
105         sh=[sh;s];
106         sph=[sph;sp];
107         mth=[mth;sum(m)];
108         sth=[sth;sum(s)];
```

```
109    th =[ th ; msp ] ;
110    uh =[ uh ; u ] ;
111 end
112
113 subplot(411);
114 plot(mh);
115 plot(sph);
116 xlabel("Per process memory usage and set point");
117 subplot(412);
118 plot(sh);
119 xlabel("Per process swap usage");
120 subplot(413);
121 plot([mth, th ]);
122 plot(sth);
123 xlabel("Global memory, swap and set point");
124 subplot(414);
125 plot(uh);
126 xlabel("Actuator output");
```

A.1.4 Scheduler simulator

The following is the scheduler implementation with the general-purpose set-point generator, used to produce the data of Figure 6.4:

```
 1 clear; clf; clc;
 2
 3 simRounds      = 1000;
 4
 5 //Periodic tasks ' parameters
 6 Tperiodic      = [50,120];
 7 Wperiodic      = [0.5,0.8];
 8 betaperiodic = [0.5,0.7];
 9
10 //Batch tasks ' parameters
11 Abatch         = [125,150]; //Arrival time
12 Dbatch         = [300,450]; //Duration
13 Wbatch         = [60,70];
14 betabatch      = [0.1,0.1];
15
16 //Priority tasks ' parameters
17 pprio          = [0.1,0.5,0.18];  //Priority (0 lowest 1 highest)
18
19 //Event−based tasks ' parameters
20 aevent         = [0.6,0.7];
21 alpha0event  = [0.02,0.03];
22 tautrgevent  = cell(2,1);
23 //Triggering times
24 tautrgevent(1).entries = [10, 20,100,280,300];
25 tautrgevent(2).entries = [5, 15, 50, 80,150,400,550];
26
27 alphamin       = 0;          //Absolute limits for tentative alpha_i
28 alphamax       = 1;
29 bmax           = 1;          //Maximum burst
```

```
30
31  kR              = 2.5;          // Rr controller (PI), default:0.5
32  zR              = 0.5;          // Rr default: 0.5
33  kI              = 0.5;          // Rt controller (I); default: 1.5
34
35  // Initialisation
36  Nperiodic             = length(Tperiodic);
37  act_periodic          = ones(Tperiodic);
38  alpha_t_periodic      = zeros(Tperiodic);
39  alpha_periodic        = zeros(Tperiodic);
40  tauto_periodic        = zeros(Tperiodic);
41  Nbatch                = length(Abatch);
42  act_batch             = zeros(Abatch);
43  alpha_t_batch         = zeros(Abatch);
44  alpha_batch           = zeros(Abatch);
45  tauto_batch           = zeros(Abatch);
46  Nprio                 = length(pprio);
47  alpha_t_prio          = zeros(pprio);
48  alpha_prio            = zeros(pprio);
49  tauto_prio            = zeros(pprio);
50  Nevent                = length(aevent);
51  tau_last_trg_event    = zeros(aevent);
52  alpha_t_event         = zeros(aevent);
53  alpha_event           = zeros(aevent);
54  tauto_event           = zeros(aevent);
55  tau                   = 0;
56  taut                  = 0;
57  taut_periodic         = zeros(Tperiodic);
58  accCPU_periodic       = zeros(Tperiodic);
59  taut_batch            = zeros(Abatch);
60  accCPU_batch          = zeros(Abatch);
61  taut_prio             = zeros(pprio);
62  taut_event            = zeros(aevent);
63  taur                  = 0;
64  xRr                   = 0;
65  b_periodic            = zeros(Tperiodic);
66  b_batch               = zeros(Abatch);
67  b_prio                = zeros(pprio);
68  b_event               = zeros(aevent);
69  vtau                  = [];
70  vtauro                = [];
71  vtaur                 = [];
72  mtauto_periodic       = [];
73  mtaut_periodic        = [];
74  maccCPU_periodic      = [];
75  mtauto_batch          = [];
76  mtaut_batch           = [];
77  mtauto_prio           = [];
78  mtaut_prio            = [];
79  mtauto_event          = [];
80  mtaut_event           = [];
81
82
```

```
83   // Main loop
84   for t=1:simRounds
85       //Set exogenous commands
86       //Round duration SP
87       tauro = 0.5;
88       //Alpha generation
89       //manage periodic tasks
90       for i=1:Nperiodic
91           //Trigger at start of period
92           if (act_periodic(i)==0 & ...
93               modulo(tau,Tperiodic(i))<modulo(taut,Tperiodic(i)))
94               act_periodic(i) = 1; //To be reset by task
95               accCPU_periodic(i) = 0;
96           end
97           //Compute tentative alpha_i (limit request if nonzero)
98           if act_periodic(i)==1
99               alpha_t_periodic(i) = ...
100                  Wperiodic(i)/(Tperiodic(i)*(1-betaperiodic(i))*
                         tauro);
101              alpha_t_periodic(i) = ....
102                  max(alphamin,min(alphamax,alpha_t_periodic(i)));
103          else
104              alpha_t_periodic(i) = 0;
105          end
106      end
107      //Manage batch tasks
108      for i=1:Nbatch
109          //Trigger at arrival
110          if act_batch(i)==0 & tau>=Abatch(i) & taut<Abatch(i)
111              act_batch(i) = 1; //To be reset by task
112              accCPU_batch(i) = 0;
113          end
114          //Compute tentative alpha_i (limit request if nonzero)
115          if act_batch(i)==1
116              alpha_t_batch(i) = ...
117                  Wbatch(i)/(Dbatch(i)*(1-betabatch(i))*tauro);
118              alpha_t_batch(i) = ...
119                  max(alphamin,min(alphamax,alpha_t_batch(i)));
120          else
121              alpha_t_batch(i) = 0;
122          end
123      end
124      //Manage prioritised tasks
125      for i=1:Nprio
126          //Compute tentative alpha_i
127          temp=pprio(i);
128          if i==2 & t>=(simRounds/2) & t<=(3*simRounds/4)
129              temp=pprio(i)*2.5;
130          end
131          alpha_t_prio(i) = alphamin+temp*(alphamax-alphamin);
132      end
133      //Manage event-based tasks
134      for i=1:Nevent
```

```
135     //Apply alpha_t decay
136     alpha_t_event(i) = ...
137        alpha_t_event(i)*aevent(i)^(tau-tau_last_trg_event(i));
138     //Reset alpha_t when triggered
139     for j=1:length(tautrgevent(i).entries)
140         if (taut<tautrgevent(i).entries(j) & ...
141            tau>=tautrgevent(i).entries(j))
142            alpha_t_event(i)      = alpha0event(i);
143            tau_last_trg_event(i) = tau;
144         end
145     end
146     //limit request, zeroing if too low
147     if alpha_t_event(i)<alphamin
148         alpha_t_event(i) = 0;
149     end
150     alpha_t_event(i) = min(alphamax,alpha_t_event(i));
151  end
152  //Rescale alpha_t to alpha
153  alpha_t_tot    = sum(alpha_t_periodic)+ ...
154                   sum(alpha_t_batch)   + ...
155                   sum(alpha_t_prio)    + ...
156                   sum(alpha_t_event);
157  for i=1:Nperiodic
158      alpha_periodic(i) = alpha_t_periodic(i)/alpha_t_tot;
159  end
160  for i=1:Nbatch
161      alpha_batch(i) = alpha_t_batch(i)/alpha_t_tot;
162  end
163  for i=1:Nprio
164      alpha_prio(i) = alpha_t_prio(i)/alpha_t_tot;
165  end
166  for i=1:Nevent
167      alpha_event(i) = alpha_t_event(i)/alpha_t_tot;
168  end
169  //Scheduler controllers
170  //Rr controller (PI)
171  xRr = xRr+kR*(1-zR)*(tauro-taur);
172  bc  = xRr+kR*(tauro-taur);
173  //Rt controllers (I)
174  for i=1:Nperiodic
175      tauto_periodic(i) = alpha_periodic(i)*(taur+bc);
176      b_periodic(i)     = ...
177          b_periodic(i)+kI*(tauto_periodic(i)-taut_periodic(i));
178      b_periodic(i)     = max(0,min(bmax,b_periodic(i)));
179  end
180  for i=1:Nbatch
181      tauto_batch(i) = alpha_batch(i)*(taur+bc);
182      b_batch(i)     = ...
183          b_batch(i)+kI*(tauto_batch(i)-taut_batch(i));
184      b_batch(i)     = max(0,min(bmax,b_batch(i)));
185  end
186  for i=1:Nprio
187      tauto_prio(i) = alpha_prio(i)*(taur+bc);
```

```
188     b_prio(i)       = b_prio(i)+kI*(tauto_prio(i)-taut_prio(i));
189     b_prio(i)       = max(0,min(bmax,b_prio(i)));
190   end
191   for  i=1:Nevent
192     tauto_event(i) = alpha_event(i)*(taur+bc);
193     b_event(i)      = ...
194         b_event(i)+kI*(tauto_event(i)-taut_event(i));
195     b_event(i)      = max(0,min(bmax,b_event(i)));
196   end
197   //Task pool
198   //Periodic tasks
199   for  i=1:Nperiodic
200     if act_periodic(i)==1
201         //With delta b for the moment
202         taut_periodic(i)   = ...
203             b_periodic(i)*(1+0.05*rand());
204         accCPU_periodic(i) = ...
205             accCPU_periodic(i)+taut_periodic(i);
206         if accCPU_periodic(i)>=Wperiodic(i)
207             act_periodic(i)    = 0; //accCPU reset by alpha mgr
208             taut_periodic(i)   = 0; //the process releases the
                    CPU
209         end
210     end
211   end
212   //Batch tasks
213   for  i=1:Nbatch
214     if act_batch(i)==1
215         //With delta b for the moment
216         taut_batch(i)    = b_batch(i)*(1+0.05*rand());
217         accCPU_batch(i) = accCPU_batch(i)+taut_batch(i);
218         if accCPU_batch(i)>=Wbatch(i)
219             act_batch(i)     = 0; //accCPU reset by alpha mgr
220             taut_batch(i)    = 0; //the process releases the CPU
221         end
222     end
223   end
224   //Prioritised tasks
225   for  i=1:Nprio
226     //With delta b for the moment
227     taut_prio(i) = b_prio(i)*(1+0.05*rand());
228   end
229   //Event-based tasks
230   for  i=1:Nevent
231     //With delta b for the moment
232     taut_event(i) = b_event(i)*(1+0.05*rand());
233   end
234   //Round time
235   taur = sum(taut_periodic)+...     .
236         sum(taut_batch)   +...
237         sum(taut_prio)    +...
238         sum(taut_event);
239   //Collect vectors for plotting
```

```
240    vtau              = [ vtau ; tau ];
241    vtauro            = [ vtauro ; tauro ];
242    vtaur             = [ vtaur ; taur ];
243    mtauto_periodic   = [ mtauto_periodic ; tauto_periodic ];
244    mtaut_periodic    = [ mtaut_periodic ; taut_periodic ];
245    maccCPU_periodic  = [ maccCPU_periodic ; accCPU_periodic ];
246    mtauto_batch      = [ mtauto_batch ; tauto_batch ];
247    mtaut_batch       = [ mtaut_batch ; taut_batch ];
248    mtauto_prio       = [ mtauto_prio ; tauto_prio ];
249    mtaut_prio        = [ mtaut_prio ; taut_prio ];
250    mtauto_event      = [ mtauto_event ; tauto_event ];
251    mtaut_event       = [ mtaut_event ; taut_event ];
252    taut              = tau ;
253    tau               = tau+taur ;
254 end
255
256 // Plotting  results
257 subplot(611);
258    plot( vtau , vtauro , 'r' );
259    plot( vtau , vtaur , 'b' );
260 subplot(612);
261    plot( vtau , maccCPU_periodic , 'b' );
262 subplot(613);
263    plot( vtau , mtauto_periodic , 'r' );
264    plot( vtau , mtaut_periodic , 'b' );
265 subplot(614);
266    plot( vtau , mtauto_batch , 'r' );
267    plot( vtau , mtaut_batch , 'b' );
268 subplot(615);
269    plot( vtau , mtauto_prio , 'r' );
270    plot( vtau , mtaut_prio , 'b' );
271 subplot(616);
272    plot( vtau , mtauto_event , 'r' );
273    plot( vtau , mtaut_event , 'b' );
```

A.2   An implementation example

This appendix contains a portion of the I+PI scheduler as it is implemented in the Miosix kernel, with the purpose of providing an example of how the proposed controllers can be easily translated into their implementation counterparts. Only the code performing the burst computation was reported, as it is the core part of I+PI. The feedforward and reinitialisation parts are here not reported. Also, the classes presented here have been simplified by removing all data fields and member functions that are not necessary to understand the operation of the scheduler. The full source code is available at the Miosix site http://miosix.org, or directly at the git repository http://gitorious.org/miosix-kernel, under the miosix/kernel/ scheduler/control directory.

```
1 // Each thread contains an instance of this class , it contains the
2 // state variables that the scheduler needs to schedule the thread
```

```
 3  class ControlSchedulerData
 4  {
 5  public:
 6      ControlSchedulerData():
 7          bo(bNominal*multFactor), alfa(0), SP_Tt(0), Tt(bNominal),
 8          next(0)
 9      {}
10
11      int bo;            // Old burst time, kept multiplied by multFactor
12      float alfa;        // CPU share, sum of alfa of all threads=1
13      int SP_Tt;         // Processing time set point
14      int Tt;            // Real processing time
15      Thread *next;      // Next thread in list
16  };
17
18  // Every thread has a corresponding instance of this class
19  class Thread
20  {
21  private:
22
23      // Status flags for a thread
24      class ThreadFlags
25      {
26      public:
27          // Returns true if it is not blocked
28          bool isReady() const;
29      };
30
31      ControlSchedulerData schedData;
32  };
33
34  // This class contains the control scheduler code
35  class ControlScheduler
36  {
37  public:
38
39      // Called every time a context switch needs to be performed
40      static void IRQfindNextThread();
41
42  private:
43
44      // I+PI code, called by IRQfindNextThread() at the round end
45      static void IRQrunRegulator(bool allThreadsSaturated);
46
47      static Thread *threadList;           // Linked list of threads
48      static unsigned int threadListSize; // Number of threads
49
50      static Thread *curInRound;           // Currently running thread
51
52      static Thread *idle;                 // Idle thread
53
54      static int SP_Tr;                    // Round time set point
55
```

```
56      static int Tr;                          // Measured round time
57
58      static int bco;                         // PI state variable
59
60      static int eTro;                        // PI state variable
61
62      // Controller parameters
63      static const float kpi=0.5f;
64      static const float krr=0.9f;
65      static const float zrr=0.88f;
66      static const int multFactor=static_cast<int>(1.0f/kpi);
67      // Scheduler constants (numbers are in seconds)
68      static const int bNominal=static_cast<int>(CLOCK*0.004f);
69      static const int bMin=static_cast<int>(CLOCK*0.0002f);
70      static const int bMax=static_cast<int>(CLOCK*0.02f);
71      static const int bIdle=static_cast<int>(CLOCK*0.5f);
72  };
73
74  void ControlScheduler::IRQfindNextThread()
75  {
76      if(cur!=idle)
77      {
78          // Not preempting the idle thread, store actual burst
79          // time of the preempted thread, increment round time
80          int Tt=AuxiliaryTimer::IRQgetValue();
81          cur->schedData.Tt=Tt;
82          Tr+=Tt;
83      }
84
85      // Find next ready thread to run
86      for(;;)
87      {
88          // Move to the next thread in the round,
89          // if it's not already the end of the round
90          if(curInRound!=0) curInRound=curInRound->schedData.next;
91
92          // If it's the end of the round, need to run the I+PI
93          // code to compute the bursts for the next round
94          if(curInRound==0)
95          {
96              // Check these two statements:
97              // - If all threads are not ready, the scheduler must
98              //   be paused and the idle thread is run instead
99              // - If the inner integral regulator of all ready
100             //   threads saturated then the integral regulator of
101             //   the outer regulator must stop increasing because
102             //   the set point cannot be attained anyway.
103             bool allThreadNotReady=true;
104             bool allReadyThreadsSaturated=true;
105             for(Thread *it=threadList; it!=0; it=it->schedData.next)
106             {
107                 if(it->flags.isReady())
108                 {
```

```
109              allThreadNotReady=false;
110              if(it->schedData.bo<bMax*multFactor)
111              {
112                  allReadyThreadsSaturated=false;
113                  // Found a counterexample to both
114                  // statements, no need to scan the
115                  // list further.
116                  break;
117              }
118          }
119      }
120      if(allThreadNotReady)
121      {
122          // No thread is ready, run the idle thread
123          curInRound=0;
124          cur=idle;
125          ctxsave=cur->ctxsave;
126          AuxiliaryTimer::IRQsetValue(bIdle);
127          return;
128      }
129
130      // End of round reached, run the I+PI scheduler
131      curInRound=threadList;
132      IRQrunRegulator(allReadyThreadsSaturated);
133  }
134
135  // Regardless of where we are in the round, see if the
136  // thread is suitable to be run
137  if(curInRound->flags.isReady())
138  {
139      // Found a READY thread, so run this one
140      cur=curInRound;
141      ctxsave=cur->ctxsave;
142      int burst=curInRound->schedData.bo/multFactor;
143      AuxiliaryTimer::IRQsetValue(burst);
144      return;
145  } else {
146      // If we get here we have a non ready thread that
147      // can't run, so regardless of the burst calculated by
148      // the scheduler we do not run it and set Tt to zero.
149      curInRound->schedData.Tt=0;
150  }
151  }
152 }
153
154 void ControlScheduler::IRQrunRegulator(bool allThreadsSaturated)
155 {
156     int eTr=SP_Tr-Tr;
157     int bc=bco+static_cast<int>(krr*eTr-krr*zrr*eTro);
158     if(allThreadsSaturated)
159     {
160         // If all inner regulators reached upper saturation,
161         // allow only a decrease in the burst correction.
```

```
162        if( bc<bco ) bco=bc ;
163    } else bco=bc ;
164
165    bco=min<int >(max( bco,−Tr ),bMax∗threadListSize );
166    float nextRoundTime=static_cast <float >(Tr+bco );
167    eTro=eTr ;
168    Tr=0; // Reset round time
169    for( Thread ∗it=threadList ; it !=0; it=it −>schedData . next )
170    {
171        // Recalculate per thread set point
172        float burstSetPoint=it −>schedData . alfa ∗nextRoundTime ;
173        it −>schedData . SP_Tt=static_cast <int >( burstSetPoint );
174
175        // Run each thread internal regulator
176        int eTt=it −>schedData . SP_Tt−it −>schedData . Tt ;
177        // note: since b and bo contain the real value multiplied
178        // by multFactor , this equals b=bo+eTt/multFactor .
179        int b=it −>schedData . bo+eTt ;
180        // saturation
181        it −>schedData . bo=
182            min( max( b,bMin∗multFactor ) ,bMax∗multFactor );
183    }
184 }
```

References

[1] P. Bailis, V. J. Reddi, S. Gandhi, D. Brooks and M. Seltzer. 'Dimetrodon: Processor-level preventive thermal management via idle cycle injection'. In *Proceedings of the Design Automation Conference*, DAC 2011, San Diego, CA, USA, 2011. IEEE Computer Society

[2] H. Hoffmann, S. Sidiroglou, M. Carbin, S. Misailovic, A. Agarwal and M. Rinard. 'Dynamic knobs for responsive power-aware computing'. In *Proceedings of the 16th International Conference on Architectural Support for Programming Languages and Operating Systems*, ASPLOS '11, pages 199–212, New York, NY, USA, 2011. ACM Press

[3] N. Balasubramanian, A. Balasubramanian and A. Venkataramani. 'Energy consumption in mobile phones: A measurement study and implications for network applications'. In *Proceedings of the 9th ACM SIGCOMM Conference on Internet Measurement conference*, IMC '09, pages 280–293, New York, NY, USA, 2009. ACM

[4] M.-R. Ra, J. Paek, A. B. Sharma, R. Govindan, M. H. Krieger and M. J. Neely. 'Energy-delay tradeoffs in smartphone applications'. In *Proceedings of the 8th International Conference on Mobile Systems, Applications, and Services*, MobiSys '10, pages 255–270, New York, NY, USA, 2010. ACM

[5] M. Salehie and L. Tahvildari. 'Self-adaptive software: Landscape and research challenges'. *ACM Transaction on Autonomous and Adaptive Systems*, 4(2): 1–42, 2009

[6] J. O. Kephart and D. M. Chess. 'The vision of autonomic computing'. *Computer*, 36:41–50, Jan. 2003

[7] J. L. Hellerstein, Y. Diao, S. Parekh and D. M. Tilbury. *Feedback Control of Computing Systems*. Wiley, Hoboken, New Jersey, USA, Sep. 2004

[8] J. L. Hellerstein. 'Why feedback implementations fail: The importance of systematic testing'. In *Proceedings of the Fifth International Workshop on Feedback Control Implementation and Design in Computing Systems and Networks*, FeBiD'10, pages 25–26, New York, NY, USA, 2010. ACM

[9] G. B. Airy. 'On the regulator of the clock-work for effecting uniform movement of equatorials'. *Memoirs of the Royal Astronomical Society*, 2:249–267, 1840

[10] J. C. Maxwell. 'On governors'. *Proceedings of the Royal Society of London*, 16:270–283, 1868

[11] E. Routh. *A Treatise on the Stability of a Given State of Motion*. Macmillan & Co., London, 1877

[12]   A. M. Lyapunov. 'Problème général de la stabilité du mouvement'. *Annales de la Faculté des Sciences de Toulouse*, 9, 1893

[13]   H. Nyquist. 'Regeneration theory'. *Bell System Technical Journal*, 11(1):126–147, 1932

[14]   H. W. Bode. 'Feedback amplifier design'. *Bell System Technical Journal*, 19:42, 1940

[15]   L. R. A. MacColl. *Fundamental Theory of Servomechanisms*. Van Nostrand, New York, 1945

[16]   J. Ragazzini and G. Franklin. *Sampled-Data Control Systems*. McGraw-Hill, New York, NY, 1958

[17]   J. Ragazzini and L. Zadeh. 'The analysis of sampled-data systems'. *Transactions of the American Institute of Electrical Engineers*, 71(2):225–234, 1952

[18]   B. C. Kuo. *Analysis and Synthesis of Sampled-Data Control Systems*. Prentice-Hall, New Jersey, 1963

[19]   K. J. Åström and B. Wittenmark. *Practical Issues in the Implementation of Self-tuning Control*, volume 20. Prentice-Hall, New Jersey, 1984

[20]   K. Gödel. 'Über formal unentscheidbare Sätze der Principia Mathematica und verwandter Systeme, I'. *Monatshefte für Mathematik und Physik*, 38:173–198, 1931

[21]   A. M. Turing. 'On computable numbers, with an application to the Entscheidungsproblem'. *Proceedings of the London Mathematical Society Series*, 2(42):230–265, 1936

[22]   A. Church. 'An unsolvable problem of elementary number theory'. *American Journal of Mathematics*, 58:345–363, 1936

[23]   M. V. Wilkes and W. Renwick. 'The EDSAC – an electronic calculating machine'. *Journal of Scientific Instruments*, 26(12):385, 1949

[24]   J. H. Wilkinson. 'The pilot ACE'. *Automatic Digital Computation*, pages 5–14, Her Majesty's stationery office, London, 1954

[25]   L. Roberts. 'Multiple computer networks and intercomputer communication'. In *Proceedings of the First ACM Symposium on Operating System Principles*, pages 3–6. ACM, Oct. 1967

[26]   T. J. Berners-Lee. 'The world-wide web'. *Computer Networks and ISDN Systems*, 25(4–5):454–459, 1992

[27]   C. A. Petri. *Kommunikation mit automaten*. Rhein.-Westfäl. Institut für Numerische und Instrumentelle Mathematik an der Univetsitat Bonn, Bonn, 1962

[28]   J. Ousterhout. 'Lecture notes for CS140 operating systems'. Stanford University, Stanford, CA, 2010

[29]   T. F. Abdelzaher, J. A. Stankovic, C. Lu, R. Zhang and Y. Lu. 'Feedback performance control in software services'. *IEEE Control Systems Magazine*, 23(3):74–90, Jun. 2003

[30]   A. Bicchi, M. Bavaro, G. Boccadamo, D. De Carli, R. Filippini, G. Grioli, *et al*. 'Physical human-robot interaction: Dependability, safety, and performance'. In *10th IEEE International Workshop on Advanced Motion Control, 2008. AMC'08*, pages 9–14, 2008

[31]   R. Filippini, S. Sen and A. Bicchi. 'Toward soft robots you can depend on'. *IEEE Robotics & Automation Magazine*, 15(3):31–41, 2008

[32]   A. Gambier, M. Wolf, T. Miksch, A. Wellenreuther and E. Badreddin. 'Optimal systems engineering and control co-design for water and energy production: A European project'. *Desalination and Water Treatment*, 10(1–3):192–199, 2009

[33]   J. Ziegler and N. Nichols. 'Process lags in automatic control circuits'. *Transactions of the ASME*, 65:433–444, 1943

[34]   K. Åström and R. Murray. *Feedback Systems: An Introduction for Scientists and Engineers*. Princeton University Press, Princeton, NJ, USA, 2008

[35]   A. V. Papadopoulos, M. Maggio and A. Leva. 'Control and design of computing systems: What to model and how'. In *Proceedings of the 7th International Conference of Mathematical Modelling, MATHMOD'12*, Vienna, Austria, Feb. 2012

[36]   L. Torvalds and D. Diamond. *Just for fun: The Story of an Accidental Revolutionary*. Harper Business, New York, NY, USA, 2002

[37]   F. Cellier and E. Kofman. *Continuous System Simulation*. Springer-Verlag, London, UK, 2006

[38]   M. Pinedo. *Scheduling Theory, Algorithms, and Systems*, 3rd edn. Springer, Jul. 2008

[39]   Z. Sun. *Switched Linear Systems: Control and Design*. Communications and Control Engineering. Springer-Verlag, London, UK, 2005

[40]   M. Maggio, F. Terraneo and A. Leva. 'Task scheduling: A control-theoretical viewpoint for a general and flexible solution'. *ACM Transactions on Embedded Computing Systems*, (in press)

[41]   G. F. Franklin, J. D. Powell and A. Emami-Naeini. *Feedback Control of Dynamic Systems*, 6th edn. Pearson, Upper Saddle River, New Jersey, USA, 2010

[42]   M. R. Guthaus, J. S. Ringenberg, D. Ernst, T. M. Austin, T. Mudge and R. B. Brown. 'Mibench: A free, commercially representative embedded benchmark suite'. In *Proceedings of the Workload Characterization, 2001. WWC-4. 2001 IEEE International Workshop*, pages 3–14, Washington, DC, USA, 2001. IEEE Computer Society

[43]   N. Weiderman and N. Kamenoff. 'Hartstone uniprocessor benchmark: Definitions and experiments for real-time systems'. *Real-Time Systems*, 4(4):353–382, 1992

[44]   M. Maggio, A. V. Papadopoulos and A. Leva. 'On the use of feedback control in the design of computing system components'. *Asian Journal of Control*, 15(1):31–40, Jan. 2013

[45]   A. V. Papadopoulos, M. Maggio, S. Negro and A. Leva. 'Enhancing feedback process scheduling via a predictive control approach'. In *Proceedings of the 18th IFAC World Congress*, volume 18, pages 13522–13527, Milan, Italy, Sep. 2011

[46]   M. Maggio and A. Leva. 'A new perspective proposal for preemptive feedback scheduling'. *Int. Journal of Innovative Computing, Information and Control*, 6(10):4363–4377, 2010

[47]   R. Jones. 'Factors affecting the efficiency of a virtual memory'. *IEEE Transactions on Computers*, 18(11):1004–1008, 1969

[48]   H. Levy and P. Lipman. 'Virtual memory management in the vax/vms operating system'. *Computer*, 18(3):35–41, 1982

[49]   W. Chow and W. Chiu. 'An analysis of swapping policies in virtual storage systems'. *IEEE Transactions on Software Engineering*, 3(2):150–156, 1977

[50]   *2.6 swapping behavior*. http://lwn.net/Articles/83588/

[51]   K. Åström and B. Wittenmark. *Adaptive Control*. Addison-Wesley Longman Publishing Co., Inc., Mineola, New York, USA, 1994

[52]   E. Camacho and C. Bordons. *Model Predictive Control*, volume 303. Springer-Verlag, Berlin, Germany, 1999

[53]   L. Ljung. *System identification – Theory For the User*. Prentice Hall, Upper Saddle River, NJ, 1999

[54]   J. Maciejowski. *Predictive Control: With Constraints*. Pearson Education, Edinburgh Gate, Harlow, Essex, England, 2002

[55]   C. Cutler and B. Ramaker. 'Dynamic matrix control-a computer control algorithm'. In *Proceedings of the Joint Automatic Control Conference*, San Francisco, California, USA, 1980

[56]   C. Garcia and A. Morshedi. 'Quadratic programming solution of dynamic matrix control (QDMC)'. *Chemical Engineering Communications*, 46(1):73–87, 1986

[57]   V. Peterka. 'Predictor-based self-tuning control'. *Automatica*, 20(1):39–50, 1984

[58]   D. Clarke, C. Mohtadi and P. Tuffs. 'Generalized predictive control–part I: The basic algorithm'. *Automatica*, 23(2):137–148, 1987

[59]   D. Clarke, C. Mohtadi and P. Tuffs. 'Generalized predictive control–part II: Extensions and interpretations'. *Automatica*, 23(2):149–160, 1987

[60]   A. Ordys and D. Clarke. 'A state-space description for GPC controllers'. *International Journal of Systems Science*, 24(9):1727–1744, 1993

[61]   J. Rawlings. 'Tutorial overview of model predictive control'. *IEEE Control Systems Magazine*, 20(3):38–52, 2000

[62]   J. Rawlings and K. Muske. 'The stability of constrained receding horizon control'. *IEEE Transactions on Automatic Control*, 38(10):1512–1516, 1993

[63]   IBM. 'An architectural blueprint for autonomic computing'. Technical report, Jun. 2006

[64]   J. Kephart. 'Research challenges of autonomic computing'. In *Proceedings of the 27th International Conference on Software Engineering*, ICSE '05, pages 15–22, New York, NY, USA, 2005. ACM

[65]   M. Maggio, A. V. Papadopoulos and A. Leva. 'SMART computing systems: Sensing, modelling, actuating, regulating, and tuning'. In *Proceedings of the 7th International Workshop on Feedback Computing*, San Jose, California (USA), 2012

[66]   A. V. Papadopoulos, M. Maggio, S. Negro and A. Leva. 'General control-theoretical framework for online resource allocation in computing systems'. *IET Control Theory & Applications*, 6(11):1594–1602, Apr. 2012

[67] J. Kephart and D. Chess. 'The vision of autonomic computing'. *Computer*, 36:41–50, Jan. 2003

[68] J. Hellerstein, V. Morrison and E. Eilebrecht. 'Applying control theory in the real world: Experience with building a controller for the .net thread pool'. *SIGMETRICS Performance Evaluation Review*, 37(3):38–42, 2009

[69] M. Maggio, H. Hoffmann, A. V. Papadopoulos, J. Panerati, M. D. Santambrogio, A. Agarwal, *et al.* 'Comparison of decision making strategies for self-optimization in autonomic computing systems'. *ACM Transactions on Autonomous and Adaptive Systems*, 7(4), Apr. 2012

[70] C. Lu, Y. Lu, T. Abdelzaher, J. Stankovic and S. Son. 'Feedback control architecture and design methodology for service delay guarantees in web servers'. *IEEE Transactions on Parallel and Distributed Systems*, 17(7), 2006

[71] H. Hoffmann, J. Eastep, M. D. Santambrogio, J. E. Miller and A. Agarwal. 'Application heartbeats: A generic interface for specifying program performance and goals in autonomous computing environments'. In *Proceeding of the 7th International Conference on Autonomic Computing*, ICAC '10, pages 79–88, New York, NY, USA, 2010. ACM

[72] R. Zhang, C. Lu, T. Abdelzaher and J. Stankovic. 'Controlware: A middleware architecture for feedback control of software performance'. In *Proceedings of the 22nd International conference on Distributed Computing Systems*. IEEE Computer Society, 2002

[73] J. L. Hellerstein. 'Why feedback implementations fail: The importance of systematic testing'. In *Proceedings of the Fifth International Workshop on Feedback Control Implementation and Design in Computing Systems and Networks*, FeBiD'10, pages 25–26, New York, NY, USA, 2010. ACM

[74] M. Maggio, H. Hoffmann, M. D. Santambrogio, A. Agarwal and A. Leva. 'Controlling software applications via resource allocation within the heartbeats framework'. In *Proceeding of the 49th International Conference on Decision and Control*, Atlanta, USA, 2010. IEEE Control

[75] K. Åström and T. Hägglund. *Advanced PID Control*. ISA – The Instrumentation, Systems, and Automation Society, Research Triangle Park, NC, 2005

[76] A. Leva, S. Negro and A. V. Papadopoulos. 'PI/PID autotuning with contextual model parametrisation'. *Journal of Process Control*, 20(4):452–463, Apr. 2010

[77] A. O'Dwyer. *Handbook of PI And PID Controller Tuning Rules*, 3rd edition, Imperial College Press, Covent Garden, London, England, Feb. 2006

[78] A. V. Papadopoulos and A. Leva. 'Antiwindup-aware PI autotuning'. In *Proceedings IFAC Conference on Advances in PID Control*. IFAC, Mar. 2012

[79] H. Hoffmann, M. Maggio, M. D. Santambrogio, A. Agarwal and A. Leva. 'SEEC: A framework for self-aware computing'. Technical Report MIT-CSAIL-TR-2010-049, Massachusetts Institute of Technology, Computer Science and Artificial Intelligence Laboratory, Cambridge, Oct. 2010

[80] L. Ljung. *System Identification: Theory for the User*. Prentice Hall PTR, Upper Saddle River, New Jersey, USA, Dec. 1998

[81] C. Bienia, S. Kumar, J. P. Singh and K. Li. 'The PARSEC benchmark suite: Characterization and architectural implications'. In *Proceedings of the 17th International Conference on Parallel Architectures and Compilation Techniques*, pages 72–81, Toronto, Ontario, Canada, Oct. 2008

[82] A. Muttreja, A. Raghunathan, S. Ravi and N. K. Jha. 'Automated energy/ performance macromodeling of embedded software'. *IEEE Transactions on Computer-Aided Design of Integrated Circuits and Systems*, 26(3):542–552, Mar. 2007

[83] V. Tiwari, S. Malik and A. Wolfe. 'Power analysis of embedded software: A first step towards software power minimization'. *IEEE Transactions on Very Large Scale Integration (VLSI) Systems*, 2(4):437–445, Dec. 1994

[84] Y. Fei, S. Ravi, A. Raghunathan and N. K. Jha. 'A hybrid energy-estimation technique for extensible processors'. *Computer-Aided Design of Integrated Circuits and Systems, IEEE Transactions on*, 23(5):652–664, May 2004

[85] K. Lahiri, A. Raghunathan and S. Dey. 'Efficient power profiling for battery-driven embedded system design'. *IEEE Transactions on Computer-Aided Design of Integrated Circuits and Systems*, 23(6):919–932, Jun. 2004

[86] R. Kumar, K. Farkas, N. P. Jouppi, P. Ranganathan and D. M. Tullsen. 'Processor power reduction via single-isa heterogeneous multi-core architectures'. *Computer Architecture Letters*, 2(1), 2003

[87] M. Maggio, H. Hoffmann, M. Santambrogio, A. Agarwal and A. Leva. 'Power optimization in embedded systems via feedback control of resource allocation'. *IEEE Transactions on Control Systems Technology*, in press, available online, DOI 10.1109/TCST.2011.2177499

[88] H. Hoffmann, J. Eastep, M. Santambrogio, J. Miller and A. Agarwal. 'Application heartbeats: a generic interface for specifying program performance and goals in autonomous computing environments'. In *ICAC '10: Proceeding of the 7th International Conference on Autonomic Computing*, pages 79–88, Washington, DC, USA, 2010

[89] Wattsup .net meter. http://www.wattsupmeters.com/

[90] J. Geromel and P. Colaneri. 'Stability and stabilization of discrete time switched systems'. *International Journal of Control*, 79(7):719–728, 2006

[91] A. Baumann, P. Barham, P. Dagand, T. Harris, R. Isaacs, S. Peter, *et al.* 'The multikernel: A new OS architecture for scalable multicore systems'. In *SOSP'09: Proceedings of the Twenty-Second ACM SIGOPS Symposium on Operating Systems Principles*, pages 29–43, 1515 Broadway, New York, NY, 2009

[92] H. Harwood and A. Shen. 'Using fundamental electrical theory for varying time quantum uni-processor scheduling'. *Journal of Systems Architecture*, 47:181–192, 2001

[93] E. A. Lee. 'Cyber-physical systems – are computing foundations adequate?' In *NSF Workshop On Cyber-Physical Systems: Research Motivation, Techniques and Roadmap*, Austin, TX, Oct. 2006

[94] Introduction to scilab. http://www.scilab.org/content/download/1754/19024/ file/introscilab.pdf

Index

Printed in the USA
CPSIA information can be obtained
at www.ICGtesting.com
JSHW011510221024
72173JS00005B/1263

9 781849 196093